MW00715142

Palgrave Studies in European Union Politics

Following on from the sustained success of the acclaimed *European Union Series*, which essentially publishes research-based textbooks, *Palgrave Studies in European Union Politics* publishes cutting edge research-driven monographs.

The remit of the series is broadly defined, in terms of both subject and academic discipline. All topics of significance concerning the nature and operation of the European Union potentially fall within the scope of the series. The series is multidisciplinary to reflect the growing importance of the EU as a political, economic and social phenomenon.

Titles include:

Heather Grabbe
THE EU'S TRANSFORMATIVE POWER

Eva Gross
THE EUROPEANIZATION OF NATIONAL FOREIGN POLICY
Continuity and Change in European Crisis Management

Hussein Kassim and Handley Stevens
AIR TRANSPORT AND THE EUROPEAN UNION
Europeanization and its Limits

Katie Verlin Laatikainen and Karen E. Smith (*editors*)
THE EUROPEAN UNION AND THE UNITED NATIONS
Intersecting Multilateralisms

Esra LaGro and Knud Erik Jørgensen (*editors*)
TURKEY AND THE EUROPEAN UNION
Prospects for a Difficult Encounter

Ingo Linsenmann, Christoph O. Meyer and Wolfgang T. Wessels (*editors*)
ECONOMIC GOVERNMENT OF THE EU
A Balance Sheet of New Modes of Policy Coordination

Hartmut Mayer and Henri Vogt (*editors*)
A RESPONSIBLE EUROPE?
Ethical Foundations of EU External Affairs

Philomena Murray (*editor*)
EUROPE AND ASIA
Regions in Flux

Costanza Musu
EUROPEAN UNION POLICY TOWARDS THE ARAB–ISRAELI PEACE PROCESS
The Quicksands of Politics

Daniel Naurin and Helen Wallace (*editors*)
UNVEILING THE COUNCIL OF THE EUROPEAN UNION
Games Governments Play in Brussels

David Phinnemore and Alex Warleigh-Lack
REFLECTIONS ON EUROPEAN INTEGRATION
50 Years of the Treaty of Rome

Sebastiaan Princen
AGENDA-SETTING IN THE EUROPEAN UNION

Palgrave Studies in European Union Politics
Series Standing Order ISBN 978-1-4039-9511-7 (hardback) and
ISBN 978-1-4039-9512-4 (paperback)

You can receive future titles in this series as they are published by placing a standing order. Please contact your bookseller or, in case of difficulty, write to us at the address below with your name and address, the title of the series and one of the ISBNs quoted above.

Customer Services Department, Macmillan Distribution Ltd, Houndmills, Basingstoke, Hampshire RG21 6XS, UK

European Union Policy towards the Arab–Israeli Peace Process

The Quicksands of Politics

Costanza Musu
*Assistant Professor of Public and International Affairs,
University of Ottawa, Canada*

First published 2010 by
PALGRAVE MACMILLAN

Palgrave Macmillan in the UK is an imprint of Macmillan Publishers Limited,
registered in England, company number 785998, of Houndmills, Basingstoke,
Hampshire RG21 6XS.

Palgrave Macmillan in the US is a division of St Martin's Press LLC,
175 Fifth Avenue, New York, NY 10010.

Palgrave Macmillan is the global academic imprint of the above companies
and has companies and representatives throughout the world.

Palgrave® and Macmillan® are registered trademarks in the United States,
the United Kingdom, Europe and other countries.

ISBN 978-0–230–55312–5 hardback

This book is printed on paper suitable for recycling and made from fully
managed and sustained forest sources. Logging, pulping and manufacturing
processes are expected to conform to the environmental regulations of the
country of origin.

A catalogue record for this book is available from the British Library.

A catalog record for this book is available from the Library of Congress.

10 9 8 7 6 5 4 3 2 1
19 18 17 16 15 14 13 12 11 10

Printed and bound in Great Britain by
CPI Antony Rowe, Chippenham and Eastbourne

To Nonna Susanna
Omnia praetereunt redeunt nihil interit

Contents

List of Tables

Abbreviations and Acronyms

AP	Action Plan
BP	Barcelona Process
CFSP	Common Foreign and Security Policy
COREU	Correspondence Européenne
CSCE	Conference on Security and Cooperation in Europe
DG	Directorate-General
DOP	Declaration of Principles
EAD	Euro-Arab Dialogue
EC	European Community
ECG	Energy Coordinating Group
EEA	European Economic Area
EEC	European Economic Community
EFP	European Foreign Policy
EMP	Euro-Mediterranean Partnership
EMU	European Monetary Union
ENP	European Neighbourhood Policy
ENPI	European Neighbourhood and Partnership Instrument
EPC	European Political Cooperation
ESDI	European Security and Defence Identity
ESDP	European Security and Defence Policy
ESS	European Security Strategy
EU	European Union
EUBAM	European Union Border Assistance Mission in Rafah
EUPM	EU Police Mission
EUPOL COPPS	EU Police Coordinating Office for Palestinian Police Support
FDI	Foreign Direct Investment
GA	General Assembly of the United Nations
GAERC	General Affairs and External Relations Council
GCC	Gulf Cooperation Council

HR	High Representative for the Common Foreign and Security Policy
IEA	International Energy Agency
MEDA	Mesures D'Accompagnement
MEPP	Middle East Peace Process
NATO	North Atlantic Treaty Organisation
OPEC	Organisation of Petroleum Exporting Countries
PA	Palestinian Authority
PEGASE	Mécanisme Palestino-Européen de Gestion de l'Aide Socio-économique
PLO	Palestine Liberation Organization
PNA	Palestinian National Authority
QMV	Qualified Majority Voting
REDWG	Regional Economic Development Working Group
RRF	Rapid Reaction Force
SEA	Single European Act
SR	Special Representative
TEU	Treaty on European Union
TIM	Temporary International Mechanism
UK	United Kingdom
UN	United Nations
UNIFIL	United Nations Interposition Force in Lebanon
USSR	Union of Soviet Socialist Republics
US	United States (of America)
WEU	Western European Union
WMD	Weapons of Mass Destruction

Acknowledgements

This book represents the culmination of a long and exciting intellectual journey. The study of the policy of the European Union towards the Arab–Israeli conflict has been both a challenge and an opportunity. In particular, it has not only allowed me to explore a complex and fascinating topic, but also to meet and engage in conversations and exchanges with some wonderful people. The time has come to thank them for their help and support.

William Wallace has been the sounding board for my initial ideas and has provided invaluable feedback and suggestions. Thanks also to Nicola Casarini, Sven Biscop, Richard Whitman, Paul Luif, Stephan Stetter and Alfred Tovias: conversations with them and the feedback they provided on various aspects of my research have helped improve this book.

My thanks also go to the numerous practitioners, civil servants and diplomats who have shared their experience, ideas and perspectives with me in London, Brussels, Rome, Tel Aviv, Jerusalem and Ottawa.

My gratitude goes to Nicole De Silva for her great editing job, and to the team at Palgrave Macmillan, and particularly to Alison Howson and Amy Lankester-Owen for their expert guidance and advice. Thanks also to the series editors Michelle Egan, Neil Nugent and William Paterson and to the anonymous reviewers for their constructive comments.

I want to thank my family and my friends, who have encouraged me over time and will be happy to see this project come to a fruitful conclusion, and my husband Patrick Leblond who offered not only encouragement and support but also expert advice and much needed feedback on various draft chapters.

1
Introduction

The Europeans will be unable to achieve anything in the Middle East in a million years.[1]

(Henry Kissinger, former US Secretary of State, 1974)

Despite what is sometimes said, the Europeans do not want to interfere in the negotiations between the parties for the sake of appearing as another mediator. They want to help the parties to settle their differences in a way satisfactory for all. When we try to make our presence felt in the region, we do so in a way that will buttress peace efforts, not complicate them.[2]

(Miguel A. Moratinos, former EU
Special Representative for the Middle East
peace process, 1998)

To anyone attempting to analyse and evaluate European policy vis-à-vis the Arab–Israeli peace process, a remarkable paradox presents itself. On the one hand we have the European Union, an entity that creates not only an economic but also a political and security community among states that had battled each other for centuries, causing uncountable casualties and destruction. Nothing could be more different from today's European Union than the semi-destroyed continent that emerged from the Second World War.

On the other hand, we have a conflict between the Arabs and the Israelis that looks very similar today to what it looked like sixty years ago: two peoples locked in a bloody conflict, seemingly unable to extract themselves from the spiral of violence and surrounded by an international community whose efforts at mediation have had very little success.

If this is the situation at first sight, a closer look allows us to study the problem from a different point of view. An analysis of EU policy towards the Middle East peace process will reveal that, while the EU as such has deeply changed from a mainly economic community of six members to an economic *and* political community of twenty-seven members with its own security and defence policy, the basic principles of EU policy towards the peace process date back to the early years of European Political Cooperation, and the limits that soon emerged still haunt EU action today and hamper its effectiveness (by which we mean the ability of the EU to influence significantly the major actors of the conflict and, ideally, their policy choices). As for the conflict, on the other hand, while the hostility between Israel and Arab states persists and has become even more entrenched, the situation on the ground has profoundly changed after the end of the Cold War, the disappearance of the Soviet Union, and the emergence of a new balance of power in the region with the United States as the sole superpower. Israel has signed two peace treaties with neighbouring states (Egypt and Jordan) and has withdrawn troops from Lebanon and Gaza, but has maintained its control over the West Bank (and in many respects over Gaza as well), has continued the expansion of its settlements, slowly eroding the territory that should be destined for the creation of a Palestinian state, and has engaged in brief but bloody wars with Hezbollah in Lebanon and Hamas in Gaza. The death of Yasser Arafat has created a leadership vacuum in the Palestinian Authority, which has, in time, contributed to the conflict between Fatah and Hamas and to the de facto political separation of Gaza and the West Bank in 2007. Iran has emerged as a major regional power, especially after the 2003 US-led invasion of Iraq. It has pushed forward its nuclear programme in defiance of international pressures and has supported Hezbollah in Lebanon and Hamas in Gaza, acting as a spoiler of the peace process by giving military and economic aid to Islamic forces that militarily engage Israel and reject a political solution to the conflict.

The EU has engaged with a conflict that is deeply affected by the shifting regional and global balance of power with an approach that has been partly laid out with the Venice Declaration of 1980 (see Chapter 2). While European ideas for a solution to the conflict have proven to a degree to be 'visionary' and have anticipated political choices that the United States has only made in the past few years, the EU has had trouble developing a coherent and effective policy, adapting to shifting realities on the ground and taking advantage of opportunities to cut for itself an autonomous role as a mediator.

The purpose of this book is to explore this paradox, that is, the EU's inability to adapt its policy to a changing situation on the ground, and, by examining forty years of EU policy towards the peace process, to answer the following question: *why has the EU been unable to develop an effective and autonomous policy towards the Arab–Israel conflict, despite its efforts and the inordinate amount of time and resources it has committed over the years?*

The book will test a set of possible complementary answers: (a) the EU failed to reach a sufficiently convergent approach among EU members; (b) the EU lacks the relevant levers and instruments to affect the Middle East peace process; (c) strategic US interests in the Middle East and the dynamics of EU–US relations have relegated the EU to a secondary role in the Middle East peace process.

EU member states[3] are directly and indirectly implicated in the Middle East conflict because of their geographic proximity, dependence on Middle Eastern oil, and security needs, as well because of the historical role played by several of them in the region (Greilsammer and Weiler 1987). The Arab–Israeli conflict, and the subsequent peace process, have been among the most strongly debated issues by member states, not only since the creation of the Common Foreign and Security Policy (CFSP) in 1991, but since the establishment of European Political Co-operation (EPC) in 1970; the peace process has been the subject of innumerable joint declarations and joint actions on the part of the EC/EU, and has always remained a high-priority issue in the European foreign policy agenda. Furthermore, it must be noted that the Middle East has often represented a problematic issue in EU–US relations, given on the one hand Europe's double dependence on the United States as a security guarantor and on Middle East oil, and on the other America's strategic interests in the region and its desire to maintain control over the development of the peace process, which has frequently clashed with Europe's attempts to cut a role for itself in the negotiations.

These few preliminary remarks are enough to establish how the question of the EU's policy towards the Arab–Israeli peace process involves composite problems and closely intertwined interests.

The quotations at the beginning of this chapter encapsulate very well the complex issues tied to the study of the development of the EU's policy towards the Middle East peace process. While trying to avoid attributing to the words of Dr Kissinger and Mr Moratinos meanings that were not originally implied, a textual analysis of their comments is highly suggestive; both quotations are indeed significant in a number of ways.

Henry Kissinger's remark was made in March 1974, after the Yom Kippur War and in the midst of the oil crisis; it was a moment of harsh tensions between the United States and Europe, as the former perceived the launching of the Euro–Arab Dialogue (an initiative undertaken by the EC mainly as a result of pressures exercised by France) as something of a 'betrayal' of transatlantic solidarity and as a danger for the American-led attempt to create a consumer front to oppose the Arab oil embargo.

In 1974 the EPC project was only four years old and there was hardly any real coordination between the EC member states in terms of foreign policy. The Middle East was one of the EPC's first fields of activity, although – as this study will show – it did not prove very successful in advancing the EC's aspiration to 'a united Europe capable of assuming its responsibilities in the world of tomorrow and of making a contribution commensurate with its traditions and its mission'.[4]

Notwithstanding the questionable successes of Europe's Middle East initiatives, the simple fact that a US Secretary of State deemed it necessary to criticise the EC's Arab policy in such a manner shows how the United States, while always supportive of European integration, also nurtured a distinct dislike for any European initiative that was not fully consonant with US strategies.

American scepticism, if not contempt, with regard to the possibility that Europe could develop an effective policy towards the Middle East appears clearly from a number of words in Kissinger's comment: the use of the expression 'the Europeans' instead of 'the EC' or 'Europe', a symptom of how EPC was far from being considered the expression of a collective European foreign policy; the words '*unable* to achieve anything' (emphasis added), which underlined the EPC's lack of any real foreign policy instruments and the

American perception that the Europeans – either as single member states or collectively as the European Community – were therefore incapable of exercising any form of influence on the Arab–Israeli conflict; and finally the last three words, 'in a million years', which on the one hand highlight American condescension towards the idea of the EC possibly taking on a role as an international actor and – in this particular instance – as a credible player in the Middle East, and on the other arguably shed light on the American determination to maintain leadership in the region.

Miguel Moratinos's statement was made almost twenty-five years later. It can be said to symbolise in a nutshell all the changes that took place in those years, but also the persistence of certain patterns.

The first element of importance is the actual role of the person making the remarks: Mr Moratinos was speaking in his capacity as EU Special Representative for the Middle East Peace Process, a position that in itself indicates the progress made by the EU in developing a Common Foreign and Security Policy, with the creation of the position of Special Representative in an attempt to enhance the coherence of the EU's policy by providing a single European referent for external interlocutors.

On the other hand, Moratinos, while describing the EU's Middle East policy, refers to 'the Europeans', using the same expression adopted twenty-five years earlier by Kissinger and thus showing how, a quarter of a century later, a common European foreign policy was still an objective to be achieved and how EU Middle East Policy continued to be the minimum common denominator among the different national policies of individual member states.

The second important point is contained in the first phrase of Moratinos's statement: 'Despite what is sometimes said, the Europeans do not want to *interfere* in the negotiations between the parties for the sake of appearing as *another mediator*' (emphasis added). It can be surmised that these words refer mainly to the old and clearly unresolved dispute between Europe and the United States with regard to the EU's role in the negotiations between Israel and the Arabs. Once again, twenty-five years later the situation appears to be little changed, with Europe still attempting to define a role for itself in the Middle East and the United States still determined to maintain its leadership and to remain the sole mediator between the conflicting parties.

The remaining words of Moratinos's statements are also highly suggestive: the phrase '[The Europeans] want to help the parties to settle their differences in a way *satisfactory for all'* (emphasis added), apart from the obvious reference to the EU's aspiration to see the Arab–Israeli conflict solved, can arguably be said to allude also to the numerous European interests in the region and to the EU's concern that a settlement of the conflict should not expose these economic, strategic and political interests to danger.

Finally, the sentence 'When we *try to make our presence felt in the region*, we do so in a way that will buttress peace efforts, not complicate them' (emphasis added) clearly indicates the EU's consciousness of its secondary role in the region, which is a consequence on the one hand of the EU's inability to express a coherent and effective policy and thus to become a reliable actor, and on the other of US hostility towards the idea of accepting the EU as a further mediator, which goes hand in hand with similar Israeli opposition to the idea of allowing the EU to play a political role beyond that of financing the Palestinian Authority.

Hampered by the differences between member states' foreign policies, by the formal limitations of the CFSP – which operates within the limits of an intergovernmental framework – and by the hostility of two of the major players in the peace process (Israel and the United States), the EU, indeed, cannot but *try to make its presence felt in the region*, but with little hope of success until both its structural deficiencies and its internal elements of incoherence are overcome.

Contribution of the book

This book conducts an analysis of European policy towards the peace process, aimed not so much at measuring the EU's success or failure in relation to the breadth of its economic involvement, but rather at identifying the factors and the interests underlying the formulation of the European Union's policy. Furthermore, European policy towards the Middle East – and in particular towards the Arab–Israeli conflict and peace process – constitutes an ideal case study for the problem of political integration within the EU (Soetendorp 2002). As pointed out above, the Middle East has been one of the most widely debated issues among member states in the past thirty years, and was one of the items discussed at the first EPC meeting in 1970. The study of European Middle

East policy, therefore, offers the opportunity of testing the ability of member states to harmonise their distinct foreign policies, to identify common interests, and to proceed along the road of further integration and towards the elaboration of a common European foreign policy.

Scholars of the European Union have often struggled with the issue of European foreign policy, trying to understand the rationale behind the creation of EPC and CFSP and studying its role as an international actor (Bretherton and Vogler 1999; Forster and Wallace 2000; Piening 1997; Regelsberger, de Schoutheete de Tervarent and Wessels 1997; Rosecrance 1997); linking the construction of a European foreign policy mechanism with the formation of a European identity (Whitman 1998); analysing its functioning and the causes of what has been referred to as its 'paralysis' (Zielonka 1998a); examining its capabilities in relation to the expectations of external interlocutors (Hill 1993; 1998) and the effects of institutional constraints on EU policies (Monar 1998a; Peterson and Shackleton 2002; Rummel and Wiedemann 1998; White 2001).

A number of scholars have studied the problem of European Middle East policy: the first works date back to the 1980s and focus on the EC's early attempts to coordinate the Member States' foreign policies and to reach a unified stance, and on US–Europe relations in the region (Allen and Pijpers 1984; Bonvicini and Coffey 1989; Garfinkle 1983; Greilsammer and Weiler 1987; Ifestos 1987; Steinbach 1980). In more recent years other scholars have focused on the issue; these works, however, have generally failed to analyse the problem of European foreign policy towards the Arab–Israeli peace process in its entirety. Instead, they have focused on specific aspects of the policy, for example, the EU's institutional limits, its economic involvement in the peace process, its policy towards the Mediterranean region (with only limited reference to the problem of the peace process) and the limitations imposed on the EU's role by American leadership in the region (Daalder, Gnesotto and Gordon 2006; Dosenrode and Stubkjaer 2002; Ginsberg 2001; Hollis 1997; Monar 1998b; Roberson 1998; Soetendorp 2002; Spencer 2001; Youngs 2006).

This book proposes to bring together in a single study different perspectives and angles of analysis and, by doing so, to achieve a better understanding of the factors and the interests underlying the formulation of the European Union's policy towards the Middle East conflict. The volume intends to fill a gap in the literature by offering a study of European policy towards the Arab–Israeli peace process that will simultaneously take into consideration the dilemma of the harmonisation of the different Member States' policies and interests; the continuation of separate national debates on foreign policy issues in parallel with convergent common declarations; the problem of the self-contained structure of CFSP, its mechanisms and its institutional and political limitations; and the questions of the EU's role as a global actor, of the diverse European interests in the Middle East, of the dynamics of transatlantic relations and of burden-sharing between the United States and the EU in the Arab–Israeli peace process.

A 'European' foreign policy?

While this study is empirical in its approach, the assumptions on which the research is based need to be clarified. The difficulty of analysing European foreign policy is already evident in the definition of the object of study itself. Is there a truly 'European' foreign policy? And what is the rationale behind it?

Such questions have haunted researchers for fifty years, and the criteria adopted for conceptualising the nature of the EU's foreign policy have differed profoundly: definitions are still very much open.

As Michael Smith puts it:

> The EC and now the EU have long established the material foundations for their presence and impact in the international arena. These foundations are the reflection of the economic and political weight of the EU, of its institutional capacity and of the ways in which it has enlarged its tasks and roles in the changing world arena. But they are not monolithic, nor do they suppress the claims or the prerogatives of the member states. There is no definite answer to the question 'does the EU have a foreign policy?' Rather there is a series of increasingly well-focused questions about the nature of EU international action and the foundation on which it is based. (Smith 1996b: 247)

Since the creation of European Political Cooperation in 1970, scholars have tried to conceptualise the idea of European foreign policy.

In 1977 Sjostedt developed the concept of *actorness*, arguing that an international actor might be defined as an entity (a) delimited from others; (b) with the autonomy to make its own law and decisions; and (c) which possesses certain structural prerequisites for action on the international level (such as legal personality, a set of diplomatic agents and the capability to conduct negotiations with third parties) (Sjostedt 1977).

This definition of an international actor contributes to resolving the dilemma that, on the one hand, actorness in the world is a quality the EU is often automatically assumed to possess, but, on the other hand, the intergovernmental nature of European foreign policy (EFP) suggests that it might be viewed as no more then the sum of decisions taken by member states.

A second concept, developed by Allen and Smith (1990), is that of *presence*. According to this notion, the EU has a variable and multidimensional presence in international affairs. A cohesive European impact on international relations must be accepted, despite the messy way in which it is produced. For Allen and Smith, the EU's presence in the international arena is characterised by two elements: (a) the EU exhibits distinctive forms of external behaviour; (b) the EU is perceived to be important by other actors within the global system (ibid.).

Thus, actorness is not only about the objective existence of dimensions of external presence, but also about 'the subjective aspects embodied in the validation of a collective self by significant others' (Rosamond 2000: 176–7).

Furthermore, as Michael Smith has underlined, the EU is not simply an 'actor' or a 'presence' but also a *process*; a set of complex institutions, roles and rules, which structure the activities of the EU itself and those of other internationally significant groupings with which it comes into contact (Smith 1996b).

Central to the debate on the nature of the EU and of European foreign policy has been the controversial idea of Europe as a '*civilian power*'. In 1972 Duchene created the term civilian power, arguing that there is no point in trying to build up a European superpower and a European army, as in our time there is more scope for civilian forms of action and influence. In his view, Europe should emerge as a model of a new type of interstate relationship, able to overcome the legacy of war, intimidation and violence. Europe should be a force for the international diffusion of civilian and democratic standards (Duchene 1972).

The notion of civilian power has prompted a fierce debate, and numerous scholars have criticised Duchene's views: Hedley Bull (1982) defined civilian-power-Europe as 'a contradiction in terms'; others have underlined the importance of military power and have accused Duchene of making a virtue out of necessity (i.e. Europe is unable to become an international actor and tries to sell its failure as a success) (Hill 1990; Zielonka 1998b: 226–8). The value of 'civilian power' has been questioned by commentators (Bull 1982; Kagan 2002; Lieber 2002) as being conditional upon an environment secured by the military power of other states (for example the United States).

Other scholars, like Zielonka (1998a), have supported the idea of the EU as a civilian power, arguing that 'aspiring to military power would be an expensive, divisive, and basically futile exercise for the Union' (228). For Karen Smith, a civilian EU is to be preferred because security in the post-Cold War world has acquired a much broader connotation than military security: 'threats to security within and between states arise from a variety of sources, including ethnic disputes, violation of human rights, and economic deprivation. And the EU is very well placed to address the long term causes of insecurity' (Smith 1998: 79).

Commenting on the development of European military capabilities, Richard Whitman has argued that this has not diminished the importance of EU 'civilian power', underlining that, so far, the EU's common security policy has been developed with the purpose of furthering the structures that facilitate civilian power, which continues to be at the heart of EU identity, relevance and effectiveness (Whitman 2002).

While this book is essentially empirical in its approach, the numerous concepts illustrated above both inform the study and constitute the basis on which the research is built. In analysing the ability of Europe to realise the objective of a common external posture towards the Middle East peace process, the volume focuses particularly on the problematic dynamics between the member states' foreign policies and the elaboration of a common European stance, on the process of interaction and socialisation among foreign ministries within the framework of political cooperation at the European level, and on whether this process has brought about a convergence of national policies (see Chapter 5).

The book utilises the concept of actorness, focusing in particular on what Sjostedt defines as 'the structural prerequisites for action on the international level' (1977: 74–109), such as legal personality and the capability to conduct negotiations with third parties. The idea of the EU as a process, that is, a set of complex institutions, roles and rules, is explored with special reference to the development of EU foreign policy instruments and to the evaluation of their effectiveness (see Chapter 6).

Finally, the vision of the EU as a model of security community in which war has been eradicated, and the question of the EU as a civilian power, are crucial in exploring the EU's relations with the Mediterranean region and its efforts to contribute to the peace process, and at the same time to interpret some of Europe's failures (see Chapters 6 and 7).

The hypotheses tested in the book

This book aims to offer a comprehensive analysis of the problem of EU policy towards the Middle East Peace Process (MEPP), tackling it from different perspectives and bringing together in a single study all the relevant elements.

The study focuses first on the problem of convergence among the different member states' policies; it examines to what extent member states have disagreed with each other in formulating a European policy towards the Middle East, and whether it is possible to detect a trend towards the attainment of a 'European perception', broadly speaking, of the Arab–Israeli problem and of the policy Europe should adopt.

Secondly, it analyses the instruments of European foreign policy from a legal–institutional point of view, studying the progressive construction of the Common Foreign and Security Policy and evaluating how EU foreign policy instruments have been used in Middle East policy.

Finally, it focuses on the crucial issue of transatlantic relations, studying the dynamics of EU–US relations in the Middle East and how they have influenced the development of EU policy towards the region.

The EU, the member states and the development of a 'European' policy towards the peace process

The first hypothesis that this book tests is that the EU has failed to develop an effective and autonomous policy towards the Arab–Israeli conflict due to failure in reaching a sufficiently convergent approach among EU members.

The Arab–Israeli conflict and subsequent peace process have been the subject of numerous joint declarations and joint actions on the part of the European Union: the Middle East policy was one of the questions discussed at the very first meeting of European Political Cooperation in 1970, and thereafter the EC/EU closely monitored the Arab–Israeli conflict, which remained a high-priority issue on the European foreign policy agenda (Allen and Pijpers 1984).

This book attempts to establish to what extent disagreement has characterised relations among member states in the context of the formulation of a European Middle East policy, and whether it is possible to detect a trend towards the attainment of a 'European perception', broadly speaking, of the Arab–Israeli problem and of the policy Europe should adopt. Harmonising the EU member states' viewpoints on the Arab–Israeli conflict is a task which has always proved difficult. As a quick overview of some member states' Middle East policies demonstrates, the individual interests and policy guidelines of the member states are still some considerable way apart despite the common interest and common efforts towards finding a just and lasting solution to the conflict.

French policy in the Middle East has privileged France's relations with the Arab world, even if it has tried at the same time to maintain good relations with Israel. Paris has often promoted an independent French policy in the area, and this independence has mainly implied conducting a policy that is independent of that of the United States. At times, such a policy has gone so far as to cause tensions with other EU member states, with autonomous French initiatives in the Middle East seemingly taken without any prior consultations with European allies.

For some European countries, such as Germany and the Netherlands, the sensitivities of relations with Israel were such that their governments have hesitated to criticise Israeli policy. For these countries the possibility of shifting national positions under the guise of a search for a common European position has proven attractive: it has allowed them to initiate a rapprochement to the Arab world while claiming this to be an 'unavoidable price' in striving for the superior objective of reaching a unified European position, and at the same time to avoid upsetting their own internal public opinions.

Great Britain has tended to follow the lines of America's Middle East policy: on the British foreign policy agenda, transatlantic relations were a much higher priority than Middle East policy, in spite of the long historical involvement of the United Kingdom in the area. London has been inclined to favour a policy that secured American approval and avoided direct confrontation with US policy in the name of Europe taking on an independent role in the peace process.

Italy's policy, on the one hand, supported a European involvement in the peace process in the framework of a broader 'Mediterranean policy', which has to be, from the Italian point of view, one of the top European priorities and must not be neglected in favour of a policy more concentrated on enlargement problems and on the 'northern dimension'; on the other hand, Italy's internal political divisions tended to make its Middle East policy unsteady and unclear.

This quick overview is enough to confirm that all EU member states continue to have their own foreign policy agendas and to set their own priorities within these agendas with regard to their Middle East policy. It is also true that – notwithstanding the existence of the CFSP – foreign policy tends to remain the domain of the nation state and that foreign policymaking within the EU is an intergovernmental process. Nevertheless, since the creation of EPC, the European states have committed themselves to cooperation in the field of foreign policy, and this commitment has been confirmed and widened in scope with the Maastricht Treaty. In this context, the Middle East peace process has been one of the main objectives of European foreign policymaking and one of the issues most discussed among the member states.

This book tries to ascertain whether the distance between individual member state policies is narrowing through the practice of discussions aimed at the elaboration of a common foreign policy, as envisaged since the creation of EPC and reasserted through the Treaty on European Union in 1991 and the creation of the Common Foreign and Security Policy (CFSP) and then of the European Security and Defence Policy (ESDP). It also seeks to verify whether member states have been able to identify common interests in a sufficient number to encourage the implementation of a *collective* European policy, which would supposedly be more effective than separate and distinct national policies, or whether their policy may only be described as a policy of *'converging parallels'*, that is, a policy that may at times converge and be harmonic with that of the other member states, but remains, and will remain, essentially a *national* foreign policy, clearly distinct from, and only occasionally similar to, those of the other member states.

The instruments of European foreign policy

The second hypothesis that will be tested in this book is the following: the EU lacks the relevant levers and instruments to affect the Middle East peace process.

One of the main charges that has been brought against European foreign policy in the years of EPC is that it was mainly a declaratory policy without much substance, conducted in a 'club-like atmosphere' (Nuttall 1992; 2000; Smith 1998); that, being the result of endless discussions among the member states, it simply represented the minimum common denominator of all the different positions present within the Community, and that the instruments at its disposal were grossly insufficient in granting it much credibility, let alone effectiveness.

With the Treaty of Maastricht, and later with the Treaties of Amsterdam and Nice, the European Union tried to equip itself with new policy instruments that would assure coherence and consistency and therefore, it was hoped, effectiveness to foreign policy (Holland 1997; Richardson 1996). Two decades of experience with European Political Cooperation had made the member states aware of the constraints that limited the existing foreign policy mechanisms, while at the same prompting them to maximise the potential of the European Community as a global actor with an influential foreign policy (Smith 1998: 63–104).

On the other hand, most member states were still determined to retain control over foreign policy and reluctant to go beyond the intergovernmental framework of EPC and proceed towards a collective foreign policy (Allen 1998). These contradictory aspirations are very well exemplified by the separation that the member states were, and are, set on maintaining between economic policy ('low politics') and foreign policy ('high politics'). This separation proved completely artificial and highly inefficient in the years of EPC: the two policies emerged as being inextricably intertwined, and member states often found themselves forced to turn to the Community's economic policy instruments in order to implement decisions taken in the separate intergovernmental framework of the European Political Cooperation (ibid.).

With the Treaty of Maastricht the member states aimed to reduce the incoherence and inconsistency caused by this separation, assuring greater coordination between the two policy areas, while at the same time preserving their sovereignty over foreign policymaking (Edwards 1996; Nuttall 2001/3; Tietje 1997). The result of these two diverging aspirations is the formalised three-pillar structure of the European Union, which includes: (a) the first pillar, referred to as the European Community; (b) the second pillar for developing Common Foreign and Security Policy; and (c) the third pillar for developing cooperation in Justice and Home affairs (Wallace 2000: 5), these last two pillars being intergovernmental (Cameron 1999).

This formalised pillar structure makes the whole foreign policy-making mechanism intricate and ponderous, and causes unresolved tensions between intergovernmentalism and Community action in foreign policy.[5]

However, the separate pillar structure was the solution the member states agreed on to ensure that foreign policymaking would remain under their control and would not slip through their hands to become the domain of Community action.

The Treaty of Maastricht and the Treaty of Amsterdam introduced new foreign policy instruments: joint actions, common positions and common strategies. Furthermore, Maastricht introduced the role of 'special envoy' – a sort of pilot project for a European diplomat[6] – appointed by the EU Council (therefore in an intergovernmental framework) with a mandate in relation to particular policy issues. The Amsterdam Treaty then created the position of a High Representative (HR) for CFSP, implemented in 1999 with the appointment to the role of Javier Solana, who also combined the functions of Secretary General of the EU Council and Secretary General of WEU.

If the creation of these new positions seems to be a response to the need for facing external interlocutors and international crises with a single European referent, the fact that both of them are appointed and respond to the Council, and therefore to the intergovernmental dimension of foreign policy, shows to what extent the member states are still reluctant to delegate foreign policymaking to the EU.

The EU has used all of the aforementioned instruments in its Middle East policy, from the declaratory common positions to the sending of a special envoy, from the enunciation of a common European strategy to the participation of the HR in the negotiations. And, together with these more properly 'CFSP' instruments (i.e. second pillar instruments), first pillar EC instruments have been used to implement decisions taken in the framework of CFSP: from trade and cooperation agreements, to association agreements, to the provision of aid and extension of loans. The Middle East Peace Process has in fact often been a sort of 'testing ground' for European foreign policy instruments and has offered the EU the opportunity to experiment with new instruments and initiatives.

Greilsammer and Weiler (1987), in analysing European Political Cooperation policymaking, have drawn a distinction between (a) an 'active' policy, which seeks to influence events directly and to posit 'Europe' as an initiator of policy and a veritable world actor; (b) a 'reactive' policy, which is less concerned with direct influence, but rather with reacting to world events in order to minimise the costs to the reactive actor; and finally (c) a 'reflexive' policy, that is, a policy mainly concerned with the actual formation of a common policy as an integrative value per se.

Indeed, this reflexive dimension of EU policy towards the peace process can be said to hold relevant weight: the peace process has sometimes been used as a means to achieve internal – that is, European – objectives, and has become an instrument for 'flexing European muscles' innocuously. The peace process, in a way, has constituted a context in which mechanisms have been tried, structures experimented with, significant experience gained, and much sought-after consensus often obtained; it has provided the European Union with a real laboratory for the testing of most of its common foreign policy and security policy mechanisms (Greilsammer 1981; Greilsammer and Weiler 1988).

The peace process has offered the EU the opportunity to experiment with new instruments and initiatives – for example, through the appointment of a special envoy to the Middle East, the monitoring of elections in the Palestinian territories, or the training of Palestinian authorities in matters of security and the fight against terrorism in the territories under its control.

Thus, how can the ineffectiveness of this policy be explained? Why has the EU failed to influence the peace process significantly? This book tries to establish whether the instruments at the EU's disposal are:

1. Insufficient: insufficient foreign policy instruments would limit the EU's range of action, even in the presence of the shared willingness among European member states to develop an influential policy towards the Middle East that would make the EU an important actor and a referent for the parties involved in the peace process.
2. Inadequate: an inadequacy of the instruments may derive from the limited military means at the EU's disposal and from its reluctance to make extensive use of them. Given the nature of the Arab–Israeli conflict and the importance of its security dimension, this would render EU policy intrinsically weak and scarcely credible, making the inclusion of the EU in the peace process as a mediator much more difficult, and limiting its role to that of aid donor and important economic partner.
3. Misused: the inadequacy of the institutions in charge and the bureaucratic complexity may negatively affect the EU's capacity to use the available instruments to their greatest effect.
4. Underutilised: an underutilisation of foreign policy instruments may be the result of a lack, on the part of the member states, of the political will to exploit the potential offered by the instruments at the EU's disposal, in favour of the pursuit of separate national policies that mirror divergent national interests.

Transatlantic relations and EU Middle East policy: Cooperation and dependence, confrontation and competition

The third hypothesis tested in this book is the following: strategic US interests in the Middle East and the dynamics of EU–US relations have relegated the EU to a secondary role in the Middle East peace process.

Indeed, in analysing EU policy towards the Arab–Israeli peace process, one cannot avoid the crucial problem: is EU Middle East policy separable at all from transatlantic relations?

The end of the Cold War has changed the world's balance of power and security order: the United States has emerged as the only surviving superpower, and the new Russia has failed to fill the gap left by the Soviet Union. The Middle East is no longer viewed in a Cold War perspective. Global intervention in the Middle East no longer projects bipolar superpower rivalry in the region: post-Cold War global intervention takes on a unipolar form, with a dominant United States using its influence in the region (Buzan and Waever 1999) to protect its interests, which include ensuring the free flow of oil at reasonable prices; regional stability and prosperity, which would help protect oil supplies, create a market for American products and reduce the demand for US military involvement in the area; the security of the State of Israel; and the consolidation of the Arab–Israeli peace process, which could guarantee Israel's security and at the same time contribute to the stability of the entire region.

The end of the Cold War also led to a redefinition of EU interests and foreign policy priorities: the fall of the Berlin Wall marked the dissolution of the political cement of the communist threat, and, following the reunification of Germany, integration became an even more important issue for European stability (Wallace 1999a). With the Maastricht Treaty and the creation of the CFSP, the European Union aimed to achieve a common foreign policy able to project onto the international arena the combined power of its member states, whose weight and influence in international affairs, it was hoped, would be stronger than that exercised by each state individually.

In the Middle East, the EU shares many interests with the United States: the promotion of the region's stability and prosperity, as well as the protection of the flow of oil supplies on which it depends heavily. Due to its geographical proximity and strong economic ties with the region, the EU risks being seriously affected by problems arising in the Middle East, such as an instability spillover, uncontrolled migration flows, proliferation of weapons of mass destruction, and the spread of terrorism (Gordon 1998). The consolidation of the Arab–Israeli peace process is one of the EU's central interests, as it would aid stability and enhance the chances of resources and efforts being directed to the economic and political development of the region. On the other hand, Europe must balance its support for the search of a just and lasting solution to the conflict between the

Arabs and Israel with its interests in the Arab world (Gompert and Larrabee 1998: 196).

The end of the Cold War and the subsequent collapse of the Soviet Union created a political vacuum in the Middle East, which could have represented a political opening for the EU. Theoretically, there was the opportunity to redefine EU–US interaction and the dynamics of burden-sharing in the region, and Europe could potentially have increased its role and influence in the Middle East peace process.

The start of the peace process in 1991, however, saw the United States (considering the inexorable decline of the Soviet Union) as the only accredited mediator (Moisi 2001; Neugart 2003; Serfaty 2000), accepted by both the Arabs (Sayigh 1991) and the Israelis (Adler 1998) and able to exert a definite political influence. Europe was invited only as a participant to the Peace Conference, and its potential role as an additional mediator was refused by the main actors involved in the process.

Although initially cut out from the core negotiations and diplomatic efforts of the peace process initiated at Madrid, the European Union nevertheless gradually expanded its role, at least in its area of comparative advantage, that is, the economic area. Over the 1990s, the EU's economic role in the peace process increased progressively, to the point that the EU became the major single aid donor to the Palestinians. The logic of the peace process – in the EU's view – was that trade and cooperation were to underpin peace, Palestinian economic development being Israel's best long-term guarantee of security. This assumption was the justification behind the European Union's massive financial assistance to the consolidation of the peace process, the underlying logic being that this was a necessary precondition for keeping the peace process on track (Richmond 2000).[7]

On the other hand, Europe's enhanced economic role in the peace process has not been matched by a similar increase in its political influence: the United States remained the only mediator between the parties, and the EU played a diplomatically and politically complementary role to that of the United States (Hollis 1997). In a way, it provided the 'basic economic foundation of the peace process', but lacked the military instruments and security institutions to make a contribution on the front of security – which remained the domain of the Unites States – and also lacked the unitary dimension of action that in such negotiations necessarily qualifies an effective mediator (Barbé 1998; Barbé and Izquierdo 1997).

The American position was ambivalent: on the one hand, the United States wanted to keep its primary role in the peace process, so as to protect its interests however it saw fit; on the other hand, it was happy to delegate a relevant part of the financial assistance to the Palestinians to the EU, as it was not willing to accept a free-riding European Union that exploited the security coverage offered by the United States without offering at least the limited assistance it was able to provide (limited diplomatically speaking, but substantial in economic terms) (Lesch 2003; Lesser 1998; Marr 1994). The United States is well aware of the fact that an economic growth of the Palestinian Authority is a necessary precondition for the consolidation of the peace process, and is willing to recognise a prominent role of the EU in this field, as long as it remains politically in line with US plans.

The United States' influence on the European Union takes different forms. At a collective level, all EU member states benefit from US presence in the region and the security guarantees that stem from that presence. The United States keeps the Sixth Fleet stationed in the Mediterranean, has substantial military assets in the region and provides enormous military assistance to friendly countries of the region (such as Egypt and Israel); all this, while protecting US security interests, guarantees a security coverage to Europe as well, and at the same time contributes to deferring the problem of a strong European defence capacity. Even France, which has always promoted a more active EU involvement in the Middle East, has come to realise, especially following the experience of the Gulf War, that the EU is not – or at least not yet – able to guarantee security either in the region, or of its own territory from the dangers deriving from instability.[8] In the period considered, and under the US security umbrella, the EU has been largely able to avoid tackling in a decisive fashion the potentially highly divisive issue of how Europe should protect itself from dangers deriving from an insecurity spillover from the Middle East.[9]

At the member states' level, American influence triggers vastly different reactions. Some member states, such as Britain,[10] Germany (Aggestam 2000: 70; Bulmer, Jeffery and Paterson 2000), the Netherlands (Tonra 2001) and Italy (De Michelis and Kostner 2003), are highly aware of the risk that a EU move from a declaratory policy towards active diplomacy always brings with itself the risk of a crisis in transatlantic relations: these countries have often pushed for a low-profile EU policy vis-à-vis the Arab–Israeli conflict, complementary to that of the United States and limited mainly to providing economic aid to the region, and particularly to the Palestinian Authority; a contribution that the United States itself welcomes for its stabilising effects.

Some countries, in particular France, are not satisfied with a US-dominated peace process and wish for a more active EU policy. French leaders have often argued that the European Union partly defines itself through emancipation from the United States' dominant influence, and that confrontation with the United States at times stimulates cohesion between Member States (Blunden 2000).

Transatlantic relations are indeed of paramount importance in understanding and evaluating EU policy towards the Middle East peace process: this book tries to analyse the dynamics of these relations and of the burden-sharing process that takes place between the EU and the United States in the Middle East, and tries to understand how, and in what measure, the United States exerts its influence over EU Middle East policy.

Structure of the book

The book will proceed as follows.

Chapter 2 provides the historical background, tracing the formulation of European policy towards the Arab–Israeli conflict from the creation of European Political Cooperation in 1969, and analysing its development until the Maastricht Conference and the introduction of the Common Foreign and Security Policy; the chapter also offers a brief overview of the structure of EPC and of the instruments the member states had at their disposal to deal with the problem of the Middle East conflict.

Chapter 3 provides an overview of the main developments in the Middle East peace process between the years 1991 and 1999. It highlights the most important changes in European foreign policymaking that took place in this period, with special reference to those innovations relevant to EU policy towards the Middle East. Lastly, the chapter analyses the evolution of the EU's strategy and initiatives towards the region, from the inception of the peace process at the Madrid Peace Conference in 1991 to the issuing of the Berlin Declaration in 1999.

Chapter 4 focuses on the EU Strategy for the Middle East peace process in the Bush era, on its role in the Quartet for Peace in the Middle East and on the struggles of diplomacy after the 2007 Annapolis Peace Conference.

Chapter 5 studies the dynamics of the relations between national foreign policies and foreign policy at the EU level towards the Middle East conflict, with the objective of establishing what has encouraged policy convergence, and to what extent a collective policy has been achieved; and what, on the other hand, has kept national policies 'parallel' and therefore separate and clearly distinct from each other.[11]

Chapter 6 conducts an analysis of the progressive, incremental construction of the edifice of Common Foreign and Security Policy, and the stratification of the instruments at its disposal, with a parallel analysis of the immediate use of these instruments in a specific foreign policy context such as the Arab–Israeli peace process.

Chapter 7 focuses on American and European policy in the Greater Middle East and on the state of transatlantic relations in this region of critical importance for both the United States and the EU. The chapter analyses the elements of convergence and divergence in American and European policies towards the region, with the objective of identifying the patterns of continuity and change that characterise the dynamics of the transatlantic relationship in this extremely contentious issue-area.[12]

The conclusion brings together the guiding threads of all the chapters and summarises the findings of the book, with the objective of answering the question posed at the beginning of this chapter: 'why has the EU spent so much time on Middle East policy, to so little effect?'

2
European Political Cooperation and the Middle East Conflict (1969–1990)

Introduction

In late May 1967, in the midst of an international crisis on the eve of the Six-Day War, an EEC Summit of the Six Heads of State or Government took place in Rome, primarily to discuss the prospect of the UK's accession to the Community, which was strongly opposed by France (Mammarella and Cacace 1998: 128–9).

The international situation called for a common Community declaration on the Middle East crisis – or at least this was the opinion of some member states – but positions were so irreconcilable that the Six came nowhere near such an achievement (Dosenrode and Stubkjaer 2002: 65): 'I felt ashamed at the Rome summit. Just as the war was on the point of breaking out, we could not even agree to talk about it', were German Chancellor Kiesinger's words following the summit (Greilsammer 1981: 64).

But this failure to reach a common position was only a prelude to what would happen a few days later, when the war broke out. Indeed, the Six achieved the remarkable result of each expressing a different position, following their traditional national policy and privileging what was perceived to be the national interest: attitudes ranged from France's strong condemnation of Israel and support for the Arabs, to Germany's support of Israel, disguised behind a formal neutrality (Greilsammer and Weiler 1987: 25).

23

The member states' different traditions and interests in the Middle East, the differing intensity of their ties with Israel and with the Arab world, and the inability to agree on a political role for Western Europe alongside the United States, all contributed to the failure to reach an agreement on that occasion (Steinbach 1980). The following two years saw hardly any attempt to harmonise the member states' policies towards the Middle East conflict (Ifestos 1987: 420); however, the inability of the EC to respond adequately and, if not unanimously, at least in harmonious coordination to major world crises was becoming increasingly evident and was a striking contrast to the increasing economic weight of the Community – especially in view of the likely imminent enlargement of the Community to include the United Kingdom, Denmark and Ireland.

The Six, and in particular France (Wallace, Wallace and Webb 1977), increasingly felt the urgency to promote an enhanced political role for Europe in the world. Arguably their failure to adequately face the Middle East crisis in 1967 was one of the main triggers of the new developments that were to take place shortly thereafter in the process of European integration.

In December 1969, with a few lines unobtrusively located at the end of the official communiqué of the Conference of the Heads of Government held at The Hague – known as The Hague Summit Declaration – the Ministers of Foreign Affairs of the European Community member states were instructed to 'study the best way of achieving progress in the matter of political unification, within the context of enlargement'.[1]

In turn, the six Foreign Ministers instructed the Belgian Political Director, Vicomte Davignon, to prepare a report which would serve as the basis for the future European Foreign Policy. The report, on which Davignon worked with the Political Directors of the other five foreign ministries, was finally presented and approved at the Luxembourg Conference of Foreign Ministers on 27 October 1970, and is known as the Davignon or Luxembourg Report.

The Hague Summit Declaration and the Davignon Report sanctioned the official birth of European Political Cooperation (EPC) – the nucleus of what more than twenty years later would become the Common Foreign and Security Policy (CFSP) – and defined its initial structure. The rationale behind the creation of the EPC was, to use the Luxembourg Report's words, 'to pave the way for a united Europe capable of assuming its responsibilities in the world of tomorrow and of making a contribution commensurate with its traditions and its mission'.[2]

The new European Political Cooperation was to be carried out through two annual meetings of the Foreign Ministers, and the work of a Committee of Political Directors and ad hoc working groups.

In fact, the activities of EPC were – at French insistence – kept as separate as possible from those of the Commission and of the Parliament, denoting France's clear intention to keep the process separate from that of the Communities and strictly within the limits of intergovernmental procedures.

This model of political cooperation basically 'relied on the principle of official collegiality to build up the consensus in preparation for foreign ministers' intergovernmental decisions' (Hill and Smith 2000: 75). The member states, in other words, were torn between two different aspirations: on the one hand, that of responding to international crisis more adequately, trying to project in the international arena the combined political weight of all the Community members through foreign policy coordination; on the other hand, that of retaining national control over crucial foreign policy decisions that were perceived to belong to a state's exclusive competence.

The first EPC ministerial meeting took place in Munich in November 1970. Together with the Conference on Security and Co-operation in Europe (CSCE), the Middle East conflict and the necessity to harmonise the Six's policy towards it were among the topics chosen to be discussed. France in particular was pressing for the issue to be discussed among the member states in the hope of influencing a shift towards a more pro-Arab stance – in line with France's own policy – in the EC (Agate and Imperiali 1984).

At the time of the meeting, though, the member states' positions were still too divergent and distant from each other for an agreement over a common public document to be reached (Hill and Smith 2000: 297). What is of interest here, however, is the fact that, since that first meeting in Munich, the Middle East conflict has been an almost permanent feature of EPC discussions, regardless of the very limited success achieved by the EC in dealing with the matter.

It can be said that certain principles and guidelines of today's European Union Middle East policy took shape as far back as in the years of EPC, and in particular between 1970 and 1980, and it is therefore worth analysing these early EC initiatives (or lack of them) in order to identify possible patterns of continuity and change that may help understand and interpret the more recent EU policy.

After The Hague Summit Communiqué, EPC progressively developed and new instruments of political cooperation were slowly added, mainly in an informal and incremental fashion; the Middle East was then very often used by the member states as a testing ground for these instruments. This chapter will conduct an analysis of EC policies towards the Middle East conflict during the years up to the creation of CFSP, but before that it will offer a brief overview of the structure of EPC and of the instruments the member states had at their disposal to deal with the issue.

A short bureaucratic digression: The structure of EPC

The Luxembourg Report (1970): The first step

The 1970 Luxembourg or Davignon Report defined the initial structure of European Political Cooperation (EPC). This embryonic form of European Foreign Policy – devoid of any kind of legal basis – was endowed with a very limited range of instruments, if any at all: the structure of EPC foresaw no more than two meetings per year of the member states' Foreign Ministers, three meetings per year of a Political Committee (consisting of the Political Affairs Directors of the national Foreign Ministries), and the creation of specialised working groups on specific issues of potential common interest. No secretariat was created, and it was clear that EPC relied 'on the principle of official collegiality to build up consensus in preparation for foreign ministers' intergovernmental decisions' (Hill and Smith 2000: 75). The burden of EPC initiatives came largely to rest on the rotating Presidency, a fact that was bound to impose limitations in terms of the continuity and coherence of EPC action.

As mentioned above, the rationale behind the creation of EPC was the urgency, felt especially by France, to promote an increased political role for Europe in the world,[3] while at the same time maintaining any form of cooperation in the field of foreign policy strictly within the limits of intergovernmental procedures.[4]

The objectives of European Political Cooperation, as stated in the Davignon Report, were to be the following:[5]

- to ensure, through regular exchanges of information and consultations, a better mutual understanding on the great international problems,
- to strengthen [member states'] solidarity by promoting the harmonisation of their views, the coordination of their positions, and, where it appears possible and desirable,
- common actions.

The Copenhagen Report (1973): Incrementalism and (in) consistency

Two subsequent Reports modified – albeit moderately – the very light structure of EPC, in essence sanctioning its incremental and 'unofficial' development. The Copenhagen Report in 1973 increased the number of Foreign Minister meetings to four a year and stipulated that the Political Committee should meet as frequently as needed (i.e. on a monthly basis); it also introduced the COREU (Correspondence Européenne) telex network among participating states, and set up a Group of Correspondents entrusted with the task of following the implementation of political cooperation.

In its last two articles (Part II, articles 11 and 12.b) the Report touched upon an issue that was destined to permanently affect the formulation of a common European Foreign Policy: the question of consistency.[6] The problem of consistency, or rather of inconsistency, affects foreign policymaking at the European level in several ways, which have been very effectively categorised by Simon Nuttall (2001/3):

- 'horizontal' consistency between the different policies of the EU;
- 'institutional' consistency between the two different bureaucratic apparatuses, intergovernmental and Community;
- 'vertical' consistency between EU and national policies.

Indeed, ever since its inception, EPC carried the seed of an inconsistency that was bound to characterise all its manifestations: its structure was light, strictly intergovernmental and entirely separate from the Community structure. On the other hand, its aim was grand, as EPC was supposed to represent the channel through which Europe would speak with 'one voice' and would finally take up the position it deserved in the world.

The member states, while acknowledging the need for increased political coordination within the framework of the EC, nevertheless wanted to make sure that each of their voices would be adequately discernible, and provided for a structure that resembled more a 'choir of voices' than 'one voice', and a potentially very discordant choir at that. National foreign policy choices and priorities could potentially block political cooperation at the European level at any time; in addition, the artificial separation of EPC and Community policies, while affording the member states the reassuring perception that EPC would safely remain within the limits of intergovernmental cooperation, soon proved to be a constant source of problems, as it was hardly possible to consistently keep external economic relations and foreign policymaking unconnected.

In order to at least alleviate these problems, therefore, the Copenhagen Report stipulated that 'for matters which have an incidence on Community activities, close contact [would] be maintained with the institutions of the Community', and that 'the Commission [would be] invited to make known its views ...'[7]

The Gymnich Formula (1974): The informal dimension of EPC

An illuminating episode in the development of EPC was the informal approval, in 1974, of the so-called Gymnich Formula, a gentlemen's agreement which provided that 'if any member of EPC [would] raise within the framework of EPC the question of informing and consulting an ally or friendly state, the Nine [would] discuss the matter and, upon reaching agreement, authorise the Presidency to proceed on that basis'.[8]

The agreement was devised to solve tensions that were arising with the United States as a consequence of America's demand to be allowed to sit in on all EPC meetings.[9] The member states had no intention whatsoever of consenting verbatim to this request, permitting the United States to be present at all levels of their policymaking, but on the other hand could not afford to badly compromise their relations with the United States. The solution devised is strongly revealing of the nature of EPC: an informal agreement, not even in written form, that allowed the Presidency to consult the United States on behalf of its partners on matters of importance. Once again, then, much of the burden of EPC initiatives was to be borne by the Presidency; however, the unofficial nature of the agreement left enough room for alternative solutions, so that, should the rotating Presidency be held by either a small country or a country with less than idyllic relations with the United States, contacts could be established through other channels, including – of course – bilateral channels.

The London Report (1981): The official birth of EPC bureaucracy

The third Report that contributed to define and codify EPC was the London Report, in 1981. The Report, in the usual 'EPC style', acknowledged developments that were already taking place and introduced a few new instruments. The former included the recognition of the so called 'troika' system in the procedures for EPC–Third Country contacts,[10] and the insistence on the principle of full association of the Commission with the work of EPC, with the objective of pursuing at least what has been referred to above as 'institutional' and 'horizontal' consistency.[11]

The new instruments introduced were a crisis procedure, which provided that the Political Committee or a Ministerial meeting could convene within forty-eight hours at the request of three member states,[12] and the setting up of an embryonic EPC secretariat, in the form of a small team of officials seconded from preceding and succeeding presidencies to aid the Presidency in office.[13] The Report also explicitly stated that EPC was an appropriate forum for discussing 'certain important foreign policy questions bearing on the political aspects of security'.[14]

The Single European Act (1986): An official basis for EPC

EPC was finally given an official basis in the Single European Act (SEA), signed in 1986 and entered into force in 1987. The SEA placed the Communities and EPC within one single document but kept EPC separate from the Community's legal order. An official EPC Secretariat to be based in Brussels was created, and the necessity to ensure consistency between EC external relations and EPC was once again reaffirmed.

European foreign policy towards the Middle East conflict (1969–1974)

These eleven years saw the first attempts of the EC to shape a unified policy towards the Middle East: from the first meetings of EPC – characterised by disagreements and the impossibility of reaching a compromise – to the Venice Declaration, a milestone of European policy towards the Arab–Israeli conflict, which contains many principles that are still valid for the EU today.

However, if, on the one hand, the Venice Declaration may be seen as a positive achievement for EPC as a form of political agreement over a difficult and controversial issue, on the other hand, a closer look at the actual developments of the EC's political initiatives in this period reveals a tendency towards a minimum common denominator, an incapacity to display solidarity within the Community, a different prioritisation of policy issues (e.g. relations with Israel, relations with the United States, relations with the Arab States), which all led ultimately to an unsuccessful and ineffective policy, if by *'effective'* policy we mean a policy that intends to influence events and does so successfully (Nuttall 1992; Regelsberger, de Schoutheete de Tervarent and Wessels 1997).

In analysing the EC policy towards the Middle East, certain crucial elements should not be overlooked: following the 1956 Suez crisis, the decline of Great Britain's and France's influence in the Middle East had proven irreversible; the Six-Day War saw the consolidation of American leadership in the area and the strengthening of the US–Israel special relationship; furthermore, the Middle East was increasingly becoming a crucial field of confrontation between the United States and the USSR in the framework of the Cold War (Brands 1994; Lesch 2003). All these factors made it very difficult for the EC to become an influential actor in the region; considering also the very limited range of instruments that EC member states had at their disposal to express a collective foreign policy and their even more limited willingness to actually make an effort to harmonise policy differences, it is not surprising that the EC's Middle East policy has been less then a success (Zielonka 1998a).

As previously mentioned, after the chaotic and uncoordinated reaction to the Six-Day War, the Six attempted to harmonise their position, and the Political Committee was instructed to study the possibility of issuing a joint paper. During the first months of 1971, however, disagreement continued to characterise discussions on Middle East policy within the Political Committee, reflecting the different positions of each of the member states; divergence spanned over issues as diverse as the refugee status, or the question of Jerusalem, and the attempt to find a common denominator resulted in each member state presenting its own report on a chosen topic and defending its own position with a noticeable lack of conciliatory spirit. By May 1971, nonetheless, mostly following ongoing pressure from France (Allen and Pijpers 1984) in the direction of obtaining some form of consensus, an agreement – or rather a compromise – was found, and the Six announced the imminent release of their first 'joint paper' on the Middle East conflict. However, this first European success was marred by German and Dutch objections to making the document's content public. The paper, which is known as the Schuman Paper and was largely based on UN Resolution 242,[15] remained unpublished, but its contents were leaked to the public in the German press, causing considerable opposition in German public opinion, which saw it as too supportive of the Arabs.

Domestic pressures caused the German Foreign Minister Scheel to assert during a visit to Israel that the document was only a 'working paper' and merely constituted a basis for further discussions among the Six (Greilsammer and Weiler 1987: 28), a declaration that in turn caused great irritation in Paris, clearly showing the limits of a common European policy towards the Middle East conflict.

In the two years that followed the Schuman Paper there were no other common initiatives on the part of the EC regarding the Middle East, but it must be noted that '*each* of the Nine continued to develop a positive reassessment of Arab demands [...] and relations with Israel continued to deteriorate' (ibid.).

In fact, a certain trend was gradually taking shape: the completely divergent positions adopted by the member states in the wake of the Six-Day War were slowly starting to converge, and especially the States more supportive of Israel were reconsidering their position towards the Arab world. This shift, well exemplified for instance by the visit of Joseph Luns of Holland to Saudi Arabia and Kuwait in January 1971, or by the toughening of Belgian policy regarding the status of Jerusalem, was strongly supported by France, who favoured a convergence of the EC member states towards its pro-Arab stance and insisted on the necessity of reaching some form of consensus before the accession of the three new member states in January 1973 (ibid.: 27). A new path in cooperation among European member states deserves to be mentioned. An upsurge of international terrorism, exemplified by the terrorist attack on Israeli athletes during the 1972 Olympic Games in Munich, gave the European governments a clear perception of Europe's exposure to cross-border terrorism and prompted an enhanced cooperation on this issue. In December 1975 the so-called Trevi Group was created by the Rome European Council, with the objective of promoting (a) cooperation in the fight against terrorism; (b) exchange of information about terrorist organisation; and (c) the equipment and training of police organisations, in particular in anti-terrorist tactics (Den Boer and Wallace 2000). This initial informal cooperation among security services and law enforcement agencies represents the original nucleus of what in the Maastricht Treaty became formalised as the third Pillar of the European Union, that is, Justice and Home Affairs.

The Nine's reaction to the October 1973 Yom Kippur War was in some ways similar to the reaction that followed the Six-Day War: each State adopted a different position along the lines of its traditional policy. What changed the situation was the subsequent oil crisis, which on the one hand persuaded some member states – in particular France and the United Kingdom – of the necessity to find a common EC position, and on the other exposed the lack of solidarity among EC members, as each country started a competition to gain the Arab States' favour (Garfinkle 1983: 4).

Immediately after the war, the Organisation of Petroleum Exporting Countries (OPEC) decided to place an embargo on the EC and, to exploit the leverage of the 'oil weapon' to the full, it differentiated EC member states into three categories, thus effectively obtaining the result of setting all countries against each other. The countries were classified as follows:

1. 'hostile countries', on which a ban on exports was imposed (the Netherlands, plus of course the United States)
2. 'neutral states', where a 5% cutback sanction was applied (Belgium, Denmark, Germany, Ireland, Italy and Luxembourg)
3. 'friendly or most favoured nations', where no sanctions were imposed (France and the United Kingdom) (Jawad 1992: 67).

A direct result of the embargo was a Joint Declaration issued by the Nine in November, which marked a clear shift towards a more distinctly pro-Arab position, inspired by the French (Dosenrode and Stubkjaer 2002: 86): the declaration made mention for the first time of the 'legitimate rights of the Palestinians' and spoke of 'the need for Israel to end the territorial occupation which it has maintained since the conflict of 1967'.[16]

The statement obtained the desired results: the OPEC decided to interrupt the 5% cutback on oil to the 'neutral States' – but maintained the embargo on the Netherlands. The Dutch appealed to the other member states to secure their supplies, but without success: Community solidarity was not important enough to risk antagonising the Arab States. The impasse and the tension between the member states was later resolved through 'secret diplomacy encouraged by the United States, resulting in allocation of oil on a pro-rata basis by the multinational oil corporations' (Ifestos 1987: 428).

Two elements emerged from the oil crisis: on the one hand, the frailty of European cohesion and the extent to which the objective of a collective foreign policy was far from being achieved; on the other hand, a conflict with the United States took shape that was to have several effects: in some ways it encouraged further European integration, especially as a result of French pressures to differentiate European policy from American policy, pursuing an autonomous stance in the Middle East, while at the same time restraining this very same process of integration, as the full extent of the EC's dependence on the United States became clear, not only in terms of security, but also in economic and political matters.

The following events deserve attention when these developments are analysed.

In December 1973 an EC Summit was held in Copenhagen; on the first day a delegation of Foreign Ministers of several Arab States arrived at the Summit and delivered a message to the EC on behalf of the Arab League. No foreigners had ever been admitted to an EC Summit before, including the Americans, and this unprecedented event, described by one author as the 'ultimate in fawning at the feet of the Arab leaders' (Feld 1978: 69), caused considerable resentment in Washington. At the conclusion of the Copenhagen Summit the EC announced its intention to enter into negotiations with oil-producing countries to promote 'comprehensive arrangements comprising co-operation on a wide scale for economic and industrial development, industrial investments, and stable energy supplies to the Member Countries at reasonable prices'.[17] This dialogue, which was to take on the name of the Euro-Arab Dialogue, was viewed quite differently by the two sides (Allen 1978): the Europeans were interested in the economic dimension, whereas the Arab countries wanted to focus on the political dimension and 'intended to use oil as a political lever in order to gain the support of the European Community in their war against Israel'.[18]

The second event took place in February 1974, when the United States government succeeded, after various delays, in convening thirteen nations[19] to the Washington Energy Conference, to work out a common programme aimed at easing the energy crisis.

Nonetheless, a clear divergence, if not conflict, between the French and American approaches to the oil crisis was taking shape: while the Americans wanted to build a 'consumer's front' to oppose the embargo, the French favoured bilateral negotiations and bargaining with oil-producing countries and the improvement of relations with the Arabs (Feld 1978: 70).[20]

France refused to take part in the Washington Conference and the Energy Coordinating Group (ECG)[21] that was created thereafter – and that would subsequently lead to the creation of the International Energy Agency (IEA).

However, while the rest of the EC member states yielded to American pressures and participated in the ECG, at the same time they also followed at least a part of France's policy. Only a few weeks after the Washington Conference, in March 1974, the Community Foreign Ministers, deliberating in the context of EPC, announced the official launch of the Euro-Arab Dialogue.

Tensions with the United States were mounting quickly: during the Washington Conference President Nixon had already underlined how 'security and economic considerations are inevitably linked and energy cannot be separated from either'.[22]

The announcement of the opening of the Euro-Arab dialogue further worsened transatlantic relations and prompted a succession of harsh public statements from the highest American authorities. President Nixon was very direct in outlining US views on the matter: '[...] The Europeans cannot have it both ways. They cannot have the United States' participation and co-operation on the security front and then proceed to have confrontation and even hostility on the economic and political fronts [...] We are not going to be faced with a situation where the Nine countries of Europe gang up against the United States which is their guarantee for security. That we cannot have'.[23]

Henry Kissinger was also extremely negative in his comments, pointing out that American allies were losing sight of the greater common transatlantic interests while concentrating on self-assertiveness (Ifestos 1987: 433). He went further, clearly stating what his opinion was of the EC's role in the Middle East: 'The Europeans will be unable to achieve anything in the Middle East in a million years.'[24]

This first phase of the European Community's efforts to take on a role in the Middle East, and the subsequent tensions that arose with the United States, somehow became paradigmatic of transatlantic relations in the region, as we shall see when analysing the nature of the same relations two decades later: certain dynamics of European and American policies and of their interrelations have changed very little since the time of the Yom Kippur War and the first oil crisis, even after the profound changes introduced to the international framework by the end of the Cold War.

As previously mentioned, after the Six-Day War the United States established its leadership in the region more clearly, and, in an effort to consolidate and expand this leadership, did not welcome any interference from the European allies. Linkage tactics between the EC's policy towards the Arabs and the security guarantees offered to Europe by the United States were used to keep the member states under pressure, and to make them realise that an autonomous EC stance in the Middle East – that is, a stance not welcomed by the United States – could only be reached at the cost of damaging US–EC relations, and of putting into question American commitments in the Old Continent.

A further crucial element in the American attitude towards European Middle East policy, beyond the resentment against any form of intrusion in something that was considered an exclusive US domain, was a basic distrust in the possibility of Europe's actually achieving anything in the Middle East, closely linked with American contempt for the EC's incapacity to achieve consensus and express a united position. All these elements are still largely present in American views, as is – it must be said – Europe's inability to act harmoniously.

In 1974 the American administration, upset by the EC's policy towards the Middle East in general and the Arab states in particular, by the reluctance with which the member states were following American 'directives' in the field of energy policy, and by the progressive shift of the EC's stance on the Arab–Israeli conflict towards pro-Arab positions, decided that a way had to be found to enable the United States to control and influence European foreign policymaking. Therefore, the United States started to exert pressure on the EC to be allowed to sit in on all EPC meetings, 'to ensure that they were able to influence any matters that the Europeans chose to discuss, which they felt impinged on their own interests' (Kohler 1982). The member states were thus faced with what was to become a permanent dilemma: prioritising between their relations with the United States and the importance of furthering European political integration. If for France, for instance, the development of a European foreign policy had meant from the start differentiation from the Americans, even at the cost of putting transatlantic relations at risk, for the United Kingdom things were – and still are – very different: its relations with the United States are considered a crucial national interest, far more critical than the construction of an independent European role in the Middle East. For this reason, the United Kingdom at first refused to support the launching of the Euro-Arab dialogue unless an agreement was found on how to associate the United States with the political cooperation procedures (Ifestos 1987: 434). The solution found in June 1974 was the aforementioned informal agreement that took the name of 'Gymnich Formula', by which the EC Presidency was to consult the United States on behalf of its partners in time for the latter to influence outcomes on matters of importance (Hill and Smith 2000: 97). In other words, the United States was to be considered a 'special case' among the third countries with which the EC entertained relations, and, even if not allowed to be present during EPC deliberations, was to be granted the possibility of having a say when decisions could be relevant for its interests.

European foreign policy towards the Middle East conflict (1975–1990)

1975–1980

The first Euro-Arab Dialogue (EAD) ministerial meeting took place in July 1974; it was followed by a number of meetings up to 1979, when the Dialogue was basically suspended as a consequence of the signing of the Camp David agreement and of the expulsion of Egypt from the Arab League. From the start, the dialogue was haunted by the different expectations of the parties involved: European aspirations to keep the Dialogue within the boundaries of economic, technical and cultural cooperation were soon to clash with the clear intentions on the part of the Arab States to exploit it for political purposes. The divergence sparked an endless confrontation between the EC and the Arab States that ultimately emptied the Dialogue of its potential significance (Garfinkle 1983: 11).[25]

The first move of the EC was to exclude both oil and the Middle East conflict from the matters to be put on the EAD's agenda. However, this strategy did not succeed in preventing these issues from conditioning the Dialogue: in 1975 the Arabs asked the EC to give up the free trade agreement it was about to sign with Israel (Jawad 1992: 94), and, as a further crucial concession with important symbolic value, they tried to put pressure on the EC to allow an independent representation of the PLO in the Dialogue: neither of these two requests were met by the EC, which managed to stand firm on its decision.

However, in the years between 1975 and 1977, the EC's relations with Israel deteriorated significantly: as criticism of Jewish settlements in the territories became harsher and the problem of the Palestinian people's rights became increasingly central in EC discussions, even traditionally pro-Israeli countries like the Netherlands, West Germany, Denmark and Luxembourg started to shift their position towards a more pro-Arab stance (Greilsammer and Weiler 1987: 35). This deterioration of EC–Israel relations was then accelerated by the victory of Begin's Likud in the Israeli elections of June 1977. The displacement of the Labour Party by Likud in effect brought an anti-West European elite to power in Israel: Begin and his government looked much more directly to the United States, rather than Europe; they cultivated links with the Jewish communities in the United States, whereas the Jewish communities in London, Paris and elsewhere in Western Europe remained more favourably oriented towards Labour and the more moderate elements in Israeli politics. Furthermore, Begin's policy of increasing the settlements in the territories and his claim to all the land of historic Israel gave the European governments a reason – or, as Greilsammer and Weiler put it, a pretext – to stiffen their position on the conflict (ibid.: 37).

In June 1977 the Nine, at the European Council in London, issued a new joint statement, worth analysing as it contains relevant points that represented an evolution of the EC's position. In fact, paragraph 3 of the London Statement declares: 'The Nine have affirmed their belief that a solution to the conflict in the Middle East will be possible only if the legitimate right of the Palestinian people to give effective expression to its national identity is translated into fact, which would take into account the need for a homeland for the Palestinian people. They consider that the representatives of the parties to the conflict, including the Palestinian people, must participate in the negotiations in an appropriate manner to be worked out in consultation between all the parties concerned.'[26]

With this Statement some of the most relevant features of what would become the distinctive European stance on the conflict were delineated:

- the Palestinian question was firmly placed at the heart of the Middle East conflict
- the idea of a homeland for the Palestinians took shape. At the time of the London Statement the concept of 'homeland' was still undefined and did not necessarily imply the concept of a sovereign state, but soon afterwards the project of a Palestinian State was to take form and become central in EC policy
- the EC claimed that the best approach to the resolution of the conflict was a comprehensive settlement rather than a process built on bilateral negotiations.

Europe's position as delineated above was very distant from Israel's: in Israel's view, the Arab world's refusal to recognise the State of Israel was the central problem (Greilsammer and Weiler 1987: 39), and not the Palestinian question; the idea of the creation of a Palestinian State was strongly rejected at the time, and bilateral negotiations that would imply mutual recognition and lead to separate peace treaties were considered the preferred option to solve the conflict with the Arabs.

A few months after the issuing of the London Statement, President Sadat's visit to Israel and the subsequent opening of Egypt–Israeli negotiations seemed to prove that the policy of bilateral contacts was the one destined to bring the most successful results. These negotiations and the preponderant role played in them by the United States relegated the EC completely to the sidelines.

When the talks eventually led to the signing of the Camp David accords and, in 1979, of a peace treaty between Israel and Egypt under American auspices, the EC offered – if unenthusiastically – its support to the peace process, underlining nonetheless that it did so 'as a first step in the direction of a comprehensive settlement'.[27]

In the following months the EC slowly distanced itself from the Camp David process as it developed the conviction that this process would not solve the Palestinian problem, which its members viewed as the core of the Middle East problem. France and Britain in particular put pressure on the other member states to launch an autonomous European peace initiative for the Middle East that would clearly distinguish itself from the American-led Camp David process: the idea was quite ambitious at this stage, and it also had the advantage, in the eyes of the Europeans, of pleasing the Arabs, who had been asking the EC to issue a new statement for some time. But the project met with the strong opposition of both Israel and the United States: Israel launched a vigorous diplomatic campaign to block the European initiative, and the United States exerted its influence to make sure that the content of the EC declaration would not harm the Camp David process, and to play down European aspirations of acting independently in the Middle East.

On 13 June 1980, the Heads of State and Government of the Nine met at the European Council in Venice and finally issued their joint resolution, known today as the Venice Declaration.[28] As was predictable following American pressures, the text of the declaration was a very 'domesticated' one, even if it did contain some very relevant points. Indeed, Paragraph 6 of the Declaration states: 'The Palestinian people, which is conscious of existing as such, must be placed in a position, by an appropriate process defined within the framework of the comprehensive peace settlement, to exercise fully its right to self-determination;' and in paragraph 7 it declares that 'the PLO will have to be associated with the negotiations'.[29]

The United States was ultimately satisfied with the content of the Declaration, as it felt that it had attained the best possible result from the EC, managing to obtain through its pressures a much more moderate statement than originally intended.

Israel's reaction, on the other hand, was extremely negative, as the document was in striking antithesis to Israeli policy in its definition – among other things – of the Palestinian problem and in its insistence on the participation of the PLO in the negotiations. Furthermore, the Palestinians themselves were not satisfied because, following the American intervention, the Venice Declaration did not recognise the PLO as the sole representative of the Palestinian people, nor did it call for the desired modification of resolution 242 with the replacement of the word 'refugees' with the word 'Palestinians' (Greilsammer and Weiler 1987: 45).

The Venice Declaration is considered a landmark in Europe's Middle East policy. As underlined, it did contain some crucial principles that still constitute the basis of the EU's policy towards the Arab–Israeli peace process (Peters 1999) more than twenty years later, but it must be noted how, alongside the achievement of the issuing of a common declaration that would sketch out a specific European stance on a highly controversial issue, the EC had also proved the extent to which it was not only largely exposed to American influence, but also prone to tend towards the objective of a minimum common denominator to enable member states to agree with each other.[30]

1980–1990

The ten years between 1980 and 1990 can hardly be considered a high point in European activism in the Middle East: not only did Israel's invasion of Lebanon in June 1982 (strongly condemned by the EC) cause the slowdown, if not the paralysis, of most initiatives in the area, including American ones; but EC member states generally went back to pursuing their own national policies in the region. The most active state was once again France; however, the presidential elections that in 1981 brought to power Francois Mitterrand – considered to be a friend of Israel and a supporter of the Camp David process – generated a change in France's Middle East policy. This change, nonetheless, was not towards a new pro-Israeli French policy, but rather towards an irresolute, uncertain and at times contradictory policy that caused the other member states to conclude that the times were not favourable for a renewed European initiative.[31]

Furthermore, some EC member states (France, Britain, Italy and the Netherlands) resolved to send a peacekeeping force to Sinai, thus expressing their support for the Camp David agreement, but also indicating the extent to which Europe was internally divided and hesitant in the formulation of its policy.

The ten-year period also saw numerous failed attempts, not at all welcomed by the United States, to revive the Euro-Arab Dialogue, which had been suspended following Egypt's expulsion from the Arab League after the signing of the Egypt–Israel peace treaty. Between 1980 and 1988, a number of preparatory meetings and ministerial meetings took place, to no avail at all, until the Dialogue was definitively broken off.

While the EAD was stalled, the EC increasingly felt the need to establish some sort of contact with the Gulf States in order to secure stable trade relations (Dosenrode and Stubkjaer 2002: 104). The Arabs were very wary of this initiative, as they wanted to avoid a division between the Gulf States and the rest of the Arab world, but a window of opportunity opened for the EC in 1981, when the six Gulf States[32] created the Gulf Cooperation Council (GCC), which was charged with economic and political tasks. Immediately the EC initiated informal talks with the GCC with the aim of creating a cooperation agreement (Jawad 1992: 166–207), but only in June 1988, after lengthy negotiations, was such an agreement signed in Luxembourg.[33]

According to Dosenrode and Stubkjaer (2002: 105), the EC initiative towards the Gulf proved a number of points:

- it underlined the EC's dependence on oil supply from the Gulf
- it stressed the need to gain access to the lucrative Gulf state markets
- it showed the lack of confidence in the ability of the United States to help its allies and secure stability in the Gulf
- it marked the end of EC paralysis
- it showed that the Gulf states enjoyed priority over the rest of the Arab states.

Neither the Euro-Arab Dialogue nor the EC–Gulf Dialogue can be seen as a huge success for the EC from a political point of view: both initiatives were promoted by the EC to secure mainly economic advantages, but met with the determination of the Arab States to use all the instruments at their disposal for political purposes. The EC was very reluctant to allow such a linkage, mainly because of strong

American pressures; on the other hand, the concurrent temptation to give in to Arab pressures in order both to secure Euro-Arab relations (and therefore steady access to oil and prosperous economic ties) and to promote an independent European role in the Middle East conflict was great, the result being mainly a hesitant and contradictory policy that gained the EC the reputation of being an unreliable friend (from the Arab point of view), a difficult and disappointing ally (from the American point of view) and a dangerous actor that had to be marginalised (from the Israeli point of view).

Conclusion

From this analysis of the first twenty-two years of EC involvement in the Arab–Israeli conflict and peace process, it is already possible to draw some critical conclusions and make some comments on the nature of Europe's Middle East policy. In fact, as we have seen, many keys to understanding EC/EU policy in this area date back to this first period, which saw the birth of an embryonic European Foreign Policy through EPC and Europe's first steps in the international arena as a new actor.

The first point to be made is probably an acknowledgement of the fact that the first 'enemies' of European foreign policy in most cases are the member states themselves, which turn to EPC and promote it when this is in line with their national foreign policy priorities (e.g. France's insistence on promoting a closer relationship with the Arab States and an independent role for Europe in the Middle East, distancing the EC's position from the United States' as much as possible), but do not hesitate to revert to bilateral contacts and initiatives when this is convenient for their national interest. Control over foreign policy was obviously still very far from being considered something that could be relinquished in the name of the higher objective of furthering European integration.

Another element that emerges is the fact that policy towards the Middle East provided the EC with an opportunity to 'experiment' with the new instruments of EPC.

In their work 'Europe's Middle East Dilemma: The Quest for a Unified Stance' Greilsammer and Weiler, in analysing the Framework for Political Cooperation, make the distinction between an *active* policy, that is, a policy that will seek to influence events directly to position Europe as an initiator of policy and veritable world actor; a *reactive* policy, that is, a policy less concerned with direct influence, but rather with reacting to world events in order to minimise costs for the reactive actor; and finally a *reflexive* policy, where the chief concern will be the actual formation of a common policy as an integrative value per se (Greilsammer and Weiler 1987: 19).

What emerges from the analysis of these twenty-two years is that EC policy towards the Middle East has been rarely 'active' (and when it has been active it has not achieved remarkable results, as in the case of the Euro-Arab dialogue or the Venice Declaration), but has more frequently, and perhaps more successfully, been 'reactive' (as it tried to minimise negative repercussions on Europe of potentially dangerous regional and international events). As for the reflexive dimension of EC Middle East policy, it appears to have acquired progressively more importance since the creation of EPC: 'in reflexive terms the Middle East has provided the real laboratory in which all mechanisms of the Framework [for Political Cooperation] were tested. And on a declaratory level, the Framework led to a convergence of European attitudes towards various issues connected with the conflict, such as Palestinian self-determination and a possible role for the PLO' (ibid.: 20).

In fact, mainly as a consequence of French insistence and pressures, in this time span the EC progressively increased its involvement in the Middle East, to the point that the Arab–Israeli conflict became one of the most discussed issues of EPC; this in turn generated a slow convergence of the member states' positions around a number of shared principles regarding possible strategies to bring peace to the region. Furthermore, it must be noted that for certain member states – Germany, for instance – 'Community discipline' constituted a very convenient explanation to justify, in both the eyes of third parties (i.e. Israel) and their own domestic public opinion, a shift in national foreign policy from a position of clear support offered to Israel to a more pro-Arab stance, which, for obvious historical reasons, was hardly welcomed.

The Arab–Israeli peace process constituted, in a way, an ideal issue-area to promote political integration at the European level: not only did some of the member states have special ties with the region because of their historical role in the Middle East (e.g. Britain and France), but events that affected the Middle East were of relevance to all member states because of the crucial importance of the region for Europe's economy, heavily dependent on Arab oil.

Given these premises, however, it must not be forgotten that all European initiatives and attempts to forge an independent role for the EC took place under the umbrella of the security framework provided by the United States, which no EC member state was prepared to renounce. American ties with Israel and the relevance of the Middle East in the context of the Cold War bipolar confrontation constituted a guarantee for Europe that it could 'flex its muscles' innocuously, without incurring the risk of being forced to take further steps and go beyond a declaratory policy towards a direct involvement 'on the ground', an involvement that the EC was neither able nor – arguably – willing to take on.

American determination to maintain complete and sole control over the Middle East peace process, and the limitation of foreign policy instruments provided by the Framework for Political Cooperation, have certainly contributed to relegating the EC to a secondary role in the region; but one has to wonder to what extent there was a deliberate willingness on the part of the member states to keep this subordinate role and avoid the direct and more complex responsibilities associated with the EC having an equal role as sponsor of the peace process alongside the United States.

3
The EU and the Middle East Peace Process: From Hope to Despair (1991–1999)

Introduction

This chapter offers an overview of the main developments of the Middle East peace process between the years 1991 and 1999; it also highlights the most important changes in European foreign policy-making that took place in this period, with special reference to those innovations relevant to EU policy towards the Middle East. Lastly, the chapter analyses the evolution of the EU's strategy and initiatives towards the region, from the inception of the peace process at the Madrid Peace Conference in 1991 to the creation of the role of the High Representative for CFSP.

The period considered will be analysed as a succession of three phases: the dates that mark the beginning and the end of each of these phases may be interpreted as turning points both in the Middle East peace process and in the EU policy's towards it: what follows is an outline of the chronological division proposed by this chapter, accompanied by explanations of the dates that define each period from both perspectives:

1991–1993

a. This phase opens with the Madrid Middle East Peace Conference, co-sponsored by the United States and the Soviet Union, and comes to a close with the beginning in Norway of secret negotiations between the Israelis and the Palestinians.

b. In 1991 the Treaty on European Union (TEU) was drafted in Maastricht and, from the original nucleus of European Political

Cooperation, the member states agreed to create the Common Foreign and Security Policy (CFSP); the Middle East was identified as one of the crucial potential areas of action for the CFSP. The TEU was ratified and came into force in 1993.

1993–1995

a. In September 1993, as a result of the Oslo negotiations, Israel and the PLO exchanged documents of mutual recognition. In Washington Rabin and Arafat signed the Declaration of Principles, which would serve as a framework for the various future stages of the Israeli–Palestinian negotiations. This phase ends with the assassination of Yitzhak Rabin and the end of the 'Oslo Spirit'.

b. In 1993, at the Washington Donors' Conference, the EU pledged 700 million ECUs to put the Palestinian economy on the path to development in five years.[1] In 1995 a Euro-Mediterranean Conference was held in Barcelona, bringing together the EU member states and twelve Mediterranean Partners (including Israel and the Palestinian Authority). The Conference approved the Barcelona Declaration, which endorsed the creation of a Euro-Mediterranean Partnership.[2]

1996–1999

a. This phase covers the three years of the Netanyahu government in Israel, during which there was a marked stalemate in the peace process that was not complete only because of strong American pressures on the Israeli government (Reich 2003: 245).

b. In 1996 the EU Council decided to appoint Miguel Angel Moratinos as Special Envoy to the Middle East Peace Process. The Special Envoy was the 'pilot project'[3] of an EU diplomat whose task would be to improve coordination of member State policies. In 1999, in a further effort in the direction of promoting political integration within the EU, the member states appointed Javier Solana, former NATO Secretary, as High Representative for the EU Common Foreign and Security Policy. Since his appointment, Mr Solana and his Policy Planning and Early Warning Unit have been closely involved in the peace process.

These phases will be analysed with the objective of offering a comprehensive view of events that are not only closely intertwined, but that often overlap chronologically, creating a confusing picture that is difficult to decipher. In fact, a number of factors come into play and need to be taken into consideration at the same time: the international and the regional context, the influence of the great powers and in particular of the United States, the different and at times diverging interests of the member states of the European Union, the evolution of the political integration process within the EU, the stratification of the foreign policy instruments at the EU's disposal, and, last but not least, the multifaceted nature of the EU's contribution (or attempted contribution) to the peace process, in the form of direct involvement in the peace process itself and indirect involvement through regional initiatives such as the Barcelona Process.

From the Madrid Peace Conference to the Oslo Accords: EU foreign policy and the beginnings of the peace process (1991–1993)

The turmoil of the years 1989–1991, which saw the reunification of Germany and the collapse of the Soviet Union, had an inevitable direct fallout on the Middle East: with the end of the Cold War and the inexorable decline of the power of the USSR, the United States rapidly emerged as the only surviving superpower. Global intervention in the Middle East no longer projected bipolar superpower rivalry in the region: post-Cold War global intervention took on a unipolar form, with the United States taking on a dominant position in the region and wielding all its power and influence (Buzan and Weaver 1999).

Furthermore, the 1991 Gulf War profoundly altered the political balance in the region, opening a window of opportunity to achieve progress in the peace process after a long impasse. The United States decided to exploit the favourable moment, and to launch a peace initiative to reach a comprehensive settlement between Israel and the Arab States (Reich 2003: 243–4).

The Gulf War prompted both the Israelis and the Palestinians to initiate peace talks. Saddam Hussein's bombing of Israeli territory with Scud missiles during the conflict had led Israel to reconsider its security needs. The Israeli government became aware that physical control of the territory through occupation was no longer a guarantee of military security, and was compelled to reconsider its strategy and the possibility of starting talks with the Palestinians. Moreover, the end of the Cold War meant that Israel no longer represented a strategic asset to the United States in the confrontation between superpowers. It was therefore in its interests to avoid antagonising the United States – its main ally – and to support the peace initiative.

Yasser Arafat's support for Saddam Hussein, on the other hand, had left the Palestinians politically isolated. The PLO had trusted the Iraqi dictator's promise to solve the Palestinian issue once the war had been won; after Saddam's defeat, the Palestinians found themselves not only heavily compromised in their relations with other Arab States who had fought against Iraq,[4] but also aware that no Arab state would or could ever solve the Palestinian issue, and that the only path to follow was now the start of direct negotiations with the Israelis. In addition, the economic situation of the Territories was rapidly deteriorating and the collapse of the Soviet Union meant that they could not rely on its political, military and economic support: 'participation in the American-sponsored peace process was perceived [by the Palestinians] as a means for regaining Arab and Western support'.[5]

These changes in the political vision and the security strategies of both Israel and the Palestinians, therefore, made possible the launching of the American peace initiative and the convening of a Middle East Peace Conference in Madrid in October 1991.

The Letters of Invitation to the Conference were issued by both the United States and the Soviet Union as co-sponsor of the event, but it was clear that this was primarily an American initiative: the United States had become the sole guarantor and manager of security in the region, and was determined to take on a primary role in the peace negotiations.

The delegations invited were those of Israel, Lebanon, Syria, Egypt and Jordan; the Palestinian delegation was to be included in the Jordanian one.

The European Community was invited as an observer alongside the Gulf Cooperation Council and the United Nations. As mentioned in the previous chapter, the EC had long claimed that to solve the Arab–Israeli conflict a Peace Conference should be convened, in order to reach a comprehensive settlement among all the parties involved. However, up to 1991 at least two of the main players (the United States and Israel – but also Egypt, at least as long as the Camp

David process was producing results) were not ready to embrace this point of view, and bilateral contacts between the parties continued to represent the main strategy pursued, despite the fact that successes were increasingly few and far between.

The European Community, on the other hand, hardly possessed the instruments or the willingness to impose its strategy. EPC, which was strictly restricted within the limits of intergovernmental cooperation, was proving to be – for reasons that will be discussed later – a highly inadequate mechanism to promote the EC as an international actor. The member states, furthermore, were still not at all in accord as to the substance of a possible European action. France favoured an initiative based on the Venice Declaration, while Germany and Britain were inclined to support the American initiative.[6] Given the fairly unsatisfactory performance of EPC during the Gulf War, to which the member states reacted without much coordination, the announced idea of a European Middle East peace initiative was finally abandoned in favour of support for the US-sponsored Madrid Conference.

Nonetheless, the EC insisted on being included in the Conference as a full participant rather then as an observer, but met with the stern opposition of Israel, which did not trust European governments and did not want to accept the EC as an additional mediator.

In the eyes of the Israeli government the EC had made three tactical errors that doomed its role as an acceptable mediator in the peace process (Ginsberg 2001: 107). It had:

- demanded that Israel make concessions to the Palestinians in advance of direct peace negotiations between Israel and the Palestinians;
- made concessions to the Palestinians that prejudged Israeli interests in advance of direct peace negotiations; and
- insisted on the United Nations as the appropriate forum for negotiations towards a comprehensive peace settlement, knowing that this was totally unacceptable to Israel.

For these reasons Israel refused to agree to the EC's full participation in the opening of the Conference and, although it accepted that the event should be located in an EC capital (Madrid), it rejected the possibility of the conference being held in either London or Paris.

The United States, for its part, was also not particularly keen on having another mediator to deal with, as in its view this would only complicate the relations with the negotiating parties, and it preferred to maintain the process firmly in its hands.

Somewhat ironically, then, when at last one of the crucial points of the EC's Middle East strategy was being accepted by the main players and all the parties, however reluctantly, were to convene to discuss a comprehensive settlement, the EC found itself relegated to a very marginal role, and excluded from the most critical negotiations.[7]

At the opening of the Conference in October 1991, the EC President-in-office, Hans Van Den Broek, in his address to the participants underlined the strong bonds existing between Europe and the Middle East, and emphasised the importance for the European Community and for the region as a whole of a peaceful solution to the conflict. Van Den Broek also stressed the importance of regional cooperation, stating, for instance, that 'elements of the process set in motion by the Conference on Security and Co-operation in Europe could serve as an inspiration and example. It shows how a modest start can bring great results'.[8]

Despite these inspired words, however, and the suggestion that Europe could serve as a model of coexistence and integration for other troubled regions, the reality of European foreign policy integration at the Community level was still quite grim. EC participation in the Conference had been a problem in itself, not only because of the abovementioned Israeli opposition to awarding the EC the status of full participant, but also because the European governments irritated the Americans by asking that they be represented as the EC at the Madrid conference, and then turning up with the EC as such and with all twelve member governments, thus adding an additional delegation without presenting a single, coherent position.

In truth, after twenty years of European Political Cooperation, the inadequacy of the European foreign policy system had become increasingly evident, and the necessity to reform and improve it was felt by many member states. Speaking at the College of Europe, in Bruges, in October 1989, the President of the European Commission had said: 'We can assume the international responsibilities only through an accelerated deepening of the Community approach, thus facilitating the emergence of a Grand Europe.'[9]

The end of the Cold War had led to a redefinition of Europe's interests and foreign policy priorities. The fall of the Berlin Wall had marked the dissolution of the political cement of the communist threat, and, following the reunification of Germany, integration had become an even more important issue for European stability (Wallace 1999a: 508). Furthermore, the post-1989 changes in the world balance of power increased the demands on Europe to advance its role as an international actor and use its weight to achieve more political influence and ensure stability around its borders (Cameron 1999: 23); the inability of the EC to react adequately to the Yugoslav crisis and to the outbreak of the Gulf War underlined the need for the EC to make qualitative progress in foreign policy, at least attempting to move on from cooperation to a common policy.

All these issues animated negotiations on the Maastricht Treaty on European Union (TEU), which took place during 1991 and during which 'the definition and implementation of a common foreign and security policy'[10] were discussed. However, the contrasts between the member states who wanted to move towards an integrated Europe and those who wanted to keep foreign policy decision-making strictly in the hands of the national governments were strong and were in the end clearly reflected in the Maastricht Treaty, especially in the establishment – within the three-pillar structure created by the TEU[11] – of the European foreign policy mechanism as an inter-governmental independent pillar of its own, and the creation at the same time of a single institutional framework.

The innovations introduced by the TEU will be analysed and discussed in detail later in this volume: what is of interest here is to highlight those changes that had a direct immediate bearing on the EU's policy towards the Middle East peace process in order to clarify the sequence of events and to better understand the nature of European initiatives.

The TEU did mark an important step by the member states of the EC (which after the ratification of the TEU became the European Union – EU) towards the creation of a common European foreign policy. European Political Cooperation evolved into the Common Foreign and Security Policy (CFSP), with the aim – as stated – of strengthening the Union's role in the international arena, and enabling it to speak 'with one voice'. 'Joint actions' and 'common positions' were created as new instruments, the possibility of appointing a special envoy to specific political areas and areas of crisis was also taken into consideration, and the Middle East peace process was identified as a possible context of action for the CFSP. The member states decided that the CFSP would be carried out within the framework of the Union's institutions, its aim being the creation of consistent policies that would be preventive rather than reactive, and that would assert the EU's political identity (Regelsberger, de Schoutheete de Tervarent and Wessels 1997: 1–14). With the Maastricht Treaty and the creation of CFSP, in other words, the European governments aimed to achieve a common foreign policy able to project onto the international arena the combined power of its member states, whose weight and influence in international affairs was, it was hoped, stronger than that exercised by each state individually.

As mentioned above, the early 1990s brought increasing pressures on the EU to enhance its role as a relevant political actor on the international stage. In the Middle East, the end of the Cold War and the subsequent collapse of the Soviet Union had created a political vacuum, which could have become a political opportunity for the EU; theoretically there was a possibility of redefining EU–US interaction and the dynamics of burden-sharing in the region, and Europe could potentially have increased its role and influence in the Middle East peace process, filling the gap left by the Soviet Union. Gerd Nonneman (2003: 37–8) has argued that:

> The Gulf War of 1990–91 brought a renewed focus on finding a solution to the Palestinian question, because the US interest in wider regional stability, and the need to maintain support in the Arab and Muslim world, required a demonstration that the war was not simply an anti-Arab or anti-Muslim affair, and that Arab grievances, too, resonated in Washington. At the same time, the emerging post-Cold War order meant that such a search for resolution would no longer be shackled by the earlier Cold War dynamic. The PLO leadership was much weakened following its failure to embrace the international action against Iraq, while Israel itself was in some quarters being described as a strategic liability rather than an asset. The result was the Madrid peace process.

As we shall see, however, the EU did not manage to take full advantage of this opportunity, for a number of reasons ranging from American reluctance to concede political space to other actors, to Israeli hostility towards the EU's involvement, to the EU member states' inability and unwillingness to make full use of the mechanisms provided by the creation of CFSP, and to formulate a coherent common policy that could be taken seriously by all the other players.

After the Madrid Peace Conference, a double tier of negotiations was opened: bilateral talks between Israel and the Palestinians, and multilateral talks between Israel and Jordan, Syria and Lebanon. The bilateral negotiations were based on direct talks between the parties, in which neither the United States nor the European Union would have a direct role. In actual fact, while the role of Europe was limited in effect to the participation of a revolving troika of 'observers' to monitor the development of the talks, the American role was significantly more important: the United States not only met with the parties separately to discuss the issues at stake, but also had the possibility of setting forth proposals aimed at supporting the dialogue. Furthermore, following the conclusion of the Peace Conference, over a dozen formal rounds of bilateral talks were hosted by the US Department of State in Washington.[12]

The multilateral negotiations, opened in Moscow in 1992, focused on more technical issues that crossed national borders.[13] The EU played a relevant role in these, as gavel holder of the Regional Economic Development Working Group (REDWG).[14] The United States, on the other hand, presided over the Water Working Group and, jointly with Russia, the working group charged with the most sensitive issues: Arms Control and Regional Security.

During these negotiations – which were not producing appreciable results or progress in the peace process –direct bilateral contacts between Israelis and Palestinians behind the scenes were initiated in Oslo: the European Community was left out of these talks, but so was the United States, informed of the results achieved only towards the conclusion of the negotiations.[15] The essence of the so-called 'spirit of Oslo' has thus been described by one of the negotiators:

> For those involved in the initial discussions in Norway the goal was to work towards a conceptual change which would lead to a dialogue based, as much as possible, on fairness, equality and common objectives. These values were to be reflected both in the character of the negotiations – including the personal relationships

between the negotiators – and in the proffered solutions and implementation. This new type of relationship was supposed to influence the type and character of Palestinian-Israeli talks which would develop between other official and semi-governmental institutions in the future, as well as future dialogue between the two peoples. (Pundak 2001: 21)[16]

From the Oslo Accords to the Barcelona Conference: The first steps of CFSP in the Middle East (1993–1995)

The outcome of the intensive diplomatic negotiations that took place in Oslo was an exchange of mutual recognition documents between Israel and the PLO, and the signing of a Declaration of Principles (DOP) that would serve as the framework for the various stages of the Israeli–Palestinian negotiations. The venue chosen for the signing of the DOP was Washington: a significant fact, as it underlined the important role played in the peace process by the United States. The United States may not have taken direct part in the talks, but nonetheless remained the sole mediator acknowledged and accepted by the PLO as well as by Israel. The role of Europe, represented at the ceremony by the EU President and by the President of the Commission, was limited to issuing statements of support.

The years between 1993 and 1995 were full of hope for the peace process: the events set in motion in Norway brought about a sequence of accords both on the Israeli–Palestinian front and on the Israeli–Jordanian one.[17] In May 1994 the Gaza–Jericho Agreement was signed in Cairo, for the withdrawal of Israeli administration and forces from Gaza and Jericho and the transfer of powers and responsibilities to a Palestinian Authority. Then, in August 1994, the so-called Transfer of Powers agreement was signed in Erez, for the early transfer of powers and responsibilities in specified spheres, in those parts of the territories not included in the Gaza–Jericho Agreement. Finally, in September 1995, the signing of the Interim Agreement – or Oslo II protocol – took place in Washington, an accord that led to the extension of autonomy in the major centres of population in the West Bank, and the holding of elections for a Palestinian Council.

As regards talks with Jordan, on the other hand, the main steps were the establishment in October 1993 in Washington of a Trilateral US–Jordan–Israel Economic Committee to discuss economic cooperation and development; the signing in July 1994 of the Washington Declaration, which put an end to the state of belligerence between the two countries; and the signing near Aqaba, in October 1994, of the Peace Treaty that established full diplomatic relations and defined international borders between the State of Israel and Jordan.

In this phase a predominant role was once again played by the United States, with the President of the United States acting as witness – and in effect as guarantor – of the Gaza–Jericho Agreement, the Treaty of Peace between Israel and Jordan, and the Oslo II accord. The European Union's involvement in the negotiations was still minimal, and only on the occasion of the signing of the Oslo II agreement was the EU invited to participate as witness.

The European Union, however, began taking on an increasingly important role in funding the peace process, in particular through an extraordinary flow of financial support for the Palestinian Authority. In October 1993, after the signing of the DOP, a Donors' Conference was convened in Washington, at which the international community pledged 2.4 billion dollars to a plan to put the Palestinian economy on its way to development in five years (1994–1998). The European Union, for its part, inaugurated a special programme, committing itself to donate 700 million ECUs[18] in support of the Palestinian economy by the end of 1997.[19] The Washington Conference also created an ad hoc Liaison Committee, of which the EU became a member, to coordinate economic assistance to the Palestinians.[20] At the signing of the Gaza–Jericho Agreement, the Vice President of the European Commission, Manuel Marin, informed Mr Arafat that the Commission would in future donate 10 million ECUs for the funding of a Palestinian police force. The underlying logic of this huge volume of external economic assistance was the assumption that Palestinian economic development was Israel's best long-term security guarantee, and a necessary precondition for maintaining the peace process on track.

Besides its economic support to the Palestinians, the EU progressively reassessed its Mediterranean policy with the objective of developing 'an overall concept on relations with the region as a whole, encompassing security, economic development and social justice aspects'.[21] After the end of the Cold War, and with the intensification of the EU's relations with the East, the southern member states increasingly requested a rebalancing of the EU's commitments towards Central and Eastern European countries and the South, as well as a revaluation of the Mediterranean region as a foreign policy priority. The Mediterranean lobby within the Community became a 'vociferous advocate of a new approach' (Gomez 1998: 140), and their pressures eventually led to the organisation of a conference in Barcelona to discuss ways of promoting a regional dialogue and cooperation, with the aim of reducing economic, social and demographic imbalances existing between the two shores of the Mediterranean.

As Sven Behrendt has pointed out, the EU's long-term strategic approach to the Mediterranean region was focused on four objectives (Behrendt and Hanelt 2000: 13–15):

1. to promote democratisation, as – in the European experience – democratic structures have proven to be efficient instruments of conflict resolution within states, and also effective in diminishing the risk of conflicts erupting between states;
2. to promote economic development and integration, an objective based on the assumption that free-market economies and liberalised international trade relations improve overall standards of living;
3. to contribute to the construction of a framework of effective regional institutions that could provide mechanisms for the peaceful resolution of conflicts;
4. to favour a broader cultural dialogue underpinning all levels of political, economic and social interaction, in order to promote a Mediterranean identity on which more stable cross-regional relations could be based.

The Barcelona Conference took place in November 1995. It approved the Barcelona Declaration, which endorsed the creation of a Euro-Mediterranean Partnership (EMP) between the fifteen EU member states and twelve Mediterranean Partners: Algeria, Cyprus, Egypt, Israel, Jordan, Lebanon, Malta, Morocco, Syria, Tunisia, Turkey and the Palestinian Authority. The United States was completely excluded from the EMP, especially as a result of France's desire to keep this process as an exclusively 'European' initiative, free from American interference.

To use the words of Commission Vice President Manuel Marin, '[...] The Euro-Mediterranean Partnership provided for the first time a clear geopolitical and economic scenario for a priority region in the Union's foreign policy, and it designed a far-reaching double structure at both the multilateral and bilateral level [...]'.[22] The EMP had three main declared objectives or pillars: to establish a common Euro-Mediterranean area of peace and stability, to create an area of shared prosperity through the establishment of a free trade area, and to promote understanding between cultures and rapprochement of the peoples in the Euro-Mediterranean region (Vasconcelos and Joffe 2000).

This initiative, which took the name of the Barcelona Process (BP), was meant from the beginning to be independent of, but parallel to, the Middle East peace process: the peace process would achieve the political breakthrough; the Barcelona Process would set up the real conditions for long-term stability and economic development (Marin 1998).[23] It would also offer a forum for the parties involved in the peace process to meet in a different context from that of the difficult and controversial negotiations on political and security issues. However, the EU has achieved this objective to only a limited extent: in effect, it soon became apparent that the formal separation between the Partnership and the peace process could not serve to prevent the de facto linkages emerging between the processes (Spencer 2001), and that any progress in the field of Mediterranean regional cooperation was continuously hampered by the difficulties encountered by the peace process. In other words, the EU's aspiration to be able to keep the process of economic cooperation and development isolated from the spillover of the political consequences of the stalemate in the peace process proved to be an illusion.

And, indeed, the atmosphere of hope generated by the progress achieved in the Arab–Israeli peace process through the Oslo accords was soon to come to an end, as the unprecedented progress in the peace process generated increasingly violent resistance from extremist political forces on both sides. In October 1994 a terrorist attack in Tel Aviv marked the start of a bombing campaign by Hamas and the Islamic Jihad against Israel, and on 4 November 1995 Prime Minister Rabin was assassinated by an Israeli right-wing extremist. The peace process did not die but certainly suffered formidable blows, and the attempts of the EU to keep the BP separated from the peace process became untenable: peace process matters became the uninvited guest at every EMP meeting, to the point of bringing it to a paralysis with the progressive failure of the Oslo accords. The deadlock in Israeli–Palestinian negotiations effectively made any constructive discussion about the establishment of a common Euro-Mediterranean area of peace and stability impossible, as the resolution of the conflict became the precondition for any concession or effort geared towards reform (Aliboni and Aly 2000).

A few additional considerations are worth mentioning: the Euro-Mediterranean Partnership attempts to address the Mediterranean as a single region in terms of economics and security, an approach which reflects the European view of the Mediterranean as a coherent geostrategic region. However, the Maghreb (North Africa) and the Mashreq (the Middle East) pose different challenges for Europe. For North Africa, the major issues are primarily in the spheres of economic development and civil society, while in the Middle East politics and the Arab–Israeli peace process are priorities for the parties involved and for Europe (Aliboni 2000). A number of commentators have argued that the attempt to deal with both issues in the same framework has not been successful and is doomed to failure (Asseburg 2003; Steinberg 1999).

From the Special Envoy to the High Representative for CFSP: The member states try to enhance the EU's role in the peace process (1996–1999)

During Benjamin Netanyahu's period in office (May 1996–May 1999) the peace process slowed down significantly, almost coming to a complete standstill. The new Israeli Prime Minister was the first Likud leader to accept the 'land for peace' idea, but, beyond this formal acceptance of the principle on which the Oslo process was based, he did all he could to delay further Israeli redeployments and to hinder the process towards a definitive peace settlement between Israel and the Palestinians (Reich 2003: 245).

However, some steps forward were made, the most relevant being the first Palestinian elections in 1996 for the appointment of the President of the Palestinian National Authority and of the Legislative Council; the signing in January 1997 of the Protocol Concerning the Redeployment in Hebron, which provided for the partial redeployment of Israeli troops from the city and a timetable for future redeployments in the West Bank; and the signing in October 1998 of the Wye River Memorandum, which consisted of steps aimed at facilitating implementation of the Interim Agreement of September 1995 (Oslo II) and a second Israeli redeployment in the West Bank. The Palestinians, on the other hand, were to implement a security plan and to abrogate the articles of the Palestinian National Charter that called for the destruction of Israel. A long deadlock in the peace process followed the signing of the Wye River Memorandum, and the next relevant step took place only after Netanyahu's defeat and the election of Ehud Barak as Prime Minister of Israel in May 1999: in September 1999 the PLO and Israel signed a Memorandum in Sharm-el-Sheikh that set out to resolve the outstanding issues of the interim status.

In this phase of the peace process the member states tried to enhance the EU's role in the Middle East, and European policy became markedly more active in nature and geared to directly influencing events through initiatives at times independent of, and at times coordinated with, the Americans.

In January 1996 the EU made a major political and financial contribution to the preparation, monitoring and coordination of the international observation of the Palestinian elections. The legal basis for the European Union's political and financial involvement in these activities was two joint actions under the CFSP approved by the Council of the European Union, which provided a total funding of 17 million ECUs.[24]

In April 1996, Israel bombarded Lebanon extensively in retaliation for attacks by Hezbollah on Northern Israel (the operation is known as 'Operation Grapes of Wrath'). The crisis in Lebanon highlighted the enduring difficulties that Europe was encountering in expressing a common policy: indeed, the first member State to react was France, and not through the mechanisms of the CFSP, or even after consulting the other member states, but with a completely autonomous initiative, much to the annoyance of the other fourteen EU members. French Foreign Minister de Charette shuttled between Jerusalem, Beirut and Damascus to help broker a deal, and when an agreement between the parties was reached France became co-chair – with the United States – of the committee to monitor the ceasefire. France's unilateral diplomatic action and its decision to proceed without consultation or coordination at EU level caused some irritation among its European partners, but a trip in the region by the EU's troika, headed by Italian Foreign Minister Susanna Agnelli, rather than improving the role of the EU, seemed to make 'a mockery of European pretensions to speak with one voice' (Peters 1999: 309).

In October, France's President Chirac toured the region visiting Israel, the Palestinian Territories, Egypt, Jordan, Syria and Lebanon; during one of his speeches he suggested that the European Union should stand alongside the United States and Russia as co-sponsor of the peace process, and that the increased involvement of France and the EU would help restore confidence in the process.[25] His trip was as much welcomed by the Arabs as it was received coldly by both Israel and the United States (Hollis 1997). However, as Joel Peters has underlined, France's initiatives in this phase did achieve one objective on the European political integration front: they 'led to increased diplomatic activism in the region by the European Union as a whole and spurred a broader and much overdue debate about Europe's potential role in the peace process' (Peters 1999: 310).

One of the immediate results of this renewed European effort to play a more relevant role in the peace process was the appointment of Miguel Angel Moratinos,[26] former Spanish Ambassador to Israel, as EU Special Envoy to the Middle East, his objective being to improve coordination of the member state policies, to reduce the inconsistencies of EU policy deriving from the system of the rotating presidency, and also to offer the EU's external interlocutors a counterpart in 'flesh and blood' rather than a vague set of principles, common declarations and contradictory initiatives.

It was also as a result of Moratinos's negotiations with the parties that the EU sent, within the context of the Hebron Protocol signing, and at the official request of the United States, a collateral letter of assurances to the Palestinians in addition to the one already sent by the United States to both the Palestinians and the Israelis. In its message, the European Union encouraged the Palestinians to reach a compromise on the deadline for Israeli withdrawal from the rural areas of the West Bank; although the letter was written in collaboration with the United States, the Palestinians appreciated the EU's additional vow to 'use all its political and moral weight to ensure that all the provisions in the agreements already reached will be fully implemented'.[27]

In April 1997, the Council adopted a Joint Action under the CFSP,[28] which regulated the establishment of a European Union assistance programme to support the Palestinian Authority in its efforts to counter terrorist activities emanating from the territories under its control, and thus fulfil Israeli security requirements.

In December 1998 the peace process between Israel and the Palestinians reached a deadlock after Netanyahu's government decided to suspend the implementation of the Wye River Memorandum, in response to what Israel viewed as insufficient Palestinian commitment to end terrorism and incitement to violence. A very tense situation arose from this decision: in Israel a vote of no confidence led to parliamentary and prime ministerial elections being called for in May 1999; as for the peace process, Arafat threatened to proclaim a Palestinian State unilaterally on 4 May 1999 in accordance with his past declarations.[29] Both the United States and the European Union made every possible effort to avoid this unilateral declaration of independence, which, in their view, would worsen the situation between Israel and the Palestinian Authority.

In March 1999, with the Berlin Declaration, the European Union reaffirmed its support of the Palestinian right to self-determination, 'including the option of a state',[30] basically offering – in exchange for Palestinian renunciation of the unilateral declaration of independence – the assurance that the European Union would in the future recognise a Palestinian State,[31] on condition that it be established through negotiations with Israel. It was, however, underlined in the Declaration that the Palestinian right to a state 'was not subject to any veto'. In April, the PLO Central Council decided to postpone the declaration of Palestinian statehood.[32]

In June 1999, in a further effort to coordinate and improve the effectiveness of the European Union's foreign policy, the European Council decided to appoint Mr Javier Solana (former Spanish Minister of Foreign Affairs and current NATO Secretary General: a figure of great international standing) as Secretary General of the Council and High Representative for the Common Foreign and Security Policy.[33] The appointment of Mr Solana was the implementation of a decision taken in 1997 and officially provided for in the Amsterdam Treaty: Article 26 of the Treaty stated that the Secretary General of the Council would add to his responsibilities the new function of High Representative for the CFSP. In a declaration annexed to the

Treaty of Amsterdam, it was agreed that a Policy Planning and Early Warning Unit in the General Secretariat of the Council should be set up, under the authority of the High Representative for the CFSP, comprising specialists drawn from the General Secretariat, the member states, the Commission and the Western European Union (WEU).[34] The hope was that joint analysis of international issues and their impact, and pooling of information, would help the Union to produce effective reactions to international developments.[35]

Since his appointment, Mr Solana and the Policy Planning and Early Warning Unit have been closely involved in the peace process. After the initial inevitable adjustments to coordinate the initiatives and to avoid the overlapping of competencies,[36] Mr Solana and the Special Representative (Mr Moratinos first and Mr Otte later) have started a fruitful cooperation, trying to improve the EU's role in the negotiations and to convince the other players – and in particular Israel – that the EU can be a reliable mediator and can contribute to brokering a deal between Israel and the Arabs.

4

The EU Strategy for the Middle East Peace Process in the Post-9/11 Era

From Camp David to the creation of the Quartet: The American search for new diplomatic geometries

The election of Ehud Barak as Prime Minister of Israel gave new impetus to the peace process. Mr Barak had been elected on the basis of a programme that promised progress in the negotiations with the Palestinians and a unilateral withdrawal from Lebanon on the basis of United Nations Security Council Resolution 425; but, if the withdrawal from Lebanon was indeed completed by June 2000, real advancements in the negotiations with the Palestinians, after the initial optimism, were harder to come by.

Shortly after Barak's election, the already mentioned Sharm-el-Sheikh Memorandum was signed with the Palestinians to resolve the outstanding issues of the interim status. Barak and Arafat set February 2000 as the target date for preparing a framework agreement for a permanent peace settlement, which was to be completed by September 2000 (Reich 2003: 246). In July 2000 a summit took place in Camp David, involving Arafat, Barak and US President Clinton. During the talks a number of crucial questions were discussed, including highly controversial issues such as the status of Jerusalem and the right of return of Palestinian refugees, but none of them were resolved.

After the failure of the Camp David summit the situation deteriorated rapidly. In September the Second Intifada – also called Al-Aqsa Intifada – started, and a vicious cycle of Palestinian violence and Israeli retaliation began. In a last attempt to bring peace to the region before the end of his mandate, President Clinton convened a peace summit in October 2000 in Sharm-el-Sheikh, where he met with representatives of Israel, the PNA, Egypt, Jordan, the UN and the EU. At the summit the decision was taken to appoint a Fact Finding Commission with the task of proposing recommendations to end the violence, rebuild confidence and resume the negotiations.[1] The Commission was to be chaired by former US Senator George Mitchell and included EU CFSP High Representative Javier Solana, Turkish President Suleyman Demirel, the Norwegian foreign minister Thorjorn Jagland, and former US Senator Warren B. Rudman.

The Sharm-el-Sheikh (or Mitchell) Committee presented its report in April 2001 to the new President of the United States, George W. Bush, but the new administration (at least until September 11) was showing relatively little interest in the Middle East and was deliberately disengaging from the previous administration's detailed involvement as main mediator between the Arabs and Israel.

In June 2001, after having vetoed a UN Security Council resolution to establish a UN observer mission, Bush dispatched CIA Director George Tenet to the Occupied Territories to negotiate a ceasefire plan. Hamas and the Islamic Jihad, however, rejected the plan, arguing that it failed to address the root causes of violence (DiGeorgio-Lutz 2003: 270).

The terrorist attacks of September 11 forced a change in American policy. In order to secure the 'coalition against terrorism' the United States had once again to concentrate on the Arab–Israeli peace process: Bush declared his support for a Palestinian State, and in November 2001 retired Marine Corps General Anthony Zinni was appointed as senior adviser to work towards a ceasefire and to implement the Tenet plan and the Mitchell Committee Report. His mission, however, failed like the previous ones, as violence continued to escalate.

In April 2002 Colin Powell, US Secretary of State, met in Madrid with the representatives of the European Union, the United Nations and Russia. The so-called 'Madrid Quartet' emerged with a common agenda partly based on the 1991 Madrid Peace Conference's agenda: a peace settlement based on an equitable resolution to the conflict, security for Israel and the Palestinians, and a major effort to address the looming humanitarian crisis within the Palestinian community. The focus of this approach was on pursuing a two-state solution to the Israeli–Palestinian conflict, with the active engagement of outside actors (Musu and Wallace 2003).

In a communiqué issued in New York in September 2002, the Quartet announced that it was working with the parties and consulting key regional actors on a three-phase implementation 'roadmap' that could achieve a final settlement within three years.[2]

In the words of Allen and Smith, '2000 was not a good year for the EU in the Middle East, despite the fact that a number of Arab states expressed a preference for much stronger EU involvement in the peace process' (Allen and Smith 2001: 107), the main reason being the deadlock in the negotiations after Camp David.

In June 2000 the European Union approved the new Common Strategy[3] on the Mediterranean Region. The document, drafted before the failure of the Camp David talks, when hopes were still high that a settlement would be reached, foresaw a possible contribution of the member states to the implementation of a final and comprehensive peace agreement between the Israelis and the Palestinians.[4] In paragraph 15 it declared: 'The EU will, in the context of a comprehensive settlement, and upon request by the core parties, give consideration to the participation of member states in the implementation of security arrangements on the ground'.[5] The breakdown of the peace process, however, rendered the EU's commitment useless, as the possibility of a 'comprehensive settlement' became more remote.

The failure of the Camp David talks also negatively influenced the Barcelona Process: Lebanon and Syria refused to attend the fourth Euro-Mediterranean conference of foreign ministers in Marseilles in September 2000, and the EU had to drop any attempt to sign a Charter of Peace and Stability for the Mediterranean as the Arab participants were not prepared to discuss the issue and no agreement was possible. Once again, economic cooperation did not prove conducive to a political settlement (Behrendt and Hanelt 2000: 21).

In 2001 tensions arose between the EU and Israel as the Israeli army, in retaliation for Palestinian terrorist attacks, proceeded to the systematic destruction of Palestinian infrastructures, most of which had been paid for by the EU. Further tensions also arose as Israel continued to export to the EU goods manufactured in the Palestinian Territories but marked as 'Made in Israel' and therefore admitted in EU territory as tariff-free on the basis of the 2000

Association Agreement[6] (the so-called 'rules of origin' problem). When Israel halted the payments of tax revenues to the Palestinian Authority, the EU approved a series of replacement loans and, in response to the 'rules of origin' problem, it threatened to withdraw the preferential tariffs that Israel enjoys. The threat, however, remained a threat, and in general the EU's action did not show great incisiveness. The dispute over the rules of origins was solved in 2004 through a technical agreement, with Israel agreeing to label products with the town of origin as well as the nationality. The marking of the town of origin allowed customs authorities in EU member states to identify and charge duty on products labelled with the name of a town in the occupied Palestinian Territories (e.g. 'made in Barkan, Israel') and to identify and not charge duties on products from 'Israel proper' (i.e. from within the pre-1967 borders), such as those marked 'made in Tel Aviv, Israel'. On the one hand, the agreement allowed Israel to continue marking these products as coming 'from Israel'; on the other, it made it possible for the EU to underline its condemnation of Israeli occupation of Palestinian territories by charging a tariff on goods produced beyond the pre-1967 Green Line (Harpaz 2004).

Arguably, the failure of the Camp David talks and the collapse of the peace process left the EU unable to react in a coordinated and effective fashion: notwithstanding High Representative Solana's participation in the October 2000 Sharm-el-Sheikh Peace Summit, the Mitchell Committee and the uninterrupted behind-the-scenes diplomatic activity of both the High Representative and the Special Envoy Moratinos, the EU's contribution to ending the violence in the area has not been particularly effective. In 2002, after a number of clashes among member states that were unable to agree on a common strategy for the peace process, and after a failed diplomatic mission during which the CFSP High Representative and the Spanish Presidency were not allowed by Israel to meet Arafat in Ramallah, the EU finally decided to renounce launching an independent peace plan and to back the US peace initiative that led to the creation of the Madrid Quartet (Soetendorp 2002: 292–3). The cumbersome structures of EU diplomacy, however, also squeezed the Commissioner for External Relations and the foreign minister of the member state holding the Council Presidency into the 'single' EU seat. The EU member states hoped that participation in the Madrid Quartet would gain the EU more visibility and influence in the peace process, and would provide Europe with a tool for influencing American policies as they are formulated.

Between multilateralism and unilateralism: Competing approaches to the Middle East

The Quartet has been praised for its 'multilateral' nature, which officially brings other actors – but particularly the European Union – into the peace process in addition to the 'old' ones (the Israelis, the Palestinians, and the United States as mediator), but has also been despised for its inability to bring about a breakthrough in the negotiations.

To be sure, the EU had played an increasingly important role in the peace process since the 1991 Madrid Conference, but participation in the Quartet arguably gave the European role a higher political relevance and resonance (Musu 2007).

The EU's presence was particularly welcomed by the Palestinians, who saw it as a potential counterbalance to an American position they perceive as permanently biased in favour of Israel. Conversely, the creation of the Quartet met with a less enthusiastic reception in Israel, where multilateralism is seen as a means to impose unwelcome decisions, and the EU is perceived as a less than friendly actor.

What remained unclear in the initial phase after the creation of the Quartet was its relevance within the overall US Middle East strategy. This was mainly because the Bush Administration, in parallel with this multilateral approach to the Arab–Israeli peace process, was elaborating new policy guidelines that favoured unilateralism in dealing with perceived threats from the region and from rogue states. The growing influence of neoconservatives on the formulation of US foreign policy in the wake of the 9/11 attacks meant that Iraq soon became a key target in the US 'war on terror'.

The American approach to the region was set out by President Bush in his 'Axis of Evil' speech in January 2002, which linked the efforts of Iraq and Iran (and North Korea) to acquire weapons of mass destruction to their sponsorship of terrorism. Though there was very weak, if any, evidence linking any of these states directly to al-Qaeda, this conceptual framework transmuted the war on terrorism into the pre-existing framework of rogue states and weapons of mass destruction, and thus into a potential war on Iraq. Iranian and Iraqi support for terrorist groups attacking Israel was an important part of their inclusion in this category.

The priority for Western Middle East policy, in this American formulation, was regime change in Iraq, combined with continued containment of Iran; the removal of a regime that encouraged Palestinian intransigence would in itself ease the Arab–Israeli conflict. The European allies would be invited to play supporting roles in the 'coalition of the willing' assembled to enforce disarmament and regime change on Iraq, and to pay for subsequent social and economic reconstruction.

European governments, on their part, sympathised with the suffering and felt the outrage that the 9/11 attacks had generated in America. But they placed this new scale of transnational terrorism within the context of the lower level of transnational terrorism their countries had suffered in the past. From their point of view as observers, too, of American strategy towards the region over previous years, largely without influence over that strategy and often critical of its sweep, there was an unavoidable undercurrent of differentiation: a feeling that the United States and the Muslim world were locked into a confrontation that could jeopardise European security while ignoring European views.

In Europe's eyes, what was needed after 9/11 was a broad diplomatic approach to the region, including an active and concerted attempt to bring the Israel–Palestine conflict back to the negotiating table and a dialogue with 'friendly' Arab authoritarian regimes. In terms of power projection and political influence, however, European governments were acutely conscious of their limited capabilities in the face of American regional hegemony.

In 2002 the clash between the European approach to the Middle East, which traditionally favours multilateralism and negotiation, and the increasingly unilateral American approach became more and more evident, bringing about a deterioration of transatlantic relations and generating mutual distrust.

The following passages, taken respectively from the 'National Security Strategy of the United States of America' adopted in September 2002 and from President Bush's 'Axis of Evil' speech of January 2002, while providing American political justification for the adoption of a pre-emptive approach to the war on terror, offer a measure of the United States' determination to pursue their chosen strategy regardless of possible disagreements with their allies:

> For centuries, international law recognized that nations need not suffer an attack before they can lawfully take action to defend themselves against forces that present an imminent danger of attack. [...] We must adapt the concept of imminent threat to the capabilities and objectives of today's adversaries. Rogue states and terrorists do not seek to attack us using conventional means. [...] The United States has long maintained the option of pre-emptive actions to counter a sufficient threat to our national security. To forestall or prevent such hostile acts by our adversaries, the United States will, if necessary, act pre-emptively.
>
> My hope is that all nations will heed our call, and eliminate the terrorist parasites who threaten their countries, and our own. Many nations are acting forcefully [...] but some governments will be timid in the face of terror. And make no mistake: If they do not act, America will.

These words indeed give a measure of the extent to which the United States had moved toward unilateralism, and seem to confirm the view that Europe and America, while sharing the same value systems (i.e. humanitarian, liberal, capitalist systems), are different political cultures, and their preferences render it difficult for them to work together as they once did when it comes to instrumentalising those values (Coker 2003: 50–1). America's decision to launch an attack against Iraq in 2003 (and the preceding diplomatic struggles at the UN) highlighted the rift between the transatlantic allies, while at the same time making painfully obvious Europe's own internal division and the persistence of national agendas that make the elaboration of a common foreign policy strenuous and, at times, impossible.

With the creation of the Quartet, on the other hand, the EU and US approaches seemed to have formally converged, at least on the aspect of Middle East policy related to the Arab–Israeli peace process. It remained, however, unclear in the early stages whether the US Administration beyond the State Department was seriously committed to this exercise, or whether national governments within the EU were fully behind their collective representatives.

The Roadmap for Peace in the Middle East

With a speech given on 24 June 2002, US President George Bush called for a new Palestinian leadership and for the creation of an independent Palestinian state that would live side by side with Israel.[7] Earlier, in April 2002, German Foreign Minister Joschka Fischer had delineated a 'seven-point plan' to achieve a peace settlement that involved Israel's withdrawal to lines close to the pre-1967 borders and the establishment of a Palestinian state. In August 2002 a three-phase 'road map' drafted by the Danish EU presidency and inspired by the Fischer seven-point plan was agreed upon at an EU foreign ministers' meeting with a view to operationalising Bush's two-state vision by adding substance and a timeframe. This European initiative had a great influence on the Roadmap for Peace in the Middle East elaborated by the Quartet in the following months (Asseburg 2003: 185).

On 30 April 2003, after the election of Mahmud Abbas (also known as Abu Mazen) as first Palestinian Prime Minister, the text of the Roadmap – a comprehensive plan for the achievement of peace between Israel and the Palestinians – was presented by the Quartet.[8]

The Quartet called for a series of steps to be undertaken by both Palestinians and Israelis. In particular the Roadmap plan called for Palestinian democratisation, a new Palestinian leadership, local elections, a written constitution, uniform and centralised security organs, and a crackdown on terrorism. As for Israel, it asked for withdrawal to the pre-intifada lines, freezing of settlement activity, and improvement of humanitarian and living conditions of the Palestinian people.

The Roadmap attempted to create a performance-based timetable (subsequently said to be non-binding), with 'phases' to build the provisional state, followed by negotiations for a final accord to be reached by 2005. Furthermore, it envisaged the organisation of an international conference to facilitate the final-status talks and an international monitoring mechanism theoretically to supervise and determine performance for the progress from one phase to the next.

The Quartet, and the Roadmap as its instrument, were meant to constitute an official 'internationalisation' of the conflict and to introduce the principle of multilateralism in the negotiations. To a degree this was a departure from the scheme traditionally preferred by Israel (and the United States), whereby negotiations would be conducted with one actor at the time (e.g. Egypt, the Palestinian Authority, Jordan, etc.) and on specific topics (security, borders, etc.) rather than in a wider context, with the participation of several actors and in a comprehensive manner, with all issues on the table at the same time.

One of the ideas more strongly supported by the EU had long been that of addressing all the problems at hand in the context of an international conference that would see the involvement not only of the 'belligerents' but also of the international community in the role of mediator and facilitator of the talks. The Roadmap, therefore, seemed to somehow endorse this European approach and transform it into the chosen path of international diplomacy.

Since the 1980 Venice Declaration, Europe had favoured a multilateral approach to the peace process, insisting that such a framework was the best suited to create the conditions for real progress. European internal division and political weakness and American pressures had resulted in this view being taken into consideration only sporadically over the years.

The creation of the Quartet can be seen as one of these occasions, as it *officially* brought into the negotiations other actors (i.e. the EU, the UN and Russia) in addition to the Israelis, the Palestinians and the traditional mediator, the United States. Participation of the Quartet in the peace process underlined the commitment of the international community to the achievement of an equitable settlement of the conflict.

Some inherent contradictions, however, rendered the Roadmap flawed from its creation and undermined its possibility to be successful from the very beginning.

'A Middle East Roadmap to Where?';[9] 'A Middle East Roadmap to Gridlock?';[10] 'A Roadmap to Mars' (Nabulsi 2004); 'A Roadmap to failure'.[11] These are some of the titles of the numerous articles and analyses published by newspapers and think tanks in the years since 2002, and they underline the doubts and criticisms that the Roadmap has raised from many sides over the years. In fact, if on paper the Roadmap was supposed to create a multilateral framework for the negotiations and to promote multilateralism as an organising principle of the peace process, in practice what it really offered was a contradictory multilateral control framework for bilateral negotiations.

Final goals and intermediate steps were approved by the Quartet and then presented to the parties to the conflict (Israel and the PA), which were then supposed to implement them, but the role of direct negotiations and the importance of achieving a negotiated settlement between the parties were clearly acknowledged.

Furthermore, and rather problematically, the Plan called for bilateral negotiations aimed at implementing pre-established steps agreed upon by the Quartet rather than by Israel and the Palestinians. The two main parties to the conflict were, in fact, not involved in developing the Roadmap, but rather the plan was presented to them for their approval.

Since then both have been trying in one way or another to redefine it. The Palestinians officially accepted the Roadmap, but regularly emphasised their inability to take certain steps in the order suggested (the PA, for example, underlined its need to build its capabilities before taking on its obligations of dismantling terrorist infrastructure). For its part, Israel accepted the Roadmap but with fourteen objections, officialised by a document circulated by the government. These objections focused largely on the need for the termination of all acts of violence, terror and incitement as a precondition for progress, the need for a new Palestinian leadership, and the centrality of bilateral negotiations on the final status.

In the months following the publication of the Roadmap, not much progress at all was made, and the tension between Israel and the Palestinians remained high. Then in June 2004 Ariel Sharon, Prime Minister of Israel, announced a plan for Israeli unilateral withdrawal from the Gaza Strip, to be realised by 2005. Despite the plan being a clear departure from the notion of multilateral negotiations initially supported by the Quartet, the reaction of the Quartet's members to the plan was positive.

The EU's CFSP High Representative commented on the plan: 'I welcome the Israeli Prime Minister's proposals for disengagement from Gaza. This represents an opportunity to restart the implementation of the Road Map, as endorsed by the UN Security Council.'[12] Both the US President and the UN Secretary General called Sharon's decision 'courageous' and referred to it as the first step towards a resumption of the peace process in accordance with the Roadmap.

Looking at it from another, if perhaps cynical, perspective, one could argue that less than two years after its creation the Roadmap had led nowhere, its stated deadline (2005) had become meaningless and its prospects of success were grim.

The Quartet and the Lebanon war: A new role for the EU in the Middle East?

Despite having been born with inherent flaws that make its implementation difficult, if not impossible, the Roadmap Plan designed by the Quartet has – to a degree – been a useful instrument over the last few years and, if only in rhetorical terms, remains the blueprint of reference when international diplomacy discusses the next steps that should be taken in the peace process.[13]

The usefulness of the Quartet has manifested itself in two ways: one more political and impalpable, the other more practical.

As mentioned by this and other chapters in this volume, the EU has long struggled both to achieve a coherent position on the issue of the Arab–Israeli conflict and, whenever such a position was actually achieved, to make it heard by the United States. European influence in the conflict has been hampered by the cumbersome structures of Brussels' diplomacy and even more by the continued predominance of different and diverging national agendas (Musu 2003). Moreover, American interests in the region have made it even more difficult for Europe to sway the policy strategy (of lack thereof) elaborated by Washington, all this obviously in the context of continued Israeli resistance to the idea of opening the door to a role for Europe in the peace process.

The novelty of the Quartet, and of the Roadmap, is that it creates a formal framework in which US–EU interaction can take place. If, on the one hand, it can be argued that the United States' strategy tends to by and large condition the workings of the Quartet, on the other hand, as sometimes happens, the initiative has taken on a life of its own and has allowed a continuous exchange of opinions between European and American diplomats. This has resulted in some European ideas being received with somewhat more favour by the United States (for example, the notion of the need to convene an international conference to address the issues) while at the same time lowering to some extent Israeli suspicions vis-à-vis the EU as a mediator.

A caveat at this point is, however, necessary: these changes have been taking place very slowly, if not imperceptibly, and the reality on the ground largely resembles that of the pre-Quartet area. Observing the movements of American diplomacy, one will notice an alternation of phases during which the United States acts alone and ignores the Quartet (see, for example, the various diplomatic trips undertaken by Secretary of State Condoleezza Rice), and phases during which the Quartet seems to take centre stage and be the engine of new initiatives.

In November 2005, for example, the Quartet was instrumental in the conclusion of an 'Agreement on Movement and Access' between Israel and the Palestinian Authority, which included agreed principles for the Rafah crossing between Gaza and Egypt. On 21 November 2005, the Council of the EU welcomed the Agreement and agreed that the EU should undertake the Third Party role proposed in the Agreement. It therefore decided to launch the EU Border Assistance Mission at Rafah, named EUBAM Rafah, to monitor the operations of this border crossing point.

This limited initiative was unprecedented in nature: for the first time EU military personnel, under the command of an Italian general, supervised an area of security concern for Israel. Only a few months before such a proposal would have been unthinkable: the EU had long voiced its wish to be involved more directly in the security dimension of the peace process, but both Israeli and American opposition had rendered this by and large unfeasible. In the particular circumstances created by the August 2005 Israeli withdrawal from Gaza, however, the EU was better suited to carry out the task of supervising the Rafah crossing, and American assurances contributed to convincing Israel to accept the EU's offer. Arguably, such a development was partly made possible by the EU's membership of the Quartet, which had created a formal framework for the EU's role and tied it to that of the United States, thus easing Israel's deep-seated reservations with regards to the EU's involvement.

The initiative was also rendered possible by the significant changes that had taken place within the EU itself, with the creation of security and military institutions that contribute to reinforcing Europe's credibility as a global actor. Both the EU's and the member states' willingness to take part in military operations have undergone a notable transformation in the past few years, rendering the description of Europe as a solely 'civilian power' quite obsolete (Merand 2008).

The operational phase of the EUBAM Mission began on 30 November 2005 and was meant to have a duration of 12 months. It was then extended twice and was supposed to be operative until May 2008, but was instead suspended (not cancelled) after the Hamas takeover of the Gaza Strip in June 2007 (see below). The mission is a civilian ESDP operation of limited scope (up to ninety police and customs officers from thirteen European countries) but, by the time of its suspension, it had facilitated the crossing of nearly 500,000 people.[14]

Alongside EUBAM Rafah, the European Union established another mission in the Palestinian Territories in 2005, known as EUPOL COPPS (Coordination Office for Palestinian Police Support), and intended to provide enhanced support to the Palestinian Authority in establishing sustainable and effective policing arrangements.

A further step in promoting the EU's role in the security dimension of the Middle East conflict was taken in the summer of 2006, while the war between Israel and Hezbollah was raging in Lebanon. France and Italy took a leading role in attempting to resolve the crisis; the diplomatic efforts of both countries, and of France in particular, were instrumental in the adoption of UN Security Council Resolution 1701, which established the guidelines for a ceasefire between the parties. In August 2006, Israel accepted (and encouraged) the deployment of a large interposition force to reinforce the existing UN mission to Lebanon (UNIFIL) as a condition for a ceasefire. At the same time, EU foreign ministers met for a so-called troop-generating conference and agreed to deploy a total of almost 7000 troops from several EU member states to Lebanon as a peacekeeping force. The mission was to continue to be run under the aegis of the UN, but the most significant military presence would be European. While it did not come under the heading of ESDP, the military presence of the Europeans in Southern Lebanon, and the fact that it was actually welcomed by Israel, reflected, more than anything else, the growing role of Europe in the search for peace and stability in the Arab–Israeli conflict.[15] On the other hand, events on the ground continued to demonstrate the difficulties that the EU and its member states face when trying to develop coherent policies and step up the level of European involvement in the Middle East. A most important case in point is the victory of Hamas in the Palestinian elections of January 2006, an event that almost paralysed not only existing European initiatives such as EUBAM and EUPOL COPPS, but the overall activities of the Quartet.

The struggles of diplomacy: Hamas, Annapolis and the challenges of the future

In January 2006 a largely surprised international community witnessed the sweeping victory of Hamas in the Palestinian elections. A by and large regular and democratic vote brought to power a group that was included in the list of terrorist organisations of both the EU and the United States and that rejected not only the principles of the Oslo accords and of the Roadmap, but the notion in general of recognising and making peace with Israel.

The event heightened Israel's feeling of insecurity and its need to receive reassurances that the international community would not support the Palestinian Authority financially or diplomatically if this meant supporting an organisation that organises terrorist attacks on Israel's soil.

The victory of Hamas exposed the EU to a double set of pressures: on the one hand, the EU's policy has long been characterised by its preference for engagement rather than isolation of difficult interlocutors (as proved, for example, by the EU's policy towards Iran); on the other, both the United States and Israel insisted on the necessity to sabotage the government of an organisation that had neither recognised Israel's right to exist nor renounced violence.

Despite its decision to boycott diplomatically the Hamas government, the EU maintained – and even increased – its high level of economic support to the Palestinians. What changed was that the money was given directly to the intended recipients through a Temporary International Mechanism created ad hoc (now known as PEGASE, Mécanisme Palestino-Européen de Gestion de l'Aide Socio-économique) instead of being channelled through the PA. The mechanism was devised to prevent the flow of economic support from going through the hands of Hamas while at the same time avoiding a complete collapse of the Palestinian Authority.

The situation, however, worsened noticeably in the following months: Palestinian institutional reforms stalled, EUBAM became largely inoperable, and the EU's other Civilian Crisis Management Mission, EUPOL COPPS, met with the same destiny.[16]

The Palestinian election results also highlighted divergences within the Quartet itself: while the EU and the United States refused to deal directly with Hamas until it recognised Israel's right to exist, Russia (also a member of the Quartet) invited members of the Hamas leadership to Moscow for talks.

For its part, the United Nations also underlined the necessity for Hamas to abandon violence and terrorism, but a leaked End of Mission Report written by UN Envoy to the Quartet, Alvaro De Soto, criticised harshly the decision to 'not talk to Hamas' as a self-defeating diplomatic choice. UN Secretary General Ban Ki-Moon underlined that the report represented Mr De Soto's personal views, but since Hamas' political victory, and even more since it seized control of the Gaza Strip in June 2007, numerous analysts have started suggesting that excluding Hamas from the peace talks means attempting to achieve peace with only a part of the Palestinian Authority, a strategy that, according to many, will in no way bring a resolution of the conflict.[17]

This tension between the reality on the ground of a divided Palestinian Authority, with a weak but internationally supported President Abbas of Fatah, and an increasingly strong but internationally ostracised Hamas, and the political choice of large parts of the international diplomatic community to boycott Hamas and not include it in the negotiations, plagued the preparations and the proceedings of the international peace conference that took place in Annapolis (Maryland) in November 2007.

In the months leading up to the conference the United States stepped up its diplomatic activity. This was as a result of multiple factors, including the difficult situation in Iraq; the rising tensions with Iran (which called for increased cooperation between Sunni Arab regimes and the West, something that would become more feasible if there were progress in resolving the Arab–Israeli conflict); and, arguably, the mounting pressure coming from the looming end of the second term in office of President George W. Bush. Once again, the hope of marking the end of a presidency with the achievement of clear progress in the Middle East peace process seemed to be driving the American strategy, as it did during the closing months of Bill Clinton's term.

This heightened level of diplomatic activity rendered more evident the ambiguous attitude that the United States had by and large maintained vis-à-vis the role of the Quartet. As mentioned before, the idea of an international conference to advance the peace process was an integral part of the Roadmap's strategy, and had always been supported and pushed forward by the European Union. To an observer of the US activity in preparation for the conference, however, the impression was that Annapolis was meant to be primarily an American initiative, and that if progress were achieved it would be mainly as a result of American mediation and efforts.

The Quartet as a whole was present at the conference, but the three other members maintained a decidedly low profile, essentially backing the US action.

After the plenary sessions at United States Naval Academy, where, apart from the Quartet members, a large number of countries were in attendance – including, importantly, Syria – the Israelis and the Palestinians had a number of bilateral meetings with President Bush to discuss the next steps in the process. Once more the Roadmap constituted the blueprint for action, but there was less talk of the Quartet's role and more of how far the US administration was ready and able to go in order to achieve results. One of the provisions of the agreement reached in Annapolis made the United States the arbiter of the commitments under the Roadmap.

The Annapolis conference in no way brought about a breakthrough in the Israeli–Palestinian peace process. Negotiations over all the crucial issues remained very much open, from the status of Jerusalem to the questions of borders, settlements, refugees and water. The 'oscillation' between bilateralism and multilateralism continues to emerge clearly: on the one hand the Quartet, after its meeting of November 2008 in Sharm-el-Sheikh, announced its intention to convoke yet another international conference in 2009. On the other, Israel started engaging in indirect bilateral negotiations with Syria (with the mediation of Turkey), with Hamas (with the mediation of Egypt), and, very discreetly and informally, with Lebanon, to hinder the rise of Hezbollah.

At the end of December 2008, however, a six months truce between Hamas and Israel in Gaza came to an end amidst recriminations from each side that the other had not kept its commitments. Israel initiated shortly afterwards a massive military operation in the Gaza Strip, with the declared objective of weakening Hamas both militarily and politically. The reaction of the EU was rather inconsistent.

While France, for example, was by and large very critical of Israel, the new Czech presidency underlined that the operation had a defensive character, and mostly blamed Hamas for having escalated violence, as did Italy. Britain, for its part, tried to exercise diplomatic pressure on Israel to achieve a ceasefire. The Bush administration, by then a few weeks away from its end, also accused Hamas of having provoked the Israeli attack through its incessant launching of rockets into Israeli territories, while the UN and Russia invoked an urgent ceasefire and lamented the large number of civilian casualties. In other words, the Quartet as a whole played an insignificant role, as its members appeared rather divided on the most appropriate stance to take.

After the inauguration of President Barack Obama the eyes of the international community turned once again to the United States as the only actor potentially able to obtain results. While the other members of the Quartet fade into the background, the question arises, inevitably, whether in the eyes of the United States the Quartet is meant to be there to take the fall in case of need, in a sort of internationalisation of diplomatic failure, or to discreetly disappear in case of success, leaving the stage to the United States as the sole recognised mediator. While it is indeed true that hardly any progress in the peace process could be achieved without the heavy involvement of the United States, there are, however, some advantages to maintaining the Quartet alive, such as a legitimisation of the negotiations' outcomes in the eyes of the international community, and also the continued existence of a framework that promotes transatlantic cooperation and can contribute to the full coordination and harmonisation of American and European policies in this area of crucial importance to both. Furthermore, the Quartet still secures for the EU some involvement in Middle East diplomacy, which it might not otherwise have, while possibly enhancing the EU's actorness[18] in the Middle East; by compelling EU member states to regularly forge a common position on such a difficult issue, the Quartet is an important vehicle to refine EU policy, cement EU cohesion, and effectively speak with one voice on the Israeli–Palestinian conflict.

5
European Foreign Policy and the Arab–Israeli Peace Process: The Paradox of 'Converging Parallels'?

Introduction

Much has been written and said about the process of political integration that has taken place among the member states of the European Union in the course of the last few decades, and particularly in the last fifteen years. Undeniably, this process has experienced – since its first timid inception in the 1970s with the introduction of European Political Cooperation (EPC) – a strong qualitative leap that has led Europe to add a defence dimension to its Common Foreign and Security Policy (CFSP), and to create the so-called European Security and Defence Policy (ESDP).

But there are two sides to the story. One is told by the creation of an ever closer union, of the progressive, incremental construction of the edifice of Common Foreign and Security Policy, of the stratification of the instruments at its disposal, of the overcoming of old taboos with the introduction of the military dimension. The other, however, draws a different picture: that of the persistence of the primacy of national foreign policies, of the difficulty for member states to overcome differences and harmonise interests, of their continuous struggle to keep foreign policy at a European level within the limits of national control. As Regelsberger and Wessels (1996: 31) argue, the difficulty lies in the 'DDS' (discrete, discretionary, sovereignty) syndrome, in the sense that coordination of foreign policy and security immediately, and most visibly, raises the issue of national sovereignty.

European policy towards the Middle East, and in particular towards the Arab–Israeli conflict and peace process, constitutes an ideal case study for the problem of political integration in the EU: in fact, as has been evidenced in previous chapters, the Middle East has been one of the most widely debated issues among member states in the past forty years, and was one of the items discussed at the first EPC meeting in 1970. European countries are directly and indirectly involved in the Arab–Israeli conflict because of their geographical proximity to the region, their dependence on Middle Eastern oil and their fears of an insecurity spillover, but also because of the special relationship that many member states have with the region as a consequence of their past as colonial powers and because of historical memories from the complex patterns of persecution of European Jews, and of occupation and collaboration during the Second World War. The study of European Middle East policy offers the opportunity to test the ability of member states to harmonise their distinct foreign policies, to identify common interests and to proceed along the road of further integration and towards the elaboration of a common European foreign policy.

The main objective of this chapter is to conduct an analysis of two opposite trends that are clearly identifiable in the process of European political integration and, especially, in European foreign policy: (a) the convergence of the member states' policies and (b) the concurrent persistence of profound differences between national policies. The central question I attempt to answer is the following: Has convergence between the EU member states reached such an advanced qualitative level as to allow the formulation of a truly collective policy towards the Middle East, or is the EU's simply a policy of *'converging parallels'*?[1] To anyone familiar with the Euclidean system of geometry, the idea of 'converging parallels' will immediately come across as a geometrical impossibility. The word *'parallel'* designates 'two or more straight lines that do not intersect [...] being an equal distance apart everywhere'. Parallel lines have the same tendency or direction but never converge. Conversely, further research will determine that the meaning of the word *'converging'* is 'to tend toward an intersecting point or a common conclusion or result'.[2]

It appears, then, that converging parallels cannot, indeed, exist; but in effect what seems to be a paradox in the world of geometry actually appears to be a reality in the world of European foreign policy, and even more so in the policy towards the Middle East.

For over forty years the member states of the EC, and then of the EU, have debated the Middle East, have issued declarations of all sorts, and have also engaged in more practical initiatives, geared to financing the Palestinian Authority, arguably not very successfully or very effectively. It is ultimately possible to identify a 'European approach', broadly speaking, to the Middle East conflict – an approach that is, in appearance if not in substance, different from that of the United States; and which, after having been clearly set out with the Venice Declaration of 1980, in many respects has not been appreciably modified since (Ortega 2003).

But behind the façade of this common approach there lies the enduring reality of distinctly different national approaches to the issue, conflicting priorities and diverse and sometimes diverging interests. It is the dynamics of the relation between national foreign policies and foreign policy at the EU level towards the Arab–Israeli conflict that this chapter attempts to analyse, with the objective of establishing what has encouraged convergence and to what extent a collective policy has been achieved, and what, on the other hand, has kept national policies 'parallel' and therefore separate and clearly distinct from each other.

Some reflections on the concept of convergence

Before analysing the specific problem of EU Middle East policy, it is worth considering the issue of convergence itself. As Helen Wallace has pointed out, 'much of the literature about EU policy integration and much of the discourse of practitioners, and indeed the formal EU texts, talk about policy convergence as either a prerequisite for agreement or a desired outcome of agreement' (Wallace 2000: 58).

On the economic front, the EU set out in the EC Treaty four convergence criteria – price stability, government finances, exchange rates and long-term exchange rates – that reflect the degree of economic convergence that member states had to achieve: each member state was called to satisfy all four criteria in order to be become part of the euro area. However, in the intergovernmental framework within which the EU's CFSP is elaborated, member states have hitherto displayed little desire to set out binding foreign policy convergence criteria that might limit their freedom of action. Acknowledging the fact that, nevertheless, coordination and convergence – albeit in an informal, incremental and non-codified fashion – do take place in the sphere of foreign policy, it remains to be seen what factors can encourage or impede them.

A first set of factors is what could be referred to as the *'exogenous variables'*, which include:

- Pressure for collective, or at least coordinated, EU action coming from the international arena as a consequence of external expectations linked to the EU's perceived role as global actor. The increasing presence of the EU as a relevant actor on the international scene and its undeniable relevance in economic terms cannot but raise expectations with regard to a potentially significant influence of the Union on the course of events;
- Pressure exerted on the EU by external interlocutors who are also actors involved in the issues at stake (in the case of Middle East policy the Arab states, the United States, the Palestinian Authority). It must be noted, however, that pressure from the actors involved may be of very diverse, if not openly contradictory, nature: pressure for increased EU involvement and action (e.g. from the Palestinians), countered by pressure for the EU to remain uninvolved (e.g. from the United States).

The second set of factors is what could be called the *'endogenous variables'*, which include:

- The similarity/dissimilarity of what member states come to define as their interests, which inform national political agendas and priorities;
- The existence of common institutions at the EU level that are responsible for the implementation of certain aspects of a given policy, decided upon in the intergovernmental framework, and that in turn also shape the policy itself;
- The progressive harmonisation of the political discourse through the practice of continuous political discussion and bargaining within the various working groups and committees and the constant contacts between diplomatic services, which have worked together for a number of years;

- The development of a common political vision, a fairly similar approach to a given geographical region, and the tendency to privilege a certain diplomatic style, which distinguish the EU from other international actors.

But, if these are the factors that may encourage convergence in the EU's Common Foreign and Security Policy, nevertheless one crucial point should not be overlooked: collective action might be triggered not by a true convergence, but rather by *congruence*. As Helen Wallace has put it, congruence can be defined as 'the compatibility of the policy actors' preferences as the basis for establishing a shared policy regime. Different policy actors may have different preferences, but none the less choose the same collective action. Congruent preferences imply conditional commitments to collective regimes. Convergence of preferences may produce longer term stability of policy regimes' (Wallace 2000: 58).

In analysing convergence in EU Middle East policy, we shall endeavour to identify the cases in which real convergence was achieved, and those in which a collective action was undertaken exclusively on the basis of different but congruent preferences. In the next section an analysis of the abovementioned endogenous and exogenous variables and of their interaction will be conducted, in order to establish whether, and to what extent, their combined pressure has brought about a true convergence in the European member states' policies towards the Middle East.

Elements of convergence in the EU's policy towards the peace process

Exogenous variables: External pressures

The EU policy towards the Arab–Israeli peace process is subject to pressures of very different kinds: there is first of all the 'general' international pressure deriving from the growing role of the EU as a global actor and consequently from expectations for an effective EU role in an area of high political instability. This pressure, in turn, generates internal EU expectations in relation to the CFSP and a demand for greater activity and decisiveness in foreign policy. As Christopher Hill put it, 'the need to deal with powerful or problematic countries such as the United States or Israel has to some extent already imposed discipline and caution on the European group' (Hill 1997: 38). Member states have also been subjected to pressures for increased European involvement in the peace process by the international community through the United Nations: if, on a political level, the UN General Secretary wants to work with the United States, the EU's involvement is nonetheless very positively perceived, both from an economic point of view and due to the prospect that the EU might contribute to mitigating the United States' unilateral approach. Europe has supported the idea of the United Nations as the proper forum to discuss the peace process in a multilateral framework from the beginning, a position in line with the EU's political culture of multilateralism and its inclination to support multilateral rules and institutions (Pollack 2003: 116).

Secondly, there is the specific pressure coming from some of the main actors involved in the Arab–Israeli dispute, namely, the Arab states (Ortega 2003; Roberson 1998). Since the early days of EPC, Arab states have tried to involve Europe in the peace process, hoping that EC/EU policy could counterbalance American policy, which they see as being biased in favour of Israel. Following the 1973 oil crisis this pressure was exercised mainly using the card of European dependence on Middle East oil, and at first resulted not only in a shift of the EC towards a more pro-Arab stance, but also in strong competition among the member states themselves to ensure oil supplies. After 1973, and the Europeans' full realisation of their dependence on oil imports, the EC/EU has undertaken a number of initiatives to institutionalise its relations with the region: from the Global Mediterranean Policy to the Euro-Arab Dialogue, the EC–Gulf Dialogue, the Barcelona process, the Common Mediterranean Strategy and the European Neighbourhood Policy. The EU has attempted to focus these initiatives mainly on the economic dimension or on wider issues of regional security, whereas the Arab states have exerted all possible pressure to widen their political significance and to force the EU to assume a more proactive role in the Arab–Israeli peace process.

However, if these are pressures for a deeper EU involvement in the peace process, pressures of an exactly opposite nature are exerted on Europe by other actors involved: the United States and Israel. The United States, which is and wants to remain the main mediator between the Arabs and the Israelis, opposed a European involvement in the peace process from day one, especially once the strong differences between American and EC/EU positions on the issue became clear. The United States has often accused the Europeans of being unable to resist the pressure coming from the Arabs and of seeking to eliminate obstacles to commerce through political accommodation (Musu and Wallace 2003).

The EU takes a completely different view on the matter, arguing that commerce may be viewed as a mean of gaining political influence, and that trade and cooperation are to underpin peace; nonetheless, it has very often had to give in to American pressures and downscale the contents of its initiatives to avoid excessive damage to transatlantic relations, which after all are more important to the EU than its Middle East policy. In the dilemma of Europe's double dependency – on the Arab countries for energy, investment capital and export markets, and on the United States for protection and diplomatic progress – it is usually transatlantic relations that have priority over other considerations.

More recently it appeared that the United States had modified its attitude towards a formal European involvement in the peace process: in 2002 Colin Powell announced the formation of a 'Middle East Quartet', formed by the United States, the EU, Russia and the UN. The focus of this approach was on pursuing a two-state solution to the Israeli–Palestinian conflict, with the active engagement of outside actors. The Quartet's three-phase implementation 'Roadmap', however, which was meant to achieve a final settlement by 2005, has failed and it still remains unclear to what extent the US Administration is seriously committed to this 'multilateral exercise', or whether the Quartet is supposed to give an illusion of international involvement in the peace process while the United States maintains its primary role in the negotiations.

Parallel to the United States' hostility to EU involvement in the peace process comes the Israeli opposition, which took shape as early as 1967, immediately after the Six-Days War, when for the first time European public opinion – especially from the left – became critical of Israel and shifted its support to the Palestinians. The fracture between Europe and Israel became deeper with the accession to power in 1977 of the Likud party, which had much stronger ties with the United States than the Labour Party, which had been traditionally much closer to Europe. Perceiving Europe's position as biased in favour of the Palestinians and influenced by the Arab states and by economic considerations, Israel has opposed EU political involvement in the peace process and made every effort to keep it within the boundaries of economic support to the Palestinian Authority. In 2005 Israel, at American insistence, accepted the EU offer to supervise the Rafah border crossing between Gaza and Egypt at the conclusion of Israel's unilateral withdrawal from the Gaza Strip. This development might indicate an improvement in Israel–EU relations, but it is far from signifying a full acceptance on Israel's part of an official involvement of the EU in the negotiations (Musu 2006b). In the eyes of the Israeli government, Europe has made over the years three tactical errors that have doomed its role as an acceptable mediator in the peace process: it demanded that Israel make concessions to the Palestinians in advance of direct peace negotiations between Israel and the Palestinians; it made concessions to the Palestinians that prejudged Israeli interests in advance of direct peace negotiations; and it insisted on the United Nations as the appropriate forum for negotiations towards a comprehensive peace settlement, knowing that this was totally unacceptable to Israel (Ginsberg 2001). In Israel's view the EU should have a secondary role and seek to achieve complementarity of policy initiatives with the United States.[3]

It is plausible to say that, given the opposite nature of the converging – or rather diverging – external pressures hitherto described, which would probably in the end nullify each other, and the natural tendency of the EU to inaction or to limited and irresolute action in foreign policy, the final result might quite easily have been an absence of initiative on the EU's part and a lack of motivation in searching for policy coordination in the Middle East,[4] were it not for a number of other endogenous factors that came into play and forced the EU to try to coordinate its policy towards the Middle East.

Endogenous variables: National interests

As previously mentioned, European countries are directly implicated in the Arab–Israeli conflict because of their geographic proximity, their dependence on oil and their security needs, as well as the historical role played by several of them in the region. Harmonising the EU's member states' viewpoints on the Arab–Israeli conflict is a task which has always proved difficult. As a brief overview of their approach to the Middle East demonstrates, the specific individual interests of the member states differ appreciably, and very often policy coordination has been obtained not on the basis of convergence but rather on the basis of congruence, that is, a sufficient compatibility of member state preferences allowing the elaboration of a common policy. The analysis will focus on four countries that have been particularly active in trying to influence EU Middle East policy: France, Germany, Great Britain and Italy. The objective is to show how, albeit for totally differing reasons, EU member states have come to support, with varying degrees of enthusiasm, the idea of a common European policy towards the Arab–Israeli peace process.

It is France that has most often taken the lead in European initiatives in the Middle East. Since the late 1960s, France's policy has been characterised by a clear pro-Arab stance and its priority has clearly been the promotion of closer relations with Arab states. Many common declarations of the EC, and then of the EU, bear the clear mark of France's influence and reflect the acceptance of the political line suggested by France, particularly with regard to the Palestinian question. This contributed, Israelis argue, to creating the first deep fractures between Israel and the EU.[5] French governments have promoted the EU's international activity as a vehicle for those initiatives which France alone cannot accomplish, and which are intended to supplement French efforts at a national level. The European presence is particularly useful in those areas of the world where French influence is weak and American hegemony is strong, where memories of France's colonial past are still strong, and where the scale of economic aid and investment required is beyond the scope of French bilateral capabilities (Blunden 2000).

France has sought to project a strong European political voice, to complement and amplify its national voice. Nicole Gnesotto has argued that 'Europe is to France what the United States is to Britain, the optimum multiplier of national power' (Gnesotto 1998). On the other hand, as France's former Foreign Minister Hubert Vedrine underlined: 'the political construction of the Union as an amplifier of French power does not oblige France to abandon sovereignty'.[6] It may be said that for France, in general terms, Europe is about 'adding', not 'subtracting'. And in specific terms it is about asserting independence from the United States.

As for the Middle East, French governments have utilised a multilateral, European approach to promote French interests. Following the Gulf War in 1991, France accelerated the Europeanisation of its foreign policy in the Arab world. It supported and promoted European initiatives in the Mediterranean to counterbalance the shift of the European centre of gravity towards the North East determined by the enlargement process, as well as to compete more effectively with the dominant American position in the region. However, this has not ruled out simultaneous and complementary invocations of privileged bilateral links with a number of countries in the Mediterranean area. To France, the EU offers effective leverage and a vehicle for reasserting French influence in the region: substantial EU aid to the Palestinian Authority has amplified the by no means insignificant French bilateral protocols. France's policy of providing financial and diplomatic support to the Palestinians has become European policy, thus placing European means at the service of a French vision of the Arab–Israeli conflict and its solution. Parallel to France's desire to protect the interests it deems more relevant for the nation, there is also the desire to develop a different and independent policy from that of the United States: this objective has long been an important priority for France, and has been pursued at times by pushing for greater European assertiveness, but on other occasions by launching autonomous French initiatives with no prior consultations with the other EU member states, as in the case of Chirac's 1996 tour of the Middle East[7] or, more recently, Sarkozy's trip to the region,[8] therefore causing tensions with the European allies and embarrassment to the EU as a whole for its inability to express a coherent policy.

Germany has made a fundamental contribution to steering integration and shaping the EU's rules and agenda priorities, as part of its attempt to shape its regional milieu (Bulmer, Jeffery and Paterson 2000). However, for obvious historical reasons, Germany's relations with Israel are a highly sensitive issue, and German governments have often hesitated to criticise Israeli policy too harshly: to use the words of Lord Weidenfeld, on the issue of Middle East policy Germany is 'torn and confused'.[9]

Germany has clear interests in the achievement of stability in the Middle East, but it hesitates to exert its diplomatic clout, especially against Israel, towards which it feels a sense of special responsibility.[10] For Germany the possibility of shifting national positions under the guise of a search for a common European position has been attractive: taking advantage of a sort of 'shield effect', it has initiated a rapprochement to the Arab world, claiming this to be an 'unavoidable price' to pay for the achievement of a unified European position and solidarity, while at the same time it has avoided upsetting domestic public opinion. Given the reconciliation and the special relationship Germany has developed with Israel since the Holocaust, this remarkable reorientation of policy would not have been conceivable outside the framework of EPC/CFSP (Overhaus, Maull and Harnisch 2002).

Germany has recently been able to capitalise on its good relations with Israel by launching peace initiatives independently or under the aegis of the EU, initiatives which would otherwise have been difficult to realise given the strained relations between Israel and the EU.[11]

The United Kingdom is, in some ways, torn between two different tendencies: on the one hand, given its historical past as a colonial power, it has a natural inclination to encourage European initiatives in the peace process and is very reluctant to accept the secondary role to which the EU is relegated. On the other hand, its close ties with the United States and the high priority given to transatlantic relations prompt the United Kingdom to exercise caution in encouraging the development of an independent EU policy towards the peace process that so often not only differs from the American policy, but goes openly against it. More than twenty years ago Geoffrey Edwards argued that 'there has been an essential duality of purpose in British policy irrespective of the political complexion of the government; this has been to influence the Arabs as far as possible to take a more conciliatory attitude and to influence the Americans to press the Israelis to the same end' (Edwards 1984: 49). This is still largely true today.

In an interview with the author, Sir Malcolm Rifkind, Former British Minister of Defence and Secretary of State for Foreign and Commonwealth Affairs, underlined how the member states – including Britain – share a genuinely common view of the preferred settlement of the Arab–Israeli conflict: security for Israel, creation of a Palestinian state, cessation of the use of terrorism on the part of the Palestinians, and of the expansion of the settlements on the part of the Israelis.[12] However, he argued, the British position differs from that of some other member states (France in particular) in that it sees increased EU involvement in the political negotiations as a 'distraction' in a domain that should be left to the Americans. The EU's involvement should be limited to those activities that are welcomed by the Arabs, the Israelis and the Americans, first among them the economic support provided to the Palestinian Authority.

Italy supports a strong European involvement in the peace process, mainly within the framework of a broader Mediterranean policy, which should, in the Italian view, be one of the top European priorities, not to be neglected in favour of a policy more concentrated on the Northern dimension and on enlargement problems (Silvestri 1998).

Italy's perception of the risk of being marginalised due to the EU's eastward enlargement has indeed increased, promoting what Mr De Michelis, former Italian Foreign Minister, has defined as 'the conscious adoption of a well-defined geopolitical perspective qualifying Italy's actions and initiatives in Europe and in the world',[13] namely, the so-called Mediterranean dimension of the European Union. This was to be a complement and balancing element to the so-called Baltic configuration resulting from the decision to expand the Union to twenty-seven members. Europe taking on a Baltic configuration threatened to relegate Italy to a more marginal role, making even Northern Italy a peripheral region and sentencing the Mediterranean to a future of instability, conflict and underdevelopment. On the other hand, explicit affirmation of Europe's Mediterranean dimension would make the exclusion of Italy from the group of guiding countries unthinkable.

Good relations with most Arab States and with the Palestinians remain by and large a constant factor in Italy's policy, but its relations with Israel have been ambivalent. Italy's policy towards Israel has spanned from the colder and critical attitude of the Forlani and Andreotti governments to the stance of the Berlusconi government, which advocated Israel's accession to the European Union. The idea of opening to Israel the possibility of accession to the EU dates back to 1991. In the aftermath of the Gulf War, and on the eve of the Madrid talks, Italy made a proposal at the European Union level by which, once an agreement had been reached by the parties, the EU would have offered Israel the opportunity of taking part in the European integration process. The first step would have been to concede to Israel, as had previously been the case with Austria, Norway, Switzerland and Sweden, the status of country belonging to the so-called European common economic space.

Mr De Michelis has described Italy's view of Europe's potential role in the peace process as follows: 'In the past decades, in phases of conflict Israel has been able to count on the Americans for economic and military support. However, when it comes to the peace process, the United States are too distant, and guarantees for Israel can only come from Europe. And this would be the most important aspect of the prospected integration at the European level, on the one hand offering European citizens the possibility of holding a European passport and of moving freely within the continent; on the other, of drawing advantage from economic integration, and the opportunities offered by a market of such considerable dimensions as the European. To the Palestinians, on the other hand, Europe should offer economic support in the form of a Marshall Plan of sorts, and a Euro-Mediterranean, Euro-Arab cooperation leading to the creation of advantageous general conditions.'[14]

To sum up, all these member states, for deeply different reasons, have encouraged the development of a common European Middle East policy: France in an effort to strengthen the EU's (and its own) international role vis-à-vis the United States, Germany in order to develop its relations with the Arab states without harming its relations with Israel, Italy in the context of its continuous insistence on the importance of a Mediterranean dimension for the EU, and the United Kingdom for historical reasons but also as a way of taking on the role of mediator between the EU and the United States in order to ease transatlantic tensions.

In addition to these specific national interests, unification is being strongly prompted by interests that are *shared* by all EU member states, namely the free flow of oil at a reasonable price to grant energy supplies to Europe; the political stability of the area to avoid an insecurity spillover and uncontrolled migration flows; regional prosperity to create a market for European products.

The combination of these centripetal and centrifugal forces – compatible national interests and convergent shared interests vs. strong and diverging national interests – generates growing pressure for the development of an effective European common policy towards the Middle East, which would allow the EU to take on an active role in the protection of its interests and an adequate say in the peace process, commensurate with its economic weight; on the other hand, though, it wields a restraining effect on the full development of this policy, pushing it towards the notorious target of a minimal common denominator, which has haunted EU foreign policy for over thirty years.

Endogenous variables: The transgovernmental network and the common institutions

In over thirty-five years of European political cooperation, EU member states have developed an intensive transgovernmental network that has profoundly changed the framework within which European governments make foreign policy: it has become normal practice within EU foreign ministries to work with diplomats seconded from other states, even in planning staff and defence policy departments. Information and intelligence are widely shared and foreign ministers meet several times a month, formally and informally (Forster and Wallace 2000).

Policy towards the Middle East is discussed at all levels of the EU foreign policy mechanism; furthermore, it is discussed both in the intergovernmental framework of Pillar II and in the framework of Pillar I, not only because Pillar I instruments are used to implement decisions taken in Pillar II, but also because the Commission is responsible for the developing and running of long-term projects of economic assistance to the region (Monar 1998a). The Middle East was actually one of the first policy areas (together with the CSCE) for which the boundaries between the EC and the EPC were broken down in the 1970s: the Euro-Arab Dialogue, for instance, had for the first time a special inter-EPC–EEC working group, which reported to both the Committee of Permanent Representatives and the Political Committee of the EPC; this EPC procedural innovation was then institutionalised with the Amsterdam Treaty twenty years later.

All this has not been without effect: in fact, it has led to a gradual harmonisation of the political discourse and the progressive softening of national differences in approach. Immersed in a process of socialisation, Foreign Ministries have slowly shifted their preferences to make them at least compatible with those of the other governments. Through constant interaction at innumerable levels, member

governments are part of a complex network of institutions and procedures that makes up EU decision-making. That interaction and
the institutional network itself inevitably play a part in determining
government strategies and in influencing the goals and objectives of
governments at the national as well as the European levels.

In parallel to this informal process of socialisation and to these
incremental changes in working practices, a more formal process of
institution-building and a stratification of the instruments at the
CFSP's disposal have taken place.

It is important here to underline the relevance of these institutions as both a vehicle and an obstacle to furthering political
integration. On the one hand, 'all evidence points to the fact that
institutions do matter, if only because they can create crucial incen-
tives to moderating divergence and inconsistency and facilitating a
common output' (Dassù and Missiroli 2002). On the other, undeniable institutional complexity (or rather confusion) continues to
handicap the EU as a global actor; the diffusion of authority within
the Union and the permanent intergovernmental bargaining produce inertia, resistance to change, and artificial compartmentalisa-
tion of policy.

The most significant innovation affecting EU policy towards the
Middle East is undoubtedly the introduction of two new figures: the
Special Envoy and the High Representative for the CFSP. The appointment in 1996 of Mr Miguel Angel Moratinos as the first EU Special
Envoy (now 'Special Representative') for the Middle East peace
process provided the EU for the first time with a single interlocutor for dealing with other regional actors, in an attempt to reduce
the difficulties and inconsistencies of the CFSP due to the rotating
EU Presidency system. The potential of this innovation, however,
has been marred by the very nature of the 'Special Representative'
mandate, which, though formally quite broad, does not include the
possibility of committing the member states to any step which has
not been previously agreed upon.[15] His action must take place in a
strictly intergovernmental framework: he is guided by, and reports
to, the Presidency (and more recently to the High Representative),
and his scope for autonomous initiative is very limited and tightly
bound to the indications received from the Council. As a consequence, Mr Moratinos encountered great difficulties (as has his suc-
cessor Marc Otte since 2003) in creating for himself a role beyond

that of 'facilitator' of the peace talks, although he took part directly in many stages of the negotiations, earning the trust and respect of all the main actors involved.

In 1999 the EU agreed to appoint Mr Javier Solana High Representative for the CFSP, a role to be added alongside that of Secretary General of the Council. Since his appointment, Mr Solana and his Policy Planning Unit have been closely involved in the Middle East peace process, representing the EU's position in the negotiations and contributing autonomous initiatives. But the familiar pattern has repeated itself, and Mr Solana's action has been hampered by the political limits of his mandate and trapped within the limits of inter-governmental consensus.

A fitting example of the EU's enhanced role as a result of the introduction of a High Representative is the inclusion of Mr Solana in the already mentioned 'Quartet', formed by the United States, the UN, Russia and the EU. However – perhaps not surprisingly – the cumbersome structures of EU diplomacy have managed to squeeze the Commissioner for External Relations and the Foreign Minister of the member state holding the Council Presidency into the 'single' EU seat. In other words, once again the member states have revealed their 'schizophrenic' attitude,[16] encouraging convergence through informal socialisation processes and formal institution-building on the one hand, while on the other trying their best to block convergence by limiting the powers attributed to the new institutions and the continuous reliance on mutual trust and consensus.

Endogenous variables: The EU's strategic culture and political vision

The paragraphs above have produced ample evidence of how difficult it is to generalise when dealing with EU foreign policy. Nonetheless – with due caution – it is indeed possible to identify certain basic principles on which the EU's stance towards the Middle East is based, and which are shared by almost all member states.

First of all, it must be stressed that, for Europe, Middle East policy overlaps with Mediterranean policy. The EU considers the Mediterranean as a coherent geostrategic region, and from this perspective it sees political instability in the Middle East as a potential danger to the political stability of the whole region. Indeed, 'the European discourse alternatively emphasises Europe's common destiny with the peoples of the region and its responsibility for furthering peace, democracy and development among its neighbours, or European security and economic interests which require both socio-economic development and political progress in the region including, prominently, the peaceful regulation of the Arab–Israeli conflict' (Perthes 2000). There is a clear link between the Middle East peace process and the EU's interest in building a safer Euro-Mediterranean regional environment.

Focusing more closely on Europe's approach to the peace process itself, it is possible to identify a number of fundamental principles on which the EU has based its policy since the signing of the Venice Declaration in 1980:

- the EU has constantly insisted on the need for all the relevant issues to be taken on simultaneously, and has repeatedly supported the idea of international peace conferences where regional actors meet in a multilateral framework. This position is consistent with the EU's political culture of multilateralism, and its emphasis on the primacy of negotiation and diplomacy over the use of force
- the EU appeals regularly to United Nations resolutions and underlines the importance of respecting international law
- the EU has always emphasised the 'legitimate right of the Palestinians' – well before the Palestinian question was recognised by the Israelis and the Americans as being central to the resolution of the Arab–Israeli dispute[17]
- The EU is a strong supporter of the two States solution and of the principle that the PLO is the legitimate representative of the Palestinian people.

To better prove this point, a study carried out in 2002 by Paul Luif of the Austrian Institute for International Affairs is of help. In his paper, Dr Luif analyses the voting behaviour of the EU member states in the General Assembly (GA) of the United Nations on a number of selected issues (including, for example, security, disarmament, decolonisation and human rights). While the decisions taken by the Security Council, rather than the General Assembly, are more significant for the conflict, an analysis of the voting behaviour of European states in the GA is helpful in order to evaluate the member states' ability to coordinate and harmonise their policies towards the Middle East.

According to Article 19 of the EU Treaty, 'Member States shall coordinate their action in international organisations and at international conferences. They shall uphold the common positions in such fora.' The UN General Assembly is indeed a prime example of EU attempts to 'speak with one voice'. Each year, from September to December, the UN General Assembly debates a wide range of issues pertaining to international relations, and passes some 300 resolutions (and a few decisions) on these issues. In the tables elaborated by Paul Luif, and reproduced here,[18] the data refer to the votes expressed by the member states with regard to Middle East issues (including the Arab–Israeli peace process).

Table 5.1 considers all the 'recorded votes' and calculates the percentage of votes where the EU member states 'spoke with one voice', that is, all EU states voted identically. Tables 5.2 and 5.3, respectively, illustrate the number of recorded votes in the UN General Assembly, including votes on parts of resolutions, motions and decisions, and the percentage of votes with EU consensus. In Table 5.4 the focal point is the EU 'majority', that is, the voting behaviour of the majority of the EU member states. With fifteen member states, if at least eight EU countries vote in the same manner, this position is used to calculate the 'Distance Index'. The 'Distance Index' sets '0' as a minimum (the EU member state always votes with the EU majority) and '100' as a theoretical maximum (the EU member state always votes against the EU majority).

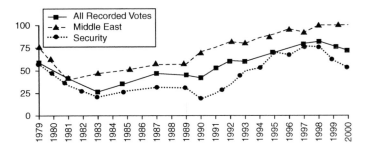

Table 5.1 EU voting behaviour in the General Assembly of the United Nations. Consensus among the EU member states in all recorded votes and selected issue areas (1979–2000)

Table 5.2 Number of recorded votes in the UN General Assembly including votes on parts of resolution, motions, decisions (1979–2002)

	1979	1981	1983	1985	1987	1989	1990	1991	1992	1993	1994	1995	1996	1997	1998	1999	2000	2001	2002
Number of all recordable votes	96	151	170	203	203	177	143	103	89	88	77	92	97	96	90	84	99	83	106
Middle East	31	35	43	51	44	37	31	34	34	20	22	21	24	25	24	22	25	25	22

Table 5.3 Percentage of votes with EU *Consensus* (1979–2002)

	1979	1981	1983	1985	1987	1989	1990	1991	1992	1993	1994	1995	1996	1997	1998	1999	2000	2001	2002
All votes	58.9	42.4	27.1	37.4	47.5	45.5	41.8	52.8	61.4	59.7	65.1	70.1	75.0	80.0	82.1	76.8	72.3	73.9	75.5
Middle East	74.2	40.0	46.5	51.0	56.8	56.8	71.0	76.5	82.4	80.0	86.4	90.5	95.8	92.0	100	100	100	84.0	95.5
Number of recordable votes	96	151	170	203	177	143			89	88	77	97	96	90	84	99	83	88	106

Table 5.4 Voting behavior of EU member states in the General Assembly of the United Nations: Distance from the EU majority for votes concerning the Middle East (1979-2002)

	1979	1981	1983	1985	1987	1989	1990	1991	1992	1993	1994	1995	1996	1997	1998	1999	2000	2001	2002
Austria	7	11	17	16	12	7	9	5	4	3	0	0	0	0	0	0	0	0	0
Finland	6	4	10	13	8	3	4	2	2	0	0		0	0	0	0	0	0	0
Sweden	6	4	10	15	9	4	5	2	2	2	0		0	0	0	0	0	0	0
Spain	35	44	28	22	19	12	15	12	11	13	3	3	2	0	0	0	0	2	0
Portugal	24	33	18	9	0	0	0	0	2	0	0	0	0	0	0	0	0	0	0
Greece	35	44	35	31	25	24	16	12	11	13	3	3	n/a	0	0	0	0	0	0
Ireland	2	5	0	2	3	0	0	0	2	3	3	3	0	0	0	0	0	0	0
Denmark	4	5	0	0	1	0	0	0	2	0	0	0	0	0	0	0	2	2	0
UK	2	0	0	0	0	1	0	2	0	0	0	0	0	0	0	0	2	2	0
France	11	2	1	2	0	0	0	0	0	6	3	3	0	0	0	0	0	0	0
Italy	2	2	0	2	1	0	0	0	0	0	0	0	0	0	0	0	2	2	0
Germany, FR	2	0	3	0	0	1	0	2	0	0	0	0	0	0	0	0	2	2	0
Netherlands	4	0	0	0	0	1	0	2	0	0	3	0	0	0	0	0	2	2	0
Luxembourg	2	2	1	0	1	0	0	0	0	0	0	0	2	2	0	0	0	0	0
Belgium	2	0	0	0	0	0	0	0	0	0	0	0	0	0	0	0	0	0	3

Note: Maximum Distance from EU Majority=100. Minimum=0.

Conclusion: 'The birds and the bats' or 'The phenomenon of the common European foreign policy'

The purpose of this chapter was to illustrate and analyse the problematic interrelation between two opposing trends in the evolution of European foreign policy: the development of a stronger convergence of member state policies as a result of the influence exercised by a number of exogenous and endogenous variables, and the undiminished strength of specific national preferences and priorities that pose a challenge to the consolidation of this convergence. With this objective in mind, the chapter focused on the case of European Middle East policy – and in particular of the policy towards the Arab–Israeli peace process, given its political relevance for the European Union and the long-standing involvement of the EU in the process.

The case study has shown how EU Middle East policy could be said to generate a paradox of *converging parallels*.

In other words, EU Middle East policy shows clear signs of convergence as a result of:

a. converging external pressures
b. the similarity of member states' interests
c. the existence of a transgovernmental network and of common institutions, which contribute to the harmonisation of the different policies
d. the development of a European perception, in broad terms, of the issue.

On the other hand, however, the attainment of a real convergence, capable of producing a truly collective policy, has been consistently hampered by the persistence of differences in the individual member states' preferences, which remain clearly distinct from, and only occasionally similar to, those of the other member states.

Therefore, this being the situation, how can convergence in European foreign policy be described?

A very suggestive idea comes to us from a search in an English language dictionary; the fifth meaning of the word 'convergence' is in fact given as follows: 'Convergent evolution: the evolutionary development of a *superficial resemblance between unrelated animals that occupy a similar environment,* as in the evolution of wings in birds and bats.'[19]

This description fits EU policy towards the peace process very nicely indeed; in fact, it strikes one as being appropriate for European foreign policy in general: EU member states have maintained, and struggle to maintain, tight control over their foreign policy in order to protect what they consider to be their national interests; nonetheless, they find ever more frequently that those interests can be better protected through a common European action, which is able to project into the international arena the combined weight of the twenty-seven members of the Union. As a consequence, more and more national governments, often prompted by totally different reasons and agendas, turn to the EU and encourage the elaboration of common European policies, creating precisely the effect of a convergence of policies that in most cases, however, will not intersect and will remain an 'equal distance apart'.

6

The Instruments of European Foreign Policy and Their Use in the Case of the Arab–Israeli Peace Process: A Case of Insufficiency, Inadequacy, Misuse or Underutilisation?

Introduction

The purpose of this chapter is twofold: to conduct an in-depth analysis of the instruments of European Union foreign policy, and to conduct an analysis of how these instruments have been used within the context of the European Union's policy towards the Arab–Israeli peace process in the years between 1991 and 2009.

The EC/EU has long been directly and indirectly involved in the Arab–Israeli dispute, and has put most of its foreign policy instruments to use in dealing with it. The varying use of these instruments on the part of the EU has reflected at times the search for an active involvement in the issue, at times the compelled response to an inescapable entanglement with the fate of a neighbouring region, and at times the purposeful search for an area of viable political harmonisation among the member states. The 'reflexive' dimension of European Middle East policy – that is, a policy mainly concerned with the actual formation of a common policy as an integrative value per se – has also very often played a primary role (Greilsammer and Weiler 1987): the Middle East peace process has frequently been used as a 'testing ground' for new European foreign policy instruments, or, in other words, as a means for achieving an internal objective, namely the development and consolidation of EPC and then of CFSP.

In general, the EU's policy has been regarded as scarcely effective (Hill 1990; Nuttall 2000; Smith 1996b; Zielonka 1998a) – where an 'effective policy' is one intended to directly and appreciably influence the other actors' actions, and therefore the course of events, and does so successfully – and constantly subordinated to that of the United States, the truly powerful mediator whose role is acknowledged and accepted by both parties: the Israelis and the Arabs (Blackwill and Sturmer 1997; Gompert and Larrabee 1998; Gordon 1998).

This chapter, analysing the instruments at the EU's disposal and how these instruments have been used in the context of the formulation of a European policy towards the Arab–Israeli peace process, will attempt to establish whether one, or possibly more than one, of the following conditions apply:

- A case of insufficiency: the EU does not have at its disposal enough instruments to deal effectively with the Middle East peace process; more instruments would enhance the EU's action and involvement, increasing its chances of success.
- A case of inadequacy: the instruments at the EU's disposal are inadequate to deal with the Middle East peace process due to the specific nature of the issues at stake; in particular, the limited military instruments available to the EU to back up and support any kind of political initiative renders the EU per se unable to act in the context of the peace process except in coordination with – and subordinate to – the United States.
- A case of misuse: foreign policy instruments are not appropriately and effectively used by the EU due to the inadequacy of the institutions in charge and the bureaucratic complexity which characterises all levels of EU policymaking.
- A case of underutilisation: the instruments at the EU's disposal are deliberately underutilised by the member states, the reasons for this being the persistent desire of the member states to maintain control over their foreign policy; their reluctance to proceed too speedily in the direction of political integration in the Union; and their inability to find common interests of sufficient number to justify, in their view, the renunciation of the particularisms of

national foreign policies and priorities in the name of the higher objective of achieving a common European policy.

An analysis of the progressive, incremental construction of the edifice of Common Foreign and Security Policy, and the stratification of the instruments at its disposal, will be matched with a parallel analysis of the immediate use of these instruments in a specific foreign policy context such as the Arab–Israeli peace process.

One objective is, through a legal–institutional analysis of the foreign policy instruments at the EU's disposal, to offer an evaluation of the scope for EU action in foreign policy, taking into consideration both the 'explicit' capabilities officially provided for in the various treaties and the 'implicit' capabilities that stem from the EU's potential power, from practice and from possible informal agreements among EU member states. The other objective is, in examining the utilisation of these instruments in a complex and highly sensitive case such as the Middle East peace process, to investigate the political dimension of certain EU failures, which are not only the result of the constraints under which the CFSP is forced to operate because of the complexities of its legal institutional rules, but also of a deliberate choice on the part of the member states, who inconsistently avail themselves of the instruments available, and intentionally keep the EU foreign policy machinery burdensome and scarcely efficient.

The next section will focus on the progressive construction of the EU's foreign policy mechanisms, from the onset of the Common Foreign and Security Policy until the creation of the European Security and Defence Policy (ESDP) and the appointment of the High Representative of the CFSP. The chapter will then proceed with a systematic analysis of the use of European foreign policy instruments in the context of the Arab–Israeli peace process from 1991 to 2009, in order to establish whether all of the available instruments have been utilised and to assess both their intrinsic effectiveness and the ability of the EU to make use of them.

An evaluation of the status of European foreign policy before Maastricht

After the creation of European Political Cooperation (EPC) in 1969 and the 1985 Single European Act (SEA) – which gave an official basis to EPC – the next crucial step in the construction of a European Foreign Policy was the Maastricht Treaty, which replaced EPC with the Common Foreign and Security Policy (CFSP).

Before engaging in an analysis of CFSP and its instruments, a recapitulation of the status of European foreign policy as it stood at the beginning of the Maastricht Intergovernmental Conference is indeed in order.

In summary, twenty years after its creation, European foreign policy had at its disposal the following instruments – instruments intended both in a strictly procedural sense and in a broader sense:

- The *will* of the member states to cooperate in the field of foreign policy. Such will can be qualified both as an active desire to promote Europe's role in the world and as a reaction to external pressures of third parties who expected the EC to take on a political role adequate to its economic weight. This is the most critical, and at the same time volatile, variable of European foreign policy, capable of hampering EPC (and then CFSP) action even if sufficient instruments are available, but at the same time capable of creating necessary instruments and procedures ex novo if deemed advisable.
- A consolidated mechanism for *consultation*, which, by 1990, had created a habit of cooperation and collaboration in the field of foreign policy among the member states, and was contributing to the progressive harmonisation of the different national policies, at least on certain issues.
- The *meetings* of the Foreign Ministers on matters of political cooperation, preferably held in the capital of the state holding the Presidency of the EC.
- The central role of the rotating *Presidency*, which became the main body responsible for initiatives in the field of foreign policy.
- A *bureaucratic apparatus,* distinct and separate from the Community's, which included the Political Committee, the various working groups, and, after the SEA, a small Secretariat.
- A tentative informal mechanism for *coordination with Community* policies, codified not only in the Reports but also in the SEA.

In the same way, it is already possible at this stage to identify those structural problems that later proved to be inherent in European foreign policy:

- An unstable and unpredictable dialectic between the foreign policies of the member states and European foreign policy, which generated a tendency towards 'minimal common denominator' objectives and a declaratory policy – the safest option in dealing with controversial issues.
- A constant reliance on informal procedures and contacts that reflected more the member states' desire to maintain control over foreign policy than a deliberate search for a new 'formula' of foreign policymaking in the framework of existing European Community institutions.
- An erratic approach to foreign policymaking ensuing from the mechanism that grants centrality of action to the rotating Presidency. External interlocutors were constantly faced with the necessity of adapting to a new Presidency and, consequently, to a potentially different view of what European priorities should be. Given the kind of foreign policymaking mechanism set up, it was indeed remarkably difficult to build a consolidated 'historic memory' of a distinctly European foreign policy approach, as every single country holding the presidency wanted to assert its own view and agenda.
- A relationship with Community institutions and policies designed in such a way as to be a constant potential source of tensions and conflicts of competences, in addition to the previously mentioned problem of inconsistency. The unrealistic ambition to keep 'low' (economic) politics and 'high' (foreign) politics separate ultimately resulted in a situation of fuzzy competences and constant necessity to resort to complicated bureaucratic manoeuvres to implement decisions and avoid the assumption of political stances that were blatantly discordant with each other.

The CFSP: The new instruments of European Union foreign policy

The problem of the (lack of) legal personality of the EU

The question of legal personality is an open problem still much debated among scholars of international law (Bekker 1994; Rama-Montaldo 1997; Von Bogdandy 1999), to the point that even the very definition of 'legal personality' is controversial. To use Bekker's words, legal personality may be defined as 'the concrete exercise of, or at least the potential ability to exercise, certain rights and the fulfilment of certain obligations' (1994: 53).

Before exploring this issue further, it is worth establishing why the possession of legal capacity is relevant at all: as Wessel puts it, 'the practical value of the possession of legal personality can be found in the fact that the entity has the required status to have certain category of rights that enable it to manifest itself on the international plane and to enter into relationships with other subjects of international law, traditionally referred to as the right of intercourse' (Wessel 2000: 511). To be more specific, certain capacities may proceed from legal personality, such as, among others, treaty-making capacity and the right to recognise other subjects of international law.[1]

Two main schools of thought may be identified in the different interpretations given of the acceptable criteria for attribution of international legal personality (White 1996): the so-called 'objective approach' claims that international legal personality simply follows from the existence of an international organisation; the 'will approach' – by and large the prevailing approach – claims that international legal personality is attributed only as a result of the will of the founding states. 'This may take the form of an explicit provision in the constitutional treaty, or it may be an *implicit* attribution, in the sense that the quality can be derived from certain external capacities of the organisation' (Wessel 1999: 245).

What is of interest for the purpose of this study is understanding what legal personality entails in term of *capacities*, and whether the EU can be said to have these capacities, if not explicitly then at least implicitly.

The Treaty of European Union (TEU), signed in Maastricht in December 1991 and ratified in November 1993, replaced EPC with the so-called Common Foreign and Security Policy, which was to be the second pillar of the new three-pillar structure of what would be called the European Union (EU).[2] The EU was not given legal personality in the Treaty, and it was maintained that only the European Community (i.e. the first pillar) and the member states could assume legal obligations with outsiders (Smith 1998). Furthermore, some member states – like Germany and the Netherlands – explicitly denied at the time that the Union could be viewed as having legal personality.

From the point of view of an 'implicit attribution', however, matters seem to be less clear-cut. While the EU was not given legal personality by the TEU, this did not mean that the member states had a uniform position on the issue: on the contrary, the question was strongly debated both before the signing of the TEU and during the *travaux préparatoires* of the Amsterdam conference, as proven by a Report of the Reflection Group on the IGC: 'A majority of members point to the advantage of international legal personality for the Union so that it can conclude international agreements on the subject matter [...] concerning CFSP [...]. For them, the fact that the Union does not legally exist is a source of confusion outside and diminishes its external role. Others consider that the creation of international personality for the Union could risk confusion with the legal prerogatives of member states'.[3] These words lead to the conclusion that at least some of the member states were forming the opinion that some of the capacities that ensue from the status of 'legal person' could indeed serve the objective of enhancing the action of CFSP.

A rather ambiguous step in this direction was taken with the Amsterdam Treaty, of which a specific article (n. 24) established for the Council the possibility of concluding international agreements,[4] therefore envisaging a treaty-making capacity for the EU (Tilikainen 2001); however, this seemingly very courageous innovation was immediately mitigated in the second part of the article, which specified that 'no agreement shall be binding on a member state [...]' (ibid.), and in a further Declaration, which underlined that 'the provisions of [Article 24] and any agreements resulting from them shall not imply any transfer of competence from the member states to the EU'.[5]

When the European Convention met in Brussels in 2002, one of its first decisions was to create a working group on legal personality, chaired by Giuliano Amato. In its report the group stated that 'there was a very broad consensus (with one member against) that the Union should in future have its own explicit legal personality. It should be a single legal personality and should replace the existing personalities'.[6] This indication translated into a specific article (n. 6) of the Draft Constitutional Treaty, 'The Union shall have legal personality.'[7] After the failure of the Constitutional Treaty to enter into force, the more limited Lisbon Treaty signed in 2007 (and still not entered into force at the time of writing) called again for the attribution of explicit legal personality to the European Union and for the elimination of the three-pillar structure in favour of a single entity.

While in the period analysed here the European Union was not explicitly in possession of legal personality, it appears clear that it has nevertheless frequently made use of the prerogatives that derive from its possession. It has used a treaty-making capacity in numerous occasions, such as in the Balkans and, as we shall see, vis-à-vis the Palestinian Authority.[8]

It has also made use of the right to recognise other subjects of international law. While the EU has not yet managed (or rather decided) to directly recognise a third state, there were attempts at *concerted* diplomatic recognition even before the coming into force of the TEU: these attempts failed in the case of the recognition of Croatia and Slovenia (as Germany acted first, unilaterally) and Macedonia (whose joint recognition was blocked by Greece). A success was registered with the collective recognition of Bosnia/Herzegovina, coordinated with the United States. Obviously in these cases the recognition of the new sovereign state was to be given by the member states acting in coordination with each other, and not directly by the EU as such. But once again, as we shall see in the analysis of EU policy towards the Palestinian Authority, the possibility of a direct recognition of a new state by the EU, far from being completely ruled out, has on the contrary been used by the EU as a means to exert its influence in a manner considered to be by far more effective than the separate, if concerted, action of the member states.

From this analysis the tension between the member states' competing views of the EU emerges more clearly than ever. One view stresses the nature of the EU as a traditional mechanism of intergovernmental cooperation, and accordingly claims that the decisions taken on the basis of the CFSP provisions must in any case be regarded as multilateral agreements among governments. In certain circumstances, nonetheless, the integrationist view effectively emerges, as the member states seem to perceive the necessity to widen the scope and strengthen the significance of certain European actions, and to proceed either to officially enlarge the competencies of the Union or to undertake initiatives that entail the attribution to the EU of at least implicit capacities.

It has been suggested that some member states might at first have been unaware of the implications of using certain legal formulations, and of establishing 'non-first pillar' policy areas in which the EU as such plays a crucial role (Wessel 2000). However, it might also be possible to surmise that the combined effect of the pressure originating from external expectations of EU performance on the international plane, and the incremental style of the construction of the European Union foreign policy, can in certain circumstances bring about sudden – if provisional and not codified – qualitative leaps in the development of CFSP action.

Who answers the phone?

Naturally, it is of no great importance to establish whether Henry Kissinger truly asked the crucial question: 'If I want to call Europe, who do I call?', but finding an answer to it is. It is indeed unclear who is in charge of the formulation of the EU's foreign policy, and the complex and burdensome interaction between different institutions, bodies and working groups, within the framework of what the member states want to keep as much as possible an intergovernmental process, cannot but puzzle any external interlocutor.

A quick and concise 'bureaucratic excursus' provides the following – confusing – picture of some of the actors involved in the CFSP at the time of its creation:[9]

- The *European Council* is the gathering of the Heads of State or Government of the Member States. It is not a formal Community institution, but has, however, been attributed a crucial role in the CFSP by the Maastricht Treaty: 'The European Council shall provide the Union with the necessary impetus for its development and shall define the general guidelines thereof.'[10] In essence, the European Council holds responsibility for setting the guidelines for the CFSP.
- The Council of the European Union is composed of ministerial representatives of each Member State and its work is organised along 'issue lines', such as foreign policy, agriculture, etc. The *Council of Foreign Ministers*, or General Affairs and External Relations Council (GAERC), is the main manager of CFSP, and its action is strictly interconnected with the European Council's action. In fact, the GAC does the preparatory and executive work that allows the European Council to function; on the other hand, the political decisions of the European Council can only

be enforced once they have been adopted by the Council of Ministers. As Geoffrey Edwards put it, 'the Council is both the ultimate arbiter of policy and an integral part of a supranational decision-making process. [...] This suggests the adaptation of the state (and the modification of the traditional principles on which it has been based) towards participation in a political system that bears strong comparison with cooperative federalist systems such as that in Germany, where responsibilities over a wide range of issues are shared' (Edwards 1996). Helen Wallace has argued that the Council can be seen as both a European institution and the 'prisoner' of the member states and that its collective identity is always vulnerable to competition between member governments, as well as competition with the Commission (Wallace 1996a: 59).

- The *Presidency* is held in turn by each member state in the Council for a term of six months; furthermore, the member state holding the Presidency of the Council also chairs the meetings of the European Council. The Presidency provides the impetus and ensures follow-up; it represents the Union in CFSP matters and is responsible for the implementation of CFSP decisions.
- The *General Secretariat* supports the action of the Presidency under the responsibility of a Secretary General.
- The *Commission*, whose role in CFSP will be dealt with more extensively below, is fully associated with the work carried out by the Council in the CFSP field.
- The *Committee of Permanent Representatives* of the member states (COREPER) is responsible for preparing the work of the Council and for carrying out tasks assigned to it by the Council.
- The *Political and Security Committee* (PSC), consisting of the Political Directors of the national Foreign Ministries, contributes to the definition of CFSP policies by delivering opinions to the Council; it also monitors the implementation of agreed policies.
- Various *working groups* carry out preparatory work or studies defined in advance on CFSP matters.

All this indeed makes for quite an extensive 'phone book', and hardly contributes to the objective of projecting a unitary image of the EU's foreign policy on the international scene.

A first step in the direction of confronting the external world with an interlocutor 'in flesh and blood' was taken in 1996 with the introduction of the role of *Special Envoy* (now *Special Representative*), a pilot project of a European diplomat. The special envoy is appointed by the Council with a mandate in relation to particular policy issues; therefore the member states maintain full control over his or her competencies.

The second, more significant, step was taken with the Amsterdam Treaty, in Article 26, where it was decided that the Secretary General of the Council would add to his or her responsibilities the new function of *High Representative* for the CFSP (HR), with the aim of working towards a new working troika, consisting of the Presidency, the High Representative, and a senior representative of the Commission. A Policy Planning and Early Warning Unit was set up under the High Representative, with personnel drawn from EU institutions, the member states and the Western European Union (WEU) (Hill and Smith 2000: 169). According to article 26, the HR was to assist the Council in matters coming within the scope of CFSP, in particular by contributing to the formulation, preparation and implementation of policy decisions, and by conducting political dialogue with third parties.[11]

Among the objectives of introducing a HR was the hope of overcoming the discontinuity of CFSP action deriving from the system of the rotating Presidency, the desire to improve the ability of the Union to react promptly to current political events, and the aspiration to facilitate the laying down of political guidelines which could transcend national interests. However, the usual reluctance to push too far in the direction of political integration prevented the setting up of a truly innovative decision-making mechanism: ultimately both the HR and the Special Representatives are appointed by the Council and have to work strictly within the boundaries of the intergovernmental framework. Some important reforms to the role of the HR were included in the failed Constitutional Treaty and later in the Treaty of Lisbon (whose ratification is so far stalled), and will be discussed in more detail below.

Practical instruments for action

During the years of EPC, European foreign policy was mainly of a declaratory nature, and the significance of the political content of the various joint declarations varied according to the ability and willingness of the member states to reach an agreement beyond the line of the lowest common denominator. The principle of consensus governed the system; however – as Simon Nuttall argued – EPC worked, within its limits, because it turned those limits to advantage: 'Foreign Ministries made sure that it remained a self contained operation, restricted to a small circle of initiates and powered by the forces of socialisation. The secret was that, in normal circumstances, those initiatives had the power to sway national policies. The Political Directors, the Heads of Department, above all the Foreign Ministers themselves, were well placed to align their countries on EPC positions if they so chose' (Nuttall 2000: 272).

The Treaty of Maastricht introduced two new foreign policy instruments: *joint actions* and *common positions*, which had to serve the purpose of providing European foreign policy with further means of action. These were meant to be qualitatively superior to what had existed in EPC, but the failure to agree on a limited, operational list of important common interests, and on qualified majority voting, made their usefulness rather limited. The distinction between these two instruments was unclear and was only clarified years later, with the Treaty of Amsterdam, which also introduced a further instrument, the *common strategy*. Thus, if common positions define the approach of the Union to a particular matter of a geographical or thematic nature,[12] joint actions address specific situations where operational action is needed,[13] and are to be implemented gradually in the areas in which the member states have important interests in common. The common strategy is not clearly defined, but could be set out as a framework that defines what the main EU interests in a region are, and by what general means they might be pursued.

The Treaty of Lisbon – if ratified – will create the instrument of 'European decisions' adopted by the Council of Ministers, which will amalgamate the joint actions, common positions and common strategies.

It is worth mentioning at this stage the laborious process behind the introduction of the principle of *qualified majority voting* (QMV) in the field of CFSP. QMV made its first timid appearance in the TEU with article J3, which indicated that, provided that an issue had already been defined by unanimity, QMV could be used to implement specific measures, and the votes of the member states would be weighted in accordance with EC procedures on QMV. The Amsterdam Treaty represents 'phase two' of the saga of QMV, a metaphor of the struggle between intergovernmentalism, integrationism and the incremental style of the evolution of CFSP. Article J.13 in fact provides for extended resorting to QMV, calling for QMV by the Council when it adopts or implements joint actions, common positions or other decisions on the basis of a common strategy previously agreed upon unanimously. In addition, the possibility of *'constructive abstention'* was introduced, allowing one or more member states to opt out of a common position without preventing the whole policy from going ahead. Needless to say, a tool allowing member states to block Council decision-making could not be absent, and was granted by providing that a council member may still declare that, for important and stated reasons of national policy, it intends to oppose the adoption of a decision to be taken by qualified majority voting. Specific criteria to define what an 'important' reason would be were not specified.

The Treaty of Nice set further criteria for proposals to be passed by QMV (number of countries and percentage of EU's population necessary), and established that the Council can act by qualified majority when appointing a special representative for the CFSP (art. 23). It also allowed for 'enhanced cooperation' (i.e. the possibility for some member states to work more closely on given issues) to take place in the field of CFSP, while at the same time retaining the possibility for any member state to require an unanimous vote on the question (therefore effectively leaving a right of veto) (art. 27C).

The Treaty of Lisbon will, if ratified, provide only limited revisions to the existing procedures of decision-making.[14] Unanimity would in fact remain the norm in decision-making in the field of CFSP except where otherwise explicitly provided for, and there would be the addition of only one new area in which member states could take decisions by a qualified majority (Whitman 2008).[15]

Qualified majority voting remains one of the most controversial issues among the member states, as its introduction and the extension of its applicability have a remarkable practical but also symbolic value, representing as they do the surrender of a stronghold of national sovereignty that many states are ready to defend tooth and nail.

The apple of discord: The relationship between the European Community and CFSP

There are two possible approaches to analysing the relationship between the European Community and CFSP: the first, and more formal, would provide a picture of the specific provisions that regulate this relationship and of the official efforts made to coordinate first- and second-pillar actions in external relations, with the commendable objective of granting consistency and coherence to European foreign policy.

On the other hand, a closer analysis would provide a bizarre picture of an anachronistic and unrealistic desire to keep economic and foreign policies separate, a desire that is nonetheless challenged by reality, which has shown how the two policies cannot but be inextricably intertwined, thus often forcing member states to turn to Community economic policy instruments[16] in order to implement decisions taken in the separate intergovernmental framework.

The Treaty on European Union stipulates that the European Commission is to be fully associated with the work carried out in the CFSP field, underlining that such association is needed to ensure the consistency of the CFSP with external economic relations and development cooperation, which are Community policies in which the Commission plays a leading role (Cameron 1997).

The President of the Commission joins the Heads of State or Government within the European Council. The Commission participates in meetings of the Council and its preparatory bodies. Like the member states, it can lay before the Council any foreign and security policy issue and submit proposals to it;[17] however, its right of initiative is not exclusive, as is usually the case with Community policies. The Treaty also provides that the Council may request the Commission to submit to it any appropriate proposals to ensure the implementation of a joint action.[18]

The relationship between the two pillars becomes particularly controversial where the *financing* of CFSP is concerned. As Jorg Monar has argued, the question of financing is indeed a crucial issue. Firstly, financing has a direct impact on the efficiency of CFSP. The lack of an adequate budgetary basis and effective budgetary procedures can endanger both the Union's capacity to act and its international credibility. Secondly, the practice of financing the CFSP has given rise to problems of democratic control of the use of EC funds, which are closely related to the persisting democratic deficit in the second pillar of the TEU. Thirdly, the present system of financing CFSP causes major tensions within the Union's dual system of foreign affairs, with its increasingly complex mixture of intergovernmental and Community methods (Monar 1997b: 35).

The Treaty of Maastricht provided that all *administrative* costs incurred by the institutions in the area of CFSP should be charged to the budget of the European Communities.[19] Two alternatives were then envisaged for *operational* expenditures: either the Council could unanimously decide that operational expenditure was to be charged to the budget of the EC, or it could determine that such expenditure was to be charged to member states (Wessel 1999: 96). With the Treaty of Amsterdam the EC budget became the 'default setting' for financing CFSP, 'apart for expenditure arising from operations having military and defence implications and cases where the Council acting unanimously decides otherwise'.[20] The trouble arises as a consequence of the fuzzy distinction between 'administrative' and 'operational' costs and the member states' desire to spare national budget. In fact, on the basis of the only identifiable distinction, which indicates vaguely that administrative costs are incurred by the institutions whereas operational costs are incurred by the implementation of CFSP provisions, the Council can decide to classify as administrative expenditure anything from the travel costs of Commission and Council personnel to the organisation of international conferences (Wessel 1999: 97). At the same time, the desire to keep CFSP intergovernmental adds more confusion and tensions as the member states struggle to find an appropriate and satisfactory scale to divide between them costs that are not charged to the EC budget.[21]

In an analysis of the relationship between the first two pillars of the EU, the complex relation between the External Relations Commissioner and the High Representative for the CFSP also calls for a few comments. It is becoming increasingly evident that the distinction between the two roles causes more and more overlapping of competencies and institutional inconsistency. Various solutions have been considered, ranging from the transformation of the High Representative into a Member of the Commission, to the more conservative idea of 'unifying the external relations bureaucracies of the Council and the Commission under the supervision of the High Representative, who would act as a Member of the Commission for matters requiring a Commission decision, and report to the appropriate body in the Council [...] for the rest' (Nuttall 2001: 8).

In May 2002 the Commission, in a Communication on the Future of Europe, put forward the option of reducing the inconsistency of the Union's institutional design (including CFSP), dismantling the current 'pillar' system. Such an option was meant to eliminate the distinction between the community area proper and the treaty provisions concerning the second and third pillars.[22] Later the same year, in the Final Report of Working Group VII on External Action, the Members of the European Convention suggested that 'in order to ensure better coherence between foreign policy decisions on the one hand, and deployment of instruments in the field of external relation on the other hand, the current roles of the High Representative for CFSP and the Commissioner responsible for external relations should be reconsidered [...] A large trend emerged in favour of a solution which would provide for the exercise of both offices by a "European External Representative". This person, who would combine the functions of HR and External Relations Commissioner, would be appointed by the Council, meeting in the composition of Heads of State or Government and acting by a qualified majority, with the approval of the President of the Commission and endorsement by the European Parliament'.[23]

A first attempt at reforming the position of the HR was made with the failed European Constitution, which included a provision for the creation of a 'European Union Minister for Foreign Affairs'. Subsequently the Treaty of Lisbon addressed the issue with slightly more modest ambitions: if ratified, the Treaty would merge the post of High Representative with that of the European Commissioner for External Relations under a new title of 'High Representative of the Union for Foreign Affairs and Security Policy'. The post-holder (appointed by the Council through QMV) would also be the Vice President of the Commission (art. 9e) and chair the Council of Ministers in its Foreign Affairs configuration. The HR would also take on the responsibility (previously exercised by the Council) for proposing and managing the Special Representatives (art. 18), and would be backed by an External Action Service.

It may indeed be argued that the stage of development achieved by the EU foreign policy machinery calls for courageous reform in the direction of a deeper integration, with the aim of not only allowing the CFSP to work efficiently and effectively, but also to avoid the risk of making CFSP a tower of Babel of discordant indications and Kafkaesque institutions that induce distrust in most external interlocutors. If and when the Treaty of Lisbon is ratified, the High Representative will become the personification, and the animus, of the new gathering together of all aspects of External Action, formally responsible for its consistency across the treaties and institutions and clearly key to achieving the ambition of greater synergy across all aspects of External Action (Whitman 2008: 5).

> Covenants, without a sword, are nothing but words, and of no strength to secure a man at all. (Thomas Hobbes, *The Leviathan*)

An account of the instruments of European foreign policy would not be complete without a reference to the construction of a European military capability in the years being considered.

As already mentioned, the London Report of 1981 explicitly stated that EPC was an appropriate forum for discussing 'certain important foreign policy questions bearing on the political aspects of security'. However, discussing problems related to security was one thing, and discussing 'defence' was quite another, given the open reluctance of some member states to extend the EU's competencies in that direction.

Since the end of the Cold War, the need to provide the EU with a military force able to support and bolster the credibility of its political and economic action was increasingly an issue among the member states. Of course, the situation was complicated by the 'complex variable geometry of diverging memberships between the EU, NATO and WEU' (Hill and Smith 2000: 194), and by the contradictory position of the United States, which wanted the Europeans to bear a greater share of the burden of Europe's security and defence, but not at the expense of NATO's supremacy in the field. There is fierce debate among EU member states about the advisability of developing an independent European military capability, as many see NATO as the only appropriate organisation to grant European security and to carry out military operations, and share the American determination to avoid the so-called 'three Ds': 'duplication' of existing capabilities and military structures, 'decoupling' from NATO and 'discrimination' against non-EU NATO allies,[24] in favour of what Lord Robertson, Secretary General of NATO, has called the 'three Is': 'indivisibility' of the transatlantic link, 'improvement' of the capabilities, 'inclusiveness' of all allies.

Article J.4 of the Maastricht Treaty specifies that the CFSP 'shall include all questions related to the security of the Union, including the eventual framing of a common defence policy, which might in time lead to a common defence'.

A few months later, in June 1992, the Western European Union issued the Petersberg Declaration, in which the different types of military tasks that the WEU might undertake were defined: military units of WEU member states could be employed for humanitarian and rescue tasks, peacekeeping tasks and tasks of combat forces in crisis management, including peacemaking.[25]

With the Amsterdam Treaty in 1997 the two threads (i.e. the EU common defence policy and the role of WEU) were tied with the incorporation of the 'Petersberg tasks' in the new Article 17 of the EU Treaty: those tasks were, therefore, now recorded as part of the EU's mission, even if the possibility of a merger between the EU and WEU was still distant.

Christopher Hill has thus described the aims of the creation of a European Security and Defence Policy (ESDP): (1) to give the EU a limited but real military capability, especially in its own region, for peacekeeping if not for peace enforcement; (2) to allow the Western European Union to be abolished, and thus the relationship between the EU and NATO to be made more honest; (3) to bind the United Kingdom into EU foreign and security policy, and thus to boost the forces of solidarity (Hill 2002).

In 1999 the Cologne European Council Declaration announced the end of the WEU by the start of 2001 and the arrival of a legitimate EU defence policy system,[26] and then the Helsinki European Council set the 'headline goal' of the establishment by 2003 of a 60,000-strong force drawn from EU states that could be deployed for a year within 60 days, and of a political body to direct it. When it became clear that the objectives outlined in the Helsinki Headline Goal were not quickly achievable, EU defence ministers approved Headline Goal 2010, extending the timelines for the EU's projects.[27] A crucial step in the establishment of the ESDP was the conclusion, in 2002, of the Berlin plus Agreement, which allows the EU to use NATO structures, mechanisms and assets to carry out military operations if NATO declines to act. Furthermore, in 2004 a European Defence Agency was created, based in Brussels.

The first deployment of European troops under the ESDP, following the 1999 declaration of intent, was in March 2003 in the former Yugoslav Republic of Macedonia (EUFOR Concordia mission, with

NATO assets). Since then the EU has organised missions in various forms in, among others, Bosnia and Herzegovina, Congo, Georgia, Indonesia, Sudan, Palestine, Ukraine-Moldova and Chad.

In 2004 the 'Military Capabilities Commitment Conference' formally launched the concept of EU Battlegroup, units of 1500 troops that would give the EU the capability to react fast and forcefully in trouble spots outside EU territory. The troops and equipment are drawn from the member states under a lead nation, and they are intended to be deployed on the ground within 5–10 days of approval from the Council. The battlegroups reached operational capacity in 2007 and could be defined as an attempt at a 'standing army' for Europe, although ambitions are more modest than those of Headline Goal 2003.

It is relevant to underline the time parallel between the progressive incremental process of the construction of an EU foreign policy and the introduction of the military dimension, as if increased EU involvement in international affairs would almost inevitably bring about the necessity to back up any political stance with a credible military capability. This axiom might not be true in every instance, but it certainly seems almost always to apply in the case of the EU's aspiration to influence the Arab–Israeli peace process.

The use of European foreign policy instruments in the case of the Arab–Israeli peace process

The chapter has hitherto conducted a critical analysis of the foreign policy instruments the EU has at its disposal; it will now proceed by examining and evaluating how the EU has used these instruments in dealing with the Middle East peace process (MEPP).

The time frame considered embraces the years between 1991 and 2009; however, reference to previous years will be necessary, as certain patterns of action and characteristics of the European Union's political stance towards the Arab–Israeli conflict took shape in the years of EPC.

Rather than following a strictly chronological order, the analysis will focus on the use of the different *typology* of instruments: (a) declaratory instruments; (b) operational instruments; (c) economic instruments; and d) strategic instruments.

The aim is not to reconstruct step by step every single initiative the EU has taken with regard to the peace process, but rather to focus on the most significant steps, trying to establish in which instances the formulation of a Middle East policy has provided the opportunity or has been a – deliberately? – missed opportunity for the EU to experiment with new instruments, to foster political cooperation among the member states and to draw closer to the objective of an efficient common foreign policy.

Declaratory instruments

European policy towards the Arab–Israeli conflict and the subsequent peace process has in effect been mainly of a declaratory nature. In the years of EPC, when joint declarations were basically the only instrument available, the member states availed themselves profusely of this instrument: in 1973, after the outbreak of the Yom Kippur war and very much as a reaction to the pressure deriving from the oil crisis, the then nine member states managed to issue a joint declaration meant to outline Europe's position, but also to 'gain Arab support with little hope of actually influencing events' (Greilsammer and Weiler 1987: 31). The declaration, on the other hand, did include important points, such as the reference to the 'legitimate rights of the Palestinians', to 'the need for Israel to end the territorial occupation which it has maintained since the conflict of 1967' and to the persuasion that 'negotiations must take place in the framework of the United Nations'.[28]

If we tentatively identify three possible objectives of such a declaration, namely (a) to actively influence the course of the crisis; (b) to endeavour a *captatio benevolentiae* towards the Arabs; and (c) to improve European cooperation at the political level, we shall see that at least two of them, (b) and (c), were to a certain extent achieved. In effect, the Arab Heads of State issued a statement expressing their satisfaction with the declaration. At the same time, with regard to European cooperation, it is possible to observe the utilisation of what has been called the 'shield effect', that is, the exploitation, on the part of some member states, of the reflexive element (the need for European unity, the superior objective of reaching a common European position) as justification for a stance which might not have been possible for individual governments to adopt independently at home (Greilsammer and Weiler 1987).[29] It would hardly be possible to argue that this joint declaration actively contributed to influencing the course of events, but it must be underlined that, under the combined pressure of the oil crisis and the perceived urgency of reaching a common European position, the EEC was able to lay down the foundations of what was to become the specific European position on the Arab–Israeli conflict.

A subsequent declaration is commonly regarded as a watershed in the EC's approach to the conflict: the Venice Declaration of 1980. The Declaration emphasised the right of the Palestinian people to full self-determination and the need to include the PLO in any peace negotiations; together with the previously mentioned request for full Israeli withdrawal and the appeal to the United Nation's deliberations on the matter, these were, and largely still are, the basic points of the EEC's stance.

Since 1980 the EEC, and then the EU, have continued to resort widely to the Joint Declaration instrument: the Maastricht European Council of December 1991 included a declaration on the Middle East, and almost every new development in the MEPP seemed to call either for a Resolution from the European Parliament, or for a Declaration from the European Council or the Council of the European Union. In these declarations the EU, within the framework of the political position adopted since the Venice Declaration, 'condemns violence', 'encourages dialogue', 'reiterates condemnation', 'reaffirms support', 'welcomes progress', and so on.

As usual, before its effectiveness can be judged, the purpose of an action must be established. In this case, if the purpose of this abundance of resolutions and declarations was to obtain at least a harmonisation of the different member states' positions on the MEPP, through the ongoing practice of political discussions and bargaining at the EU level prior to the formulation of the official declarations, then the objective was at least partly achieved, given the detectable trend towards the attainment of a 'European perception', in a broad sense, of the Arab–Israeli problem and of the policy the EU should adopt. On the other hand, if the EU intended to influence the development of the peace process directly through the use of the Declarations, it can hardly claim success.

There is, however, at least one exception to this otherwise unsatisfactory success rate of EU declaratory policy: the case of the Berlin European Council Declaration of 25 March 1999. In this instance the European Union, in coordination with the United States, was trying to persuade Mr Arafat to postpone a unilateral declaration

of independence, and calling for a resumption of final status negotiations with Israel. What deserves to be highlighted in this case
is the fact that the European Council, in order to encourage Mr
Arafat to drop the idea of a unilateral action, offered in exchange
the assurance that the European Union would in the future recognise a Palestinian State, and in the wording of the Declaration the
Heads of State or Government decided not to mention the fact that
every single member state would be ready to recognise a Palestinian
State, but rather referred to 'the EU readiness to consider recognition of a Palestinian State in due course'. What is of interest here is
the implicit reference to a 'right of intercourse' of the EU, and more
specifically to the right to recognise other subjects of international
law. As already discussed above, the EU has not been officially given
legal personality, and therefore lacks the formal right to recognise
third states; nevertheless, on this occasion an empirical analysis of
the EU's behaviour shows that the Union was making at least an
implicit use of this capacity, and it is reasonable to suppose that the
reason for choosing this course of action was the perception that an
assurance to the Palestinian Authority in such terms would be by
far more effective than the separate, albeit coordinated, initiatives
of the member states. Here again, the combined effect of external
pressures and the member states' desire to increase the EU's political influence in external affairs brought about an initiative whose
implications, if ever formalised, would have strongly significant consequences for the status of European political integration. In April,
the PLO Central Council decided to postpone the declaration of
Palestinian statehood, and it can be surmised that the EU's assurance
that it would be ready to recognise a State of Palestine in the future,
even if it were declared unilaterally, did have a role in influencing
Arafat's decision, especially considering the strong ties, particularly
of an economic nature, between the Palestinian Authority and the
European Union.

Operational instruments

The Treaty of Maastricht introduced a new operational instrument:
the joint action. This definition, which refers to a legal instrument
under Title V of the Treaty on European Union, means 'co-ordinated
action by the member states whereby resources of all kinds (human
resources, know-how, financing, equipment and so on) are mobilised

to attain specific objectives fixed by the Council on the base of general guidelines from the European Council'.[30]

Since this instrument was introduced, the Middle East peace process has been the subject of numerous Joint Actions adopted by the Council. The first two were of a more declaratory nature, expressing the Union's general and unreserved support for the peace process.[31] The third,[32] however, was indubitably more significant, as it provided the basis for the Union's major political and financial involvement in the preparation, observation, and coordination of international observation of the first Palestinian elections, and allocated a total funding of 17 million ECUs.[33]

Three days later the EU, represented by the President of the Council, Mr Felipe Gonzales, signed as a witness the Israeli–Palestinian Interim Agreement on the West Bank and the Gaza Strip (known as Taba Agreement or Oslo II). Of particular interest is Annex II of the Agreement, which is the Protocol concerning the Palestinian Elections: the Protocol provides that 'the European Union will act as the coordinator for the activity of observer delegations'[34] and specifies that 'the European Union will only bear [...] liability in relation to members of the co-ordinating body and to the European Union observers and only to the extent that it explicitly agrees to do so'. As Wessel has underlined, this latter provision 'reveals the Union's acceptance of a possible future liability on the basis of the Agreement and thus of its standing under international law' (Wessel 2000: 533). Considering that this Protocol was signed even before the Amsterdam Treaty and the introduction of Article 24 (which established for the Council the possibility of concluding international agreements), it can be argued that the EU made at least an *implicit* use of one of the capabilities that may proceed from legal personality, namely the treaty-making capacity.[35]

Arguably one of the most significant steps taken by the EU in its policy towards the peace process is the appointment in November 1996 of the position of EU Special Envoy (now Special Representative) to the Middle East peace process through the adoption of joint action no. 96/676/CFSP.[36] The Special Representative's mandate was subsequently extended and rectified with several more joint actions.[37] The main objective of this appointment was to pursue better coordination of individual member states' policies; undeniably Mr Moratinos first, and Mr Otte later, have not only contributed significantly to the preparation of common positions and the development of European initiatives aimed at promoting progress in the peace negotiations, but have also participated directly in many stages of these negotiations, earning the trust and respect of all the main actors involved. The real problem is that their action has been hampered by the very terms of the mandate, which is formally quite broad[38] but still provides that the Special Representative's action must take place in a strictly intergovernmental framework: he or she is guided by, and reports under, the authority of the Presidency, and also reports to the Council's bodies on a regular basis; as a result, his or her scope for autonomous initiative is very limited and tightly bound to the indications he or she receives from the Council. He or she cannot officially commit any member state to any step which has not been previously agreed upon, and it is therefore hard to envisage for him or her a role beyond that of 'facilitator' of the peace talks.[39]

A few further joint actions are worth mentioning. In 1997 the EU established an Assistance Programme to support the Palestinian Authority in its efforts to counter terrorist activities emanating from the territories under its control.[40] The programme was quite wide and included training in surveillance, the establishment of a technical investigation bureau with forensic capabilities, and training of management personnel of security and police agencies. It could be argued that the EU's increasing involvement in the peace process made a European contribution to the field of security inevitable, especially as the EU found itself struggling to change its role in the Middle East from 'payer' to 'player'. The aspiration to become an important player with a higher degree of political responsibility has long been significantly hindered by the EU's limited availability of military instruments: in a situation such as the Arab–Israeli peace process – or rather conflict – in which the military dimension and security concerns are of foremost importance, even the huge economic commitment the EU had pledged over the years was not sufficient to enable it to directly influence the political development of the process.

In June 2004 EU leaders declared their readiness to support the Palestinian Authority in taking responsibility for law and order, and, in particular, in improving its civil police and law enforcement capacity. In January 2005 the EU Coordination Office for Palestinian Police Support (EU COPPS)[41] was established within the office of the

EU Special Representative for the Middle East peace process, Marc Otte; in November the Council established the so-called EUPOL COPPS mission, a civilian mission in the framework of the European Security and Defence Policy (ESDP), which builds on the work of EU COPPS and aims to contribute to the establishment of effective policing arrangements under Palestinian ownership in accordance with international standards. The mission was set to start operating in January 2006, but was largely paralysed after Hamas' electoral victory, and only started operating – and only in the West Bank – after the Hamas-Fatah split of June 2007 (Asseburg 2009). EUPOL COPPS is rather small, consisting of thirty-two unarmed members of staff, twenty-seven of whom are seconded from EU member states and five are local. The Head of Mission receives guidance from the High Representative Mr Solana, through the Special Representative Mr Otte. The mission also coordinates EU Member States' and international assistance to the Palestinian Civil Police and advises on police-related Criminal Justice elements, activities in line with EU's efforts in building and reinforcing Palestinian institutions.

In November 2005 the Council of the EU agreed to establish another civilian mission in the framework of ESDP (see also Chapter 4). The mission, called EUBAM Rafah (EU Border Assistant Mission Rafah), was tasked with monitoring the operations of the Rafah border crossing point between Gaza and Egypt, in accordance with the 'Agreement on Movement and Access' signed by Israel and the Palestinian Authority following the unilateral withdrawal of Israel from the Gaza Strip. The operational phase of the Mission began on 30 November 2005 and was meant to have a duration of 12 months. On 24 May 2007 the Council adopted another joint action, extending the mandate of the mission until 24 May 2008.[42] The operations of EUBAM, however, were suspended in June 2007 due to the Hamas takeover of the Gaza Strip. After the closure of the crossing point, the mission maintained its operational capability and the European Union announced that it was prepared to redeploy its personnel at the border as soon as conditions permitted.

There are two ways to look at this operation. On the one hand, it can be seen as a qualitative step forward in the EU's involvement in the security dimension of the peace process. For the first time a small group of EU military personnel (ninety police and custom officers) were called in to supervise a checkpoint previously under Israeli control and to monitor the compliance of the Palestinian Authority with the principles of the 'Agreement on Movement and Access'. The initiative was limited, and Israel maintained the right to close the crossing point, but the EU had for the first time visible 'boots on the ground'. On the other hand, EUBAM turned out to be largely a failure: while it did succeed in facilitating the crossing of almost half a million people, it was also constantly hostage to the developments on the ground. As Colonel Faugeras, the Head of EUBAM, put it in an interview in 2009, 'EU's job was limited when it came to security. It has monitors at Rafah [...] but it is not an enforcement body; its role is to report observations to Israel and the Palestinian Authority.'[43] The consequences of this limited mandate are that EUBAM was unable to really control the security situation or the building of tunnels between Gaza and Egypt (used to smuggle everything from arms and explosives to food and cigarettes) and, when Hamas took power in June 2007, it could do nothing but temporarily shut down and wait in hope that an agreement would be reached between Israel, the Palestinian Authority, Hamas and Egypt (the EU, after all, has no relations with Hamas).

All this, despite being arguably a consequence of the nature of the mission's mandate and of the imperfect nature of the Agreement on Movement and Access itself (in 2005 only the section of the agreement that related to the crossing of people was signed, but not the section relating to the passage of goods or the security protocol, which was supposed to outline security risks and procedures), did not result in any real improvement or consolidation of the EU's credibility as a security actor in the eyes of both the Palestinians and the Israelis.

Economic instruments

The European Union has made widespread use of economic instruments for political ends in the development of its policy towards the Middle East and the Mediterranean. The EU is gavel holder of the Regional Economic Development Working Group (REDWG) within the multilateral framework of the peace process initiated in 1991 at the Madrid Peace Conference, and co-organiser of the working groups on environment, water and refugees.

Furthermore, the EU has since 1995 promoted regional dialogue and cooperation through the Euro-Mediterranean Partnership[44] (or

Barcelona Process, BP), which operates at both bilateral and multilateral levels with the declared long-term goal of progressively establishing an area of regional security and free trade.

At the bilateral level, the strategy of the BP has consisted of concluding Euro-Mediterranean Association Agreements between the Union and its Mediterranean partners,[45] and establishing national indicative programmes for financial assistance under the Community's MEDA programme.[46] As the Agreements are of a 'mixed' type (drawing on both European Community and member states' competences – the latter concerning the second and third EU pillars), after signature they have to undergo a lengthy ratification process by the national parliaments of the EU member states.

On the multilateral or regional track, since 1995, the EU and its Mediterranean Partners have developed an architecture of regularly meeting coordination bodies including Euro-Mediterranean Foreign Ministers conferences. The Euro-Mediterranean Committee for the Barcelona Process, composed of representatives of the EU and the Mediterranean Partners,[47] would meet on average every three months, to ensure the overall guidance of the established work programme on regional cooperation. Together with rotating EU Presidencies, the Commission was responsible for the coordination, preparation and monitoring of this process for the Union; furthermore, it was entrusted with the appraisal and implementation of political and security, economic and financial, social and cultural partnership activities in the fields described by the Barcelona Work Programme and by subsequent decisions of Euro-Mediterranean Foreign Ministers, particularly those that are financed from the EU budget.

The Barcelona Process was meant develop separately from the peace process, but to contribute to it indirectly by offering confidence-building measures and an alternative forum in which the parties involved in the peace process could continue to meet even when the peace process was stalled. This strategy, as this study has already pointed out, has not proved to be completely successful: even though the parties did meet in the framework of the Barcelona Process, progress in the various fields has always been dependent on the state of the peace process, and when the latter has been either in difficulties or completely in ruins the Barcelona Process has been directly and negatively affected almost to the point of paralysis.

In 2004 the EU developed the European Neighbourhood Policy (ENP) with the objective of avoiding the emergence of new dividing lines between the enlarged EU and its neighbours, and of strengthening the prosperity, stability and security of all concerned. The ENP applies to the EU's immediate neighbours by land or sea, including the Mediterranean partners of the BP, and it is based on deepening the EU's bilateral relations with neighbouring states (partly as a means of using the bilateral approach to overcome the blockages inherent in region-wide policies such as the BP). The central elements of the ENP are the bilateral Action Plans (APs) agreed between the EU and each partner, which set out an agenda of political and economic reforms with short and medium-term priorities. At the beginning of 2009 the EU had signed Action Plans with the following Mediterranean Partners: Israel, Jordan, Morocco, Tunisia, the Palestinian Authority, Egypt and Lebanon. The implementation of the Action Plan with the Palestinian Authority, however, was suspended following the election of Hamas in January 2006.

The APs carry the advantage of bringing the political and economic instruments of the EU closer together under the Commission, which is thus able to create approaches better tailored to the individual circumstances of each partner. While the Barcelona Process remained the cornerstone of the Partnership with the Mediterranean, the Neighbourhood Policy was supposed to give the EU the possibility of working more flexibly to meet the interests of each country. In 2007 the MEDA programme, which was the principal financial instrument of the EU for the implementation of the Barcelona Process, was replaced by the European Neighbourhood and Partnership Instrument (ENPI), a more flexible, policy-driven instrument designed to target sustainable development and approximation to EU policies and standards.

A critique that can be directed at these initiatives (BP and ENP) is that they have become too cumbersome and bureaucratic, not to mention confusing to external interlocutors, who have trouble understanding the function of each and the difference between them. Matters have been further complicated by the announcement, on the part of the French presidency in 2008, of the creation of a 'Union for the Mediterranean'. In the intentions of French President Sarkozy, the Union for the Mediterranean was supposed to represent the creation of a new single European Mediterranean policy; the idea, however, had mixed responses, especially because it was not clear how this Union would fit with the existing initiatives and whether it would end up adding another layer to the already confused picture of the EU's policies vis-à-vis the region (Emerson 2008). At the time of writing, the official position of the European Union's website is that the Union for the Mediterranean 'aims to infuse new vitality into the partnership, offering more balanced governance and increased visibility'.[48]

In past years the EU's direct economic support of the peace process has been enormous: the EU is the largest donor of non-military aid to the MEPP, and it is also the first donor of financial and technical assistance to the Palestinian Authority.[49]

The election of a Hamas-led government in January 2006 created serious problems for the EU: while the decision was taken to boycott Hamas (which is on the EU's list of terrorist organisations), a complete suspension of economic assistance to the Palestinians was likely to bring about a humanitarian crisis in the Territories. Direct aid to the Palestinian Authority was suspended, but the EU created instead a Temporary International Mechanism (TIM) to channel needs-based funds directly to the Palestinian population, bypassing Hamas entirely, to enable the people to survive. In 2008 the TIM was replaced by PEGASE (Mécanisme Palestino-Européen de Gestion de l'Aide Socio-Économique), which channels EU assistance to support a three-year Palestinian Reform and Development Plan prepared by the Palestinian Authority.[50] If EU support has been a lifeline for the Palestinian people, providing much needed economic support meant to prevent a complete collapse and humanitarian catastrophe in the occupied territories, the new mechanism, on the other hand, moves the focus of EU efforts to crisis management and away from institution-building and development, two goals that remain crucial to ensure the viability of the future Palestinian state.

Tables 6.1–6.3 illustrate EC support to the Palestinians in the years 2000–2008.[51]

While, as already underlined, EU political relations with Israel have been and remain rather difficult and are marked by Israeli reluctance to accept the EU as a mediator in the peace process, the Union is nevertheless the first trading partner and a major economic, scientific and research partner of Israel.

Table 6.1 EC Support for the Palestinians (2000–2006)

				€ million			
	2000	2001	2002	2003	2004	2005	2006	Total 00–06
Direct support to Palestinian Authority	90	40	120	102	90.25	76		518.25
Infrastructure projects	0.8	0.97	38.3	0	0	40.55		80.62
Institution building	16.89	5.76	21.50	12	6	17	12	91.15
Support to refugees through UNRWA	40.24	57.25	55	57.75	60.65	63.67	64.41	398.97
Humanitarian and food aid	33.60	41.95	69.24	61.61	61.11	65.28	104	436.79
ISR/PS civil society and support for peace process	22.90		10	7.50	10	10		60.340
SMEs, East Jerusalem, Human rights, NGOs, other projects	20.77	2.55	11.86	30.04	26.22	5.86	17.75	97.30
Emergency support, incl. TIM							141.75	141.75
TOTAL	225.20	148.48	325.90	270.90	254.23	278.36	339.91	1825.23

Table 6.2 EC assistance to the Palestinians in 2007

EC Assistance to the Palestinians in 2007 (last updated 17 December 2007)	(Commitments in million EUR)
Temporary International Mechanism	350
New scheme for private sector arrears	20
Institution Building	5.7
UNRWA's General Fund	66
UNRWA-specific projects (Camp Improvement for Palestine Refugees in Lebanon; Scholarships for Palestine Refugees in Lebanon; Nahr el Bared)	13.8
Food Aid and Humanitarian Aid (ECHO)	66.3
Food Security	10
Social and Health projects in East Jerusalem	2
Support to civil society, e.g., Partnership for Peace, Democracy and Human Rights	9.2
Support to Palestinian–Israeli negotiations towards a peace agreement (support to civil police; work of Quartet Representative Blair)	7.5
TOTAL	**550.5**

Table 6.3 EC assistance to the Palestinians in 2008 (Commitments in million EUR)

PEGASE (Palestinian Reform and Development Plan: Recurrent Expenditure)	258
PEGASE (Palestinian Reform and Development Plan: Development projects)	53
UNRWA (General Fund, SHC programme and UNRWA reform)	76
Nahr el Bared (Emergency aid for populations affected by the conflict in Lebanon)	13
Humanitarian and Food Aid *through UNRWA, WFP, NGOs (ECHO)*	66
Civil Society *(Partnership for peace)*	5
CFSP actions (support to EUPOL COPPS and EUBAM Rafah)	15
TOTAL	**486**

Note: last updated January 2009.

Relations between the two are regulated by the Association Agreement, signed in 1995 and ratified in 2000. Under the Association Agreement, each party granted the other preferential economic, commercial, technological and research status. In 2005 the European Union adopted an Action Plan (AP) with Israel in the context of the new European Neighbourhood Policy.[52] The AP covered a time frame of three years and was aimed at building the foundations for developing EU–Israel relations further.

The EU is Israel's largest market for exports and its second largest source of imports after the United States. In 2007, for example, Israel imported goods from the EU with a value of €14 billion, and exported goods with a value of €11.3 billion. Israel has a substantial trade deficit vis-à-vis the EU, which has stabilised in recent years at about €4 billion.[53]

In recent years a vast public debate has taken shape around the possibility of imposing sanctions on Israel to force it not only to loosen its tight grip on Palestinian territories and improve Palestinians' living conditions but also to stop the construction of new settlements and retire from all territories occupied in 1967.[54] The EU has been accused of not making sufficient use of political conditionality, and there have been pressures (not only from the public but also from the European Parliament itself[55]) for the EU to impose sanctions on Israel or at least make the strengthening of ties conditional upon progress on the front of the peace process. The EU has occasionally taken into consideration the idea of withholding economic benefit from Israel when the peace process was stalled, and Israel did not respond to pressures (see, for example, Chapter 4). However, so far the official position of the Commission has been that:

> The EU's policy is based on partnership and cooperation, and not exclusion. It is the EU's view that maintaining relations with Israel is an important contribution to the Middle East peace process and that suspending the Association Agreement, which is the basis for EU-Israeli trade relations but also the basis for the EU-Israel political dialogue, would not make the Israeli authorities more responsive to EU concerns at this time. It is also a well-known fact that economic sanctions achieve rather little in this respect. Keeping the lines of communication open and trying to convince our interlocutors is hopefully the better way forward.[56]

Given the difficult relations with Israel, the weight of history (particularly for some EU member states) and the secondary role of the EU in the peace process, the Union has elected until now to privilege the building of a closer relationship with Israel over the strong use of political conditionality. Not all member states have been in agreement with this choice,[57] but this line nevertheless prevailed, arguably also as a result of Israeli and American pressures. After the Gaza war of December 2008–January 2009, new calls were made on the EU to block the previously announced upgrading of relations with Israel, which would entail the development of a new Action Plan within the framework of the European Neighbourhood Policy. The 9th Meeting of the EU–Israel Association Council was first postponed and, when it finally took place in June 2009, did not proceed to draw up and approve a new Action Plan. The formal position is that EU–Israel relations will continue to be governed by the existing Action Plan, which expired in April 2009. To all effects the upgrading of relations with Israel has been put on hold for the time being, and both the Commissioner for External Relations, Benita Ferrero-Waldner, and a number of EU Foreign Ministers have suggested, in a more or less veiled fashion, that the upgrade will only go ahead if there is movement on Israel's part with regards to its policy towards the occupied territories.[58] While it is too early at the time of writing to evaluate the impact of this decision, these latest developments seem nevertheless to underline a slight change in the EU's policy, possibly compounded by the shift in the US discourse with President Obama's strongly worded request for a complete and immediate freeze of settlements on Israel's part.[59]

Strategic instruments

While it would be excessively ambitious to claim that the EU has been able to devise a comprehensive and coherent strategy with regard to the Middle East peace process, in this context it is nevertheless worth mentioning the adoption of a number of 'Strategies' that have in one way or another been relevant in the formulation of the EU's policy towards the peace process.

In June 2000 the EU adopted the Common Strategy for the Mediterranean Region. As pointed out earlier, the EU's Barcelona Process had found in the Middle East peace process, from which it is at least formally separate, the main obstacle to its progress. With the

Common Mediterranean Strategy the EU not only acknowledged the inevitable link between any possible progress in the field of regional cooperation and a successful outcome of the peace process, but in paragraph 15 went as far as to state: 'The EU will, in the context of a comprehensive settlement, and upon request by the core parties, give consideration to the participation of member states in the implementation of security arrangements on the ground.' Once again the member states found themselves confronted with the old dilemma: either step up the level and quality of Europe's involvement through coordination of the national policies and full employment of the instruments at EU's disposal, or renounce the aspiration to play a significant role and to exert political influence on the parties involved. And once again the solution devised was a compromise between the two options: in fact, although the Strategy did take into consideration the hypothesis of participating in the implementation of security arrangements on the ground, it was nevertheless contingent upon a full peace agreement being in existence,[60] therefore acknowledging implicitly that the EU Common Strategy was not going to contribute directly to achieving the final settlement itself.

In 2003 the European Council adopted the 'European Security Strategy' drawn up under the authority of the EU's High Representative for the Common Foreign and Security Policy, Javier Solana. The document identifies the global challenges and key threats to the security of the Union and clarifies its strategic objectives in dealing with them; it underlines the importance of building security in the EU's neighbourhood and promoting an international order based on effective multilateralism. The abovementioned European Neighbourhood Policy addressed many of the strategic objectives set out in the 2003 European Security Strategy.

A further document worth mentioning is the 2006 Regional Strategy Paper for Southern Mediterranean and Middle East,[61] whose purpose is to provide a strategic framework for programming the regional Mediterranean allocation of the European Neighbourhood and Partnership Instrument (ENPI), which replaced the previous MEDA financial instrument for the region. The paper underlines the strategic importance of the Mediterranean region to the EU in both economic and political terms, and identifies three priority objectives for the EU: a common Euro-Mediterranean area of justice, security and migration cooperation; a common sustainable economic area, with a focus on trade liberalisation, regional trade integration, infrastructure networks and environmental protection; and a common sphere for sociocultural exchanges.

Conclusion

This chapter has offered a legal institutional analysis of EU Common Foreign and Security Policy instruments, with a subsequent examination of how these instruments have been used by Member States in shaping the EU's policy towards the Arab–Israeli peace process. The ultimate purpose was to establish whether CFSP instruments are misused or underutilised by the member states, and whether they are quantitatively insufficient or qualitatively inadequate. The following conclusions can be drawn on the basis of the analysis conducted.

The instruments of EU foreign policy do indeed appear to be inadequate to deal with certain foreign policy issues, especially those in which the security dimension is of primary importance. In particular, the limited availability of military instruments appears to have a very negative effect on the EU's chances of influencing the Middle East peace process and becoming an acknowledged and accepted mediator. For many years the lack of military instruments seriously diminished the credibility of EU policy, and the parties involved – Israel without a doubt, but also the Arabs – continued to turn to the United States, which is the security manager of the region and whose military power contributes to making it a credible mediator, as well as the only accepted one. In 2003, in an interview with this author, Sir Brian Crowe – Former Director-General for External and Politico-Military Affairs, General Secretariat of the Council of the European Union – argued that the EU is very unlikely to develop the amount of military power that would be needed to emerge effectively from the sidelines and contribute to the security dimension of the peace process; however, he continued, if the goal of building a European military force is achieved, the EU might in the future be able to participate in peacekeeping operations in the context of a UN or NATO-sanctioned initiative in the area, thus adding a crucial dimension to its participation in the peace process. In this respect the events of the summer of 2006, when several EU member states were heavily involved in the negotiations to achieve a ceasefire between Israel and Hezbollah and subsequently committed to send a large number of troops to reinforce the UN mission in Lebanon (UNIFIL), seem to confirm Sir Crowe's prediction. On 25 August 2006, EU foreign ministers agreed to deploy a total of almost 7000 troops to Lebanon as a peacekeeping force. The mission was to continue to be run under the aegis of the UN, but the most significant military presence was going to be European. The agreement to deploy, however, was only reached after several discussions around the rules of engagement, with France particularly being concerned that those should be quite clear and not include the direct disarming of Hezbollah by UNIFIL.[62]

Three years after the deployment of this 'beefed-up' UNIFIL, it remains rather doubtful whether this presence of European troops along the Israeli border has contributed to improving Israeli perceptions of the EU as a security actor. The limited rules of engagement of UNIFIL do not allow the force to engage Hezbollah or to effectively prevent its rearmament. Weapons continue to be smuggled through the border with Syria, and ramps for missiles that can target Northern Israel have been simply moved by Hezbollah further north, into the area outside UNIFIL's competence (i.e. north of the Litani river).[63] While Israel is aware that the problem lies with the rules of engagement themselves, several Israeli politicians and officers have expressed perplexities as to European willingness to engage in dangerous operations in the area and fear that, even in the event of an Israeli–Palestinian agreement, an interposition force of Europeans would not truly guarantee Israeli security.[64]

If one looks beyond the issue of military instruments, CFSP instruments do not appear to be insufficient: the EU has at its disposal a wide variety of declaratory, operational, economic and strategic instruments. All of these instruments have been largely, if not always successfully, used by the EU in its policy towards the Middle East peace process. Moreover, the member states have also made implicit use of certain capabilities that derive from an 'implicit attribution' of legal personality to the EU, namely the treaty-making capacity and the right to recognise other subjects of international law. An empirical examination of the EU's behaviour can actually provide the grounds for the argument that the member states have on some occasions 'forced' the formal limits of the EU and operated as if the Union were an international legal person.

The inadequacy of the institutions in charge, and the bureaucratic complexity which characterise all levels of EU policymaking, have led to a misuse of CFSP instruments (i.e., the instruments are not appropriately and effectively used by the European governments). This is quite clear, for instance, in the case of the Special Representative and of the High Representative, whose mandates are at the origin of overlapping of competencies and inefficiencies, and in the difficult and often inefficient coordination of first- and second-pillar action in external relations.

Finally, it can be argued that the instruments at the EU's disposal are not underutilised by the member states, but are rather left undeveloped. There are different reasons behind this behaviour, such as the persistent desire of the member states to maintain control over their foreign policy, their reluctance to proceed too speedily in the direction of political integration in the Union, and the inability to find common interests of sufficient number to justify, in their view, the renunciation of the particularisms of national foreign policies and priorities, for the sake of the higher objective of achieving a common European policy. Once again, the cases of the Special Representative and the High Representative are particularly significant. Their potential role is not fully exploited by the member states to enhance the EU's role in the international arena. Rather, their scope for action is strictly regulated by the rules of intergovernmental cooperation, and their inability to commit the member states to any type of action arguably symbolises the continuing unwillingness of most European governments to give up what they consider should be the domain of the nation state.

7
Transatlantic Relations and the Middle East: Patterns of Continuity and Change

Introduction

This chapter focuses on American and European policy in the Greater Middle East[1] and on the state of transatlantic relations in this region of crucial importance for both the United States and the EU (Musu and Wallace 2003). The guiding thread is an analysis of the elements of convergence and divergence in American and European policies towards the whole region, with the objective of identifying the patterns of continuity and change that characterise the dynamics of the transatlantic relationship in this extremely contentious issue-area. The reason for this wider geographical focus lies in the close interrelation existing between the two policies (i.e. toward the peace process and towards the whole region), which are inextricably connected and need to be analysed in parallel in order to understand the dynamics of reciprocal influence. The central argument of the chapter is that strategic US interests in the Middle East and the dynamics of EU–US relations have relegated the EU to a secondary role in the Middle East peace process.

As has already emerged from the analysis conducted in previous chapters, the Middle East has indeed always been a highly controversial issue in transatlantic relations, sparking off some of the harshest instances of confrontation between the United States and Europe (Allen and Smith 1984; Garfinkle 1983; Steinbach 1980). This was the case in 1973 during the oil crisis, when Europe's Arab policy in response to the oil boycott outraged the American administration, which considered it an interference with both its small-steps strategy towards the Arab–Israeli dispute and its construction of an 'oil consumers front' by means of a new International Energy Agency; and contrasts arose again less than ten years later, in 1980, when the EC's Venice Declaration on the Arab–Israeli conflict caused discontent – to say the least – in Washington, where Europe's emphasis on the centrality of the Palestinian question and on the legitimacy of the PLO was seen as extremely untimely and potentially damaging to the peace process that had started in Camp David. It may be argued that some of the patterns of US–European interaction in the Middle East already began taking shape at the time of the events mentioned above, with the United States progressively deepening its engagement in the region and becoming the main mediator in the Arab–Israeli conflict, and the EC confined to a subordinated role, constrained and conditioned in its action by internal divisions, institutional inadequacies and a heavy dependence on Middle Eastern oil, but also by American reluctance to share the 'driving seat' in the peace process and by the rigid dynamics of the Cold War – of which the Middle East was hostage – which allowed Europe very little leeway, caught as it was in the middle of a confrontation between superpowers.

In the last twenty years, a number of successive crucial events have transformed both the Middle East and the interrelations between the United States and the EU in the region (Gompert and Larrabee 1998; Gordon 1998). The end of the Cold War deeply modified the balance of power in the area, leaving the United States as the sole superpower. The Gulf War transformed the dynamics of interregional relations, creating a window of opportunity for a resolution of the Arab–Israeli dispute and strengthening the role of the United States as the only accepted mediator. The ratification of the Treaty of Maastricht and the creation of the Common Foreign and Security Policy (CFSP) and of the European Security and Defence Policy (ESDP) marked an acceleration in the process of European political integration and in the transformation of the EU into a global actor, increasing its aspirations – and also its chances – of playing a more relevant role in the Middle East.

The election of George W. Bush in 2000 and his initial apparent disengagement from the Arab–Israeli conflict created a brief political vacuum that the EU, nonetheless, proved unable or unwilling to fill (Stein 2002). The September 11th attacks, though, forced the Bush

Administration back into Middle East policy, and the 'war on terror' and the attack on Iraq made necessary a reappraisal of their overall strategy and approach to the region as a whole (Gordon 2003). The redefinition of American strategy had an immediate effect on the EU's role, on the one hand opening up some windows of opportunity for a greater European involvement in the Middle East, and in particular in the peace process, while on the other hand reducing Europe's margin for action with regard to some specific issues – such as its policy towards rogue states – given the increasingly unilateralist approach adopted by the American administration.

In this framework, this chapter will focus on the elements of *convergence* and *divergence* in US and EU policies towards the Middle East, and will address the following issues:

- To what extent are the basic interests of the United States and the EU similar and compatible?
- On what issues can convergence between US and EU policies towards the Middle East be said to exist?
- Is convergence actually generated by a shared political vision or rather by the EU's inability to challenge American supremacy?
- Are American and European approaches to the Arab–Israeli peace process and to the Greater Middle East irreconcilable, or rather different but complementary?

Furthermore, the chapter looks at the patterns of *continuity* and *change* that characterise the dynamics of the transatlantic relationship in the Middle East, and tries to answer the following questions:

- What elements – of convergence and divergence – are long-term features in American and European policies towards the region, and have 'resisted' untouched by all the upheavals of the last decades, including the failure of the Oslo process, the election of President Bush, the September 11th attacks and the war in Iraq? May elements such as the EU's inability to overcome its internal divisions in formulating its Middle East policy, its reluctance to forsake the security umbrella offered by the United States in the region, or the US and the EU approaches to the peace process or to countries like Iran and Iraq (dual containment strategy versus critical engagement) be included in this category?

- What events have actually brought about significant changes in US and EU policies, modifying the trend of continuity in transatlantic relations in the Middle East? Can we include in this category phenomena such as the progressive building of a European political identity and the institutional consolidation of the EU with the introduction of the High Representative for CFSP and the creation of ESDP? Or – during George W. Bush's presidency – the change in American priorities with the adoption of the 'Bush Doctrine' and the strategy for the war on terror, which have seemingly pushed the United States towards unilateralism in dealing with perceived threats from the region and with rogue states, while on the other hand encouraging the United States to adopt a multilateral approach to the Arab–Israeli peace process, thereby possibly creating an opportunity for strengthened cooperation with the EU through the so called 'Madrid Quartet'?

The analysis will cover the trends of the last twenty years and will close with the end of the second George W. Bush Presidency. While the Obama Presidency might bring some important changes to the dynamics that have prevailed until now, it is too soon to offer any in-depth analysis or evaluation.

EU and US policies towards the Middle East: Elements of convergence and divergence

The first step in the direction of identifying the elements of convergence and divergence in EU and US policies towards the Middle East is to analyse their respective interests in the region in order to establish whether they differ, and, if so, to what extent. This analysis of US and EU interests in the Middle East is essential in understanding their long-term strategies on the one hand, and, on the other, to what extent the pursuit of different policies is an expression of different underlying interests, or rather of a different perception of the strategies necessary to pursue interests that are, on the whole, quite similar.

The complexities of both American and European relations and ties with the Middle East are such that any categorisation of their interests in the region will necessarily be incomplete; for the purpose of this analysis, however, three main interests can be identified:

- The settlement of the Arab–Israeli conflict
- The free flow of oil
- Regional stability and prosperity.

As this chapter will show, these are all interests shared by both the United States and the EU; however, a closer analysis of the policies pursued by each will reveal how the strategies and policy choices differ, and at times diverge.

These shared American and European interests are threatened by various dangerous trends, which may in turn be categorised as follows:

- Regional instability
- The threat posed by rogue states and by the diffusion of weapons of mass destruction (WMD)
- The spread of terrorism.

The analysis conducted in this section will be structured as follows: first it will focus on the Arab–Israeli peace process, devoting special attention to the different approaches of the United States and the EU towards this issue and to the reasons behind their differing policies; it will then focus on the problem of free access to oil and on the importance of regional stability. Finally it will analyse the factors that constitute a threat to these European and American interests and their different policy responses.

EU and US interests in the Middle East: The settlement of the Arab–Israeli conflict

An analysis of American and European approaches to the problem of the Arab–Israeli conflict shows that divergence is more about policies and priorities than it is about interests: the settlement of the Arab–Israeli conflict is undeniably a shared interest of both the United States and the European Union, as the political instability and potential dangers that derive from the continuation of this dispute affect the United States and the EU alike (Khalilzad 1998; Perthes 2000). However, the view they have of the conflict and of the appropriate strategies for solving it, and their relations with the parties involved, diverge markedly to say the least.

Much has already been said about EU and US policy towards the Arab–Israeli peace process in previous chapters, but in this context it is worth mentioning some specific aspects of these policies that can help to compare and contrast EU and US *attitudes*.

The most standard characterisation that is normally given of the different American and European attitudes is that the United States is more supportive of Israel whereas the EU tends to be more supportive of the Arab side (Blackwill and Sturmer 1997; Dosenrode and Stubkjaer 2002; Hadar 1996). Apart from the clear oversimplification and the obvious difficulty in labelling any policy as an 'EU' unitary policy or stance, this description does hold a grain of truth.

There are many reasons for American support of Israel, some of the main factors being:

- The presence in the United States of a strong, organised and well-funded Jewish lobby, able to exercise its influence both on the US Congress and on the President, who cannot afford to neglect the broad Jewish electorate[2]
- Sympathy for the Jewish community tied to the catastrophe of the Shoah
- An underlying cultural affinity between the two countries, both new, immigrant-absorbing, democratic societies (Gordon 1998: 29)
- The common Israeli and American interest in regional peace, security, openness and prosperity[3]
- Israel's potential as a useful strategic regional partner for the United States, thanks to its role in fighting opponents of American interests and influence in the area such as Syria, Iran and Iraq
- The possibility of US–Israel military collaboration, through enhanced cooperation on counterterrorism, various forms of defence against ballistic missiles, American use of Israeli air space or collaboration between intelligence agencies (the precondition for this cooperation, –however, being an easing of the Arab–Israeli conflict that would allow the open involvement of Israel in military operations in the region).

On issues linked to the peace process between Israel and the Arab states and between Israel and the Palestinians, American and Israeli positions are often aligned: according to the American vision, the United States' function should be that of facilitating talks and negotiations between the two parties, not imposing predetermined solutions.[4]

An effective description of America's perception of its role in the peace process is given by Middle East expert Stephen Cohen: 'In [...] the Arab–Israeli conflict there is such a struggle of wills within the competing parties, and between the competing parties, and the forces for and against change are so evenly balanced, that only a third party – with a clear vision – can swing things toward compromise. That is America's role. [Also] the parties themselves are always going to be focused on the immediate costs of doing something because the positive outcomes seem remote or even unlikely to them. Which is why they'll need [America's] push'.[5]

This role of the United States as facilitator is also the one favoured by Israel, which does not welcome the idea of a mediator that wants to enforce its strategy against the will of the negotiating parties. The United States have indeed been quite reluctant to exercise strong pressures on Israel, for domestic reasons (the Jewish vote and the pressures of the Jewish lobby) and also because of their perception of the issues at stake (American understanding of Israeli security concerns) – particularly on questions such as the withdrawal from the Golan Heights or the problem of the return of the Palestinian refugees and their descendants to Israel; furthermore, there is a degree of flexibility on America's part regarding United Nations resolutions on issues such as the status of Jerusalem, which in Washington's view can only be determined by direct negotiations among the parties involved; the United States does not actually consider the UN an appropriate forum for debating issues that are the object of direct negotiations between Arabs and Israelis.

As for the European Union, the first comment to make is the usual disclaimer that applies most of the time to EU foreign policy, that is, that the member states do not share a common position, but rather a series of varying positions which, at times, converge more strongly. This is indeed one of the main impediments to a truly effective and high-profile involvement of Europe in the peace process, to which a number of other factors must be added, including Europe's image as being too supportive of the Arabs, which causes Israel to be wary of an extensive EU involvement in the negotiations; the diplomatic strategy favoured by the EU, which is rejected by the Israelis; and the European Union's limited availability of military instruments, which has long rendered the EU unable to contribute directly to the security dimension of the negotiations (even though most of its member states have participated in UN peacekeeping forces).

It must not be forgotten that, even though there are long-established Jewish communities in Europe, they are by far not as numerous, well-organised or influential as the American Jewish communities.[6] On the other hand, Europe has a significant Muslim presence (ca. 15–17 million people, including Turkish immigrants), which has accustomed rising generations to its diverse culture (Vaisse 2008). Political dialogue, social interaction, and economic and financial interdependence have contributed to building links between elites; integration, however, has not always taken place easily or successfully, and very often Muslim immigrants and their descendants represent the poorest layer of the population. The Muslim communities have only recently started to organise themselves politically and do not exercise political influence directly over the various governments; obviously, though, the very presence of these large communities (e.g. 5 million Muslims in France) does pose a constraint on European governments' actions (*Strategic Survey* 2003: 106–7) and creates concerns for potential internal instability and security problems, originating also from possible discontent regarding policies towards the Arab–Israeli conflict.[7] These factors do contribute to generating a certain cautiousness in the EU's policy towards the Arab world, which, coupled with the historical ties of many member states with the region, the close economic relations between the EU and a number of Arab states and the peculiarity of Europe's relations with Israel because of the historical legacy of the past, causes Israel to perceive Europe as biased in favour of the Arabs and to be, by and large, opposed to an EU role in the peace process.

A further important fact is that the European diplomatic approach to the peace process differs significantly from that of Israel and the United States. Europe has followed a well-defined policy with clearly identifiable guidelines: focus on immediate results rather than on the process and the negotiation themselves,[8] reiterated appeals to United Nations resolutions, and emphasis repeatedly placed on the need for the issues on the floor to be taken on globally, within the context of international peace conferences.

This different approach to the peace process creates a deep fracture between the EU and both Israel and the United States: the Israeli diplomatic approach – supported by the United States – is in fact geared to affording the utmost priority to bilateral contacts,[9] possibly supported by an external party acting as facilitator. Bilateral contacts are considered by Israel to be not only necessary, but almost a precondition for each set of talks.[10] The origin of the Israeli diplomatic strategy may lie in part in the will to discuss different issues separately, optimising negotiating power and potential leverage;[11] on the other hand, a further crucial objective is to meet with the counterpart in a context where mutual recognition and mutual acceptance as legitimate interlocutors are indubitable. Together with security, diplomatic recognition is incontrovertibly a central priority of Israeli policy.

The EU's repeated requests for an immediate Israeli withdrawal from the West Bank and (until Israel's 2005 unilateral withdrawal) Gaza and from the Golan Heights have caused Israel to consider Europe not to be sufficiently understanding and supportive with regard to its need for security guarantees, deemed vital for the very survival of the State of Israel. Besides, the EU's inability to guarantee security and to contribute directly to the military dimension of the peace process has long relegated the EU automatically to a secondary role in the negotiations until a final settlement is reached. The EU's role has continued to be linked to the development of financial assistance to the Palestinian Authority: in other words, the EU has made use of economic instruments for political ends, as has so often been the case since the creation of EPC.

The American position vis-à-vis Europe's role continues to be rather ambivalent: the United States is wary of a strong European involvement in the peace talks, and is keen on safeguarding its primary mediation role in the peace process, partly in order to protect American interests most effectively. Yet the United States is also happy to leave Europe with the burden of financial assistance to the Palestinian Authority: Washington does not welcome the idea of a free-riding EU that exploits the security coverage offered by the United States – the sole security manager of the region – without offering at least the limited assistance within its power; diplomatically limited, but substantial in economic terms. Furthermore, the United States is aware that economic growth of the Palestinian Authority is a necessary precondition for the consolidation of the peace process, and is willing to acknowledge a prominent role for the EU in this field, as long as it remains politically in line with American strategy (Gompert and Larrabee 1998; Perthes 2000).

The creation of the Middle East Quartet in 2002 (discussed in detail in Chapter 4) has established a formal framework for the EU and the United States to interact and coordinate their policies towards the peace process. Some ideas, including the concept of a 'Roadmap' and the idea of convening an international conference, originated in Europe but were then transformed into a Quartet strategy. This has seemingly brought about a convergence of strategy between the EU and the United States, and has also helped the EU to be accepted by Israel for the first time as a contributor to security arrangements, albeit in an extremely limited fashion (see, for example, the creation of the ill-fated EUBAM force or, in a different context, Israel's acceptance of a largely European beefed-up UNIFIL force in southern Lebanon). Serious doubts, however, still remain over to what extent the United States believes in the Quartet project. Both during the preparation of the 2007 Annapolis conference and during the last twelve months of the Bush presidency the relevance of the Quartet was rather weak, and Washington appeared mostly intent on securing for itself the traditional exclusive role of mediator, to the detriment of the possible role of the other members of the Quartet.

The victory of Hamas in the Palestinian elections of 2006 saw the EU and the United States aligned in their decision not to recognise the Islamist organisation (which is in both countries' list of terrorist organisations) as a legitimate representative of the Palestinian people, although by the end of 2008 several European governments were more openly making the case for a policy change regarding Hamas, and France even admitted to informal contacts with the Islamist movement.[12]

While the Obama presidency might bring changes to how Washington views a role for the EU in the peace process beyond that of 'provider', this transformation of the burden-sharing dynamic was still far from being concrete at the end of George W. Bush's second term.

EU and US interests in the Middle East: The free flow of oil

Europe and the United States share a dependence on oil from the Middle East to guarantee their economic prosperity, and would both suffer greatly if access to such an important energy supply were to be limited, as they would from a sudden rise in oil prices (Haass 1999; Khalilzad 1998: 191–217; Yorke 1999). Concerns over access to oil have influenced the formulation of policies by both the EU and the United States towards the whole region. The need to ensure the free flow of oil has often been one of the vital reasons behind interventions of a military nature, from the Suez invasion to the Earnest Will Operation during the Iran–Iraq war, when the United States escorted ships loaded with Kuwaiti oil, and on to Operations Desert Storm and Iraq Freedom[13] against Saddam Hussein's Iraq.

It has been underlined that, while the free flow of oil is a shared interest for the United States and Europe, their dependence on Middle Eastern oil is not the same (Gordon 1998: 31): European Union member states – with the exception of Great Britain, which has its own oil reserves – depend on imported supplies to the measure of more than 80% of their energy, and almost 35% of the oil imported by Europe comes from the Middle East and North Africa, against a 25% share of the United States' imported oil.[14]

However, it should not be forgotten that the global oil market is essentially a single market and that US imports have increased rapidly over the last twenty years, while European imports have remained relatively stable. Indeed, American dependence on OPEC oil in the mid-1990s was far higher than that of Britain or Germany (for which North Sea oil provided a secure supply), though considerably lower than in France or Italy. Furthermore, overall American oil consumption and imports rose steadily throughout the 1990s, as higher taxation and energy conservation in Europe held oil consumption and dependence levels stable (Claes 2001: 70–4).

American interests in oil imports from the Middle East are in fact at least as strong as Europe's. Oil plays a key role in US energy security, providing 49% of the total annual energy requirements of the United States. The United States is actually the world's number one consumer of oil, with a consumption of 21 million barrels of oil per day, or one-quarter of the world's total. Of these 21 million barrels, the United States imports 12 million; its domestic production is declining, while its consumption is rising.[15]

The United States depends on the Gulf/Middle East region for only about one-fifth of its direct oil imports, as the US imports primarily from Mexico, Canada and Venezuela,[16] whose geographic proximity allows for minimal transport costs. However, given that oil is a fungible commodity, the United States is ultimately dependent on Arab/Gulf oil as a consequence of the entire world's dependence on Gulf oil. Considering the Middle East/Gulf region's hefty percentage of world oil production, any disruption in Gulf oil supply would force those countries that directly import high quantities of oil from the Gulf to try to buy from different suppliers, including those from which the United States imports heavily. Such competition would inevitably cause a dramatic increase in the price of crude oil for all consumers, and thus impact on the US economy.

The cost for the United States of past oil price shocks and supply manipulation by the OPEC cartel has been enormous. Estimates place the cumulative costs from 1972 to 1991 at over 4 trillion 1993 US dollars. According to a study drafted in 1995 for the Office of Transportation Technology of the US Department of Energy (Greene and Leiby 1995), future oil price shocks would be just as harmful to the US economy as those of the past. As the report says, '[...] fundamental economics ordains that the potential market power of the OPEC cartel depends on its market share, the ability of consumers to reduce oil use in response to higher prices, and the ability of the rest of the world producers to expand oil supply in response to a reduction by the cartel. Not only is OPEC's market share rising towards its historic high point, but recent studies provide no evidence of increases in the price elasticities of world oil supply and demand.[17] Greater market share and continuing oil dependence on OPEC oil will give the cartel the opportunity to raise oil prices. Studies reaffirm that oil price increases cause gross national product (GNP) to fall and prices to rise and suggest no significant differences between the impacts on the US economy of the 1990 price shock and those of 1973–74 and 1979–80 [...]'. The reason for this situation is that little has changed compared with the past. According to the US Department of Energy figures, the cost of oil as a percentage of US GNP was 1.5% in 1973 and also in 1992. Oil imports covered 35% of US oil consumption in 1973 and peaked at 46.5% in 1977. US petroleum imports were 44% in 1993, 46% in 1994, 55.5% in 2001[18] and 57% in 2007.

One of the pillars of American oil policy has been the construction of a close relationship with Saudi Arabia (Pollack 2002: 77–102), whose supplies represent a relevant share of the oil imported by the United States, providing about 14% of total US crude imports and 7%

of US consumption. Essentially, the global oil market consists of two main consumer regions (the Atlantic and the Asia Pacific) and one main producer region (the Middle East); among global oil producers, Saudi Arabia, with its substantial oil reserves and excess production capacity, occupies a central place. Russian oil cannot be more than a partial substitute for Saudi oil, in part because the poor extraction technologies used in the Soviet period have degraded the remaining reserves, which are in any event far smaller than Saudi reserves. As for oil from the Caspian region, not only are the necessary pipelines still under construction, but strong doubts remain as to whether its resources will ever be able to replace Saudi oil.[19]

Over the years the United States and Saudi Arabia have become strategic partners and have a record of close cooperation: apart from ensuring the stable supply and price of oil on the world market, during the Cold War Saudi Arabia played a key role in meeting a number of US foreign policy objectives, including assistance in the effort to expel the Soviet Union from Afghanistan.[20] During the 1991 war against Iraq, Saudi Arabia was a key member of the allied coalition that expelled Iraqi forces from Kuwait, while on the other hand Saudi officials expressed opposition to the US-led attack on Iraq in 2003.

American partnership with Saudi Arabia has proved to be difficult to reconcile with the United States's close relationship with Israel. Saudi Arabia supports Palestinian national aspirations, strongly endorses Muslim claims in the old city of Jerusalem, and has been increasingly critical of Israel since the outbreak of the Palestinian uprising in the occupied West Bank and Gaza in September 2000. At the same time, however, Saudi Arabia has supported US policy by endorsing Israeli–Palestinian peace agreements. In March 2002, then Crown Prince Abdullah proposed a peace initiative calling for full Israeli withdrawal from occupied territories in return for full normalisation of relations between Arab states and Israel. The plan was endorsed by the Arab League at a summit conference. Over a year later President Bush, then Crown Prince Abdullah, and four other Arab leaders met at Sharm-el-Sheikh, Egypt, where the attendees endorsed the Quartet's Road Map (Prados 2006: 8).

For its part, the EU maintains its relations with Saudi Arabia and with other Gulf states[21] through the Gulf Cooperation Council (GCC). Despite the existence of this formal framework for coordination of European policy towards Gulf states, however, the political content of the GCC is rather minimal, and relations between the EU and Gulf countries have concentrated mostly on the conclusion of a free trade agreement. The GCC is currently the EU's sixth largest export market and the EU is the GCC's first trading partner. EU imports from the GCC consist mostly of fuels and derivatives (70% of total EU imports from the GCC countries). GCC countries currently benefit from preferential access to the EU market under the EU's Generalized System of Preferences (GSP).[22]

As Ana Echague has underlined, 'GCC states complain that they are treated by the EU only as sources of energy, when the GCC seeks a broader strategic partnership to offset US power, especially in relation to the Arab-Israel conflict. Some European officials complain, conversely, that dialogue is already far too dominated by efforts to coordinate positions on Palestine and that this issue invariably displaces all debate and cooperation on energy' (Echague 2007: 13).

The ongoing availability of reliable sources of oil, therefore, remains crucial for the prosperity of the United States as well as Europe's.[23] (See Tables 7.1, 7.2 and 7.3) The United States uses economic and diplomatic means to guarantee this availability,

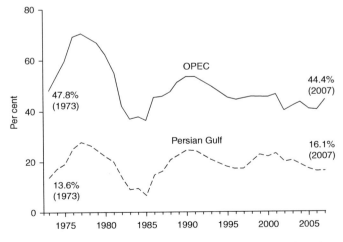

Table 7.1   US imports from OPEC and Persian Gulf as share of total imports (1973–2007)

Source: Energy Information Administration.

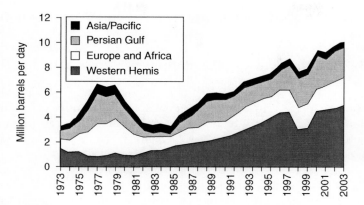

Table 7.2 US crude oil imports by area of origin (1973–2004)
Source: Energy Information Administration.

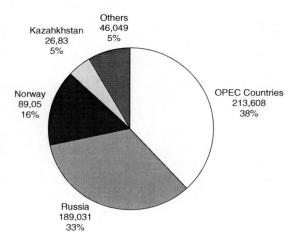

Table 7.3 Imports of crude oil in EU27 by trading partners (2006)
Source: European Commission.

backed up by a huge military force and by the credible threat that it is ready to use it should the need arise. The European Union has chosen to pursue policies that are geared to avoiding the direct hostility of the Arab world, and, through the use of economic instruments for political purposes, it has tried to build close relations with crucial oil producer states in an attempt to be shielded from possible oil supply crises.

EU and US interests in the Middle East: Regional stability and prosperity

A further interest shared by the United States and Europe is regional stability and prosperity, which would protect the supply of oil, reduce the demand for US military involvement in the area, and create a market for American as well as European products.

First of all, one relevant factor that emerges from the analysis of European and American interests in the Greater Middle East should be highlighted. Europe tends to focus its attention on the Mediterranean region,[24] the stability of which influences Europe's prosperity more directly, and where its economic interests, as well as its historical and political links, are stronger. In American policy, on the contrary, there is little consciousness of the Mediterranean as a coherent geostrategic region (Lesser 1998). American policymakers tend to focus on Persian Gulf countries and on the Arab–Israeli conflict.

For European governments, the Mediterranean is the near south, and the Middle East an integral component of the EU's Mediterranean Partnership policies. For the United States, the Mediterranean has long represented the southern flank of NATO, and the essential west–east corridor through which to project power across the Middle East and Central Asia. The predominant pattern of European policies is based on differentiated relations with particular states and groups of states; American policymakers, in contrast, have designed strategic concepts for the entire region, awarding clear priority to security concerns and instruments.

The European Union tends to pursue its objectives in the region – such as the achievement of regional political stability, the maintenance of good relations with countries in the region, and the strengthening of trade relations that contribute to the economic development of the Middle Eastern countries, thus reducing the risk of an instability spillover for Europe – by means of economic policy tools. Through the Euro-Mediterranean Partnership (EMP), the European Union attempts to promote close political, economic and social cooperation with ten countries of the Mediterranean area, including Israel and the Palestinian Authority, with the declared long-term goal of 'progressively establishing an area of regional security and free trade'.[25] The EMP extends as far as Jordan and Syria, incorporating the complex politics of the Arab–Israel conflict within a partnership primarily designated as economic. Through the EMP, the EU also attempts to counterbalance certain dangerous trends that undermine the stability of the region, such as the very limited south–south trade and the absence of region-wide institutions promoting cooperation on economic, political or security issues. Since 2004 the European Neighbourhood Policy (which is examined in more detail in Chapter 6) has been added to the EMP as an instrument for dealing with countries of the region. Unlike the EMP, the ENP is based on bilateral agreements between the EU and countries in Europe's neighbourhood, and Egypt, Israel, Jordan and the Palestinian Authority have all signed Action Plans with the EU.

Regional instability in the Middle East is the result of a number of factors, which include strong demographic growth, poor economic growth, the spreading of Islamic extremism, the scarcity of resources such as water, and almost non-existent regional cooperation. The European approach to countering these threats has relied on 'civilian power' instruments: diplomacy, trade, financial assistance. The American approach has relied on all these plus the ability to project credible military power.

The EU – given its geographical proximity to the region – is particularly vulnerable to problems such as uncontrolled migration flows generated by the region's economic underdevelopment and the scarcity of jobs: immigration places pressure on European borders, generating security problems, and the presence of large communities of immigrants in Europe increases social tensions. As said before, approximately 15 million Muslims live within the European Union (approximately 5 million in France and 1.4 million in Great Britain), and their presence is largely a result of the massive influx of workers and other migrants from the Middle East and from former colonial territories in Africa.[26] Through regional cooperation and dialogue, the EU attempts to contribute to the economic and social development of the region, thus hoping to ease the tensions that cause social instability and prompt migration towards Europe. While it is not the purpose of this book to discuss in detail the Euro-Mediterranean

Partnership, it is worth mentioning here that there is ample debate as to how far this strategy has been successful, considering structural problems such as the organisation of the Partnership itself, which sees the EU negotiating as a single bloc with each South-Mediterranean partner (and therefore from a position of negotiating strength that prevents the southern partners from gaining real economic advantages), or the fact that the South-Mediterranean partners have pursued the strategy of linking every political concession to the progress of the Arab–Israeli peace process, and therefore the Partnership has ultimately come to a stalemate with the collapse of the Oslo process (Youngs 2006).

The United States is less affected by problems such as immigration flow from North Africa and the Middle East, and more concerned with the security of friendly states in the area to guarantee access to oil and prevent the emergence of a hostile regional hegemonic state that may threaten their interests. The instrument of choice in pursuing this policy is military and financial assistance, and the projection of power: apart from providing Israel with military and economic assistance worth over three billion dollars a year,[27] every year the United States provides substantial support to both Egypt[28] and, to a lesser extent, Jordan.[29] Furthermore, the presence of the US Sixth Fleet in the Mediterranean and of numerous US military bases throughout the area constitutes a constant tangible reminder to every state in the region of America's determination to protect its interests with all means available, including military power.

After 9/11 the Bush administration started considering the idea of launching long-term programmes to improve the stability of Arab states and reduce the appeal of extremist ideology by advancing democratic transformation in the region. In this context two projects are worth mentioning. The first is the US Middle East Partnership Initiative (MEPI), established by then Secretary Powell in 2002, to create educational opportunity at a grass roots level, promote economic opportunity and help foster private sector development, and to strengthen civil society and the rule of law throughout the region. The MEPI was received with many reservations in the Arab world and its achievements have been limited, partly as a result of the hostility of autocratic Arab governments to any greater independence or activism in the non-governmental sector.

The second project is the Broader Middle East and North Africa Initiative (BMENA), a multilateral development and reform plan aimed at fostering economic and political liberalisation in a wide geographical area of Arab and non-Arab Muslim countries. The initiative, an American 'brainchild', was adopted by the Group of Eight Industrialized Nations (G-8) at their June 2004 summit in Sea Island, Georgia, and was seen by the Bush Administration as representing a milestone in the war on terrorism. The two key elements were the launching of a 'Partnership for Progress and a Common Future with the Region of the Broader Middle East and North Africa' and a plan for the G-8 countries to support reform in Arab countries.

When, in February, an early draft of the US proposal was leaked to an Arabic newspaper, *al-Hayat*, it raised an outcry among Arab leaders that the United States was attempting to impose external political models on the region. Reception among European states was also rather cold, if not outright negative. The reasons for European preoccupation can be summarised thus. Firstly, some states (particularly France) were worried that the Americans would 'hijack' pre-existing European regional initiatives (such as the EMP) while exploiting their existence and their achievements to promote their own interests and agenda. Secondly, Europeans were worried by a partnership with the United States that could constrain their options while at the same time creating a negative backlash as a result of American unpopularity and tarnished image in the region. Additionally, the fact that the initiative had been drawn up without consultation with Arab states or civil society undermined, in Europe's eyes, the chances of success of the whole project.

A further preoccupation that the Europeans voiced, arguably based partly on the, by then, nine-years-old experience with the Barcelona Process, was the fact that in the initial American project there was little connection between reform efforts and progress on the Arab–Israeli conflict. The argument brought forward by European officials was that, while it was true that Arab political stagnation fuels radicalism, the Arab–Israeli conflict was also a major source of radicalisation and therefore deserved equal attention in the priorities on the BMENA initiative. European pressures on the United States in this respect were reflected in the official BMENA statement from the G8's Sea Island summit, which did indeed refer to progress in the Arab–Israeli peace process as one of the crucial priorities in the road towards the achievement of stability in the region.

Despite the initial excitement and debate caused by the BMENA initiative, soon the initiative lost much of its steam and turned into a rather low-profile forum with limited achievements, a fate that it seems to share with previous regional initiatives such as the EU's Barcelona Process. It is, however, worth underlining in this context the importance of the debate that took place between the United States and the EU on the importance that should be assigned to tackling the Arab–Israeli issue when attempting reform and stabilisation of the Middle East. As Wittes and Youngs put it, 'The well-known European line persisted that Washington's imbalanced position on the Arab–Israeli conflict complicates other areas of policy in the Middle East. The European conviction remains strong that support for democratic reform is unlikely to prove fruitful until the Arab–Israeli peace process makes significant progress, a development that in turn requires a more even-handed US attitude' (Wittes and Youngs 2009: 4).

Threats to US and EU interests: Rogue states and weapons of mass destruction

The danger posed by rogue states and by the diffusion of weapons of mass destruction (WMD) represents a very strong threat to both American and European interests in the Greater Middle East; however, the political reading of this threat and the policy choices adopted are not only different, but at times significantly divergent.

It is worth recalling briefly the origins of the concept of 'rogue state', developed in the United States at the end of the Cold War by Colin Powell (the then Chairman of the Joint Chiefs of Staff) as part of an argument which justified the continuation of heavy investment in conventional forces after the demise of the Soviet Union. The new doctrine characterised hostile (or seemingly hostile) Third World states with large military forces and nascent WMD capabilities as 'rogue states' or 'nuclear outlaws' bent on sabotaging the prevailing world order. Such regimes were said to harbour aggressive intentions vis-à-vis their less powerful neighbours, to oppose the spread of democracy and to be guilty of circumventing international norms against nuclear and chemical proliferation. Furthermore, they were seen as supporting and sponsoring terrorist actions against American citizens and interests abroad (Klare 1995). From 1990 on, the general model of a rogue state ruled by an 'outlaw regime' armed with chemical and nuclear weapons became central in American national security discourse. The strategy devised called for American readiness to react militarily to the threat posed by rogue states through the rapid concentration of power and the use of superior firepower to shock and disable enemy forces at the very beginning of hostilities. This, in turn, required the continued possession of technological superiority and a capability for strategic mobility, that is, the rapid deployment of US forces and equipment to distant battle zones (ibid.). The Middle East states originally identified as rogue states were Iran and Libya;[30] from August 1990 (i.e. from the invasion of Kuwait) Iraq was added to the list.

American and European strategies to protect their interests against the menace represented by these states in the region are not alike: whereas the United States espouses regime change and economic sanctions as key tools for containing and coercing difficult regimes, Europeans emphasise the benefits of international political pressure linked to multilateral negotiation and engagement. Moreover, while the EU may be more sensitive to the regional dynamic, and to the perceptions and sensitivities of regional actors, the United States views the dangers linked to rogue states and the diffusion of WMD in a global perspective, and its policymaking is geared to countering the threats to which the international order is exposed (Yorke 1999: 12).

The distance between European and American strategies towards the American-defined rogue states also emerges symbolically from the names of the respective policies elaborated: whereas during the 1990s the United States promoted the so-called 'Dual Containment'[31] towards Iran and Iraq, with the aim of weakening both countries through strict economic sanctions and diplomatic isolation (Saltiel and Purcell 2002), most EU member states[32] favoured a 'Critical Engagement' approach, at least with Iran and Libya, in order to promote dialogue and trade relations which – in their view – would afford them the leverage to moderate difficult government behaviour. Interestingly, the expression 'rogue states' is absent from the 2003 European Security Strategy, which delineated both the threats facing the EU and the strategy that should be adopted to counter them.[33]

In the past few years the attention of both the United States and the EU has focused progressively more closely on Iran as a threat to international peace and security, particularly since Teheran has announced its intention to develop an independent nuclear programme and has started developing the necessary technology.

The main sources of friction in US–Iranian relations may be broken down into three categories: (1) Iranian attempts to acquire weapons of mass destruction; (2) Iranian support of violent opposition to Israel (military, economic and political support to Hezbollah, Hamas and Palestinian Islamic Jihad); and (3) Iranian aspirations to regional hegemony, which have increased and become more assertive since the US-led coalition has removed Saddam Hussein from power in Iraq, therefore leaving a power vacuum in the region that Iran is eager to fill.[34] The American policy of containment towards Iran, also rooted in the history of US relations with Iran, in the trauma of the 1979 Revolution and in the hostage crisis, is not without critics, both at home and abroad. What is viewed as particularly dubious is the effectiveness of coercive diplomacy and unilateral sanctions in compelling Iranian leaders to give up WMD options. Many experts believe that, even with US sanctions in place, Iran has enough money to spend freely on WMD development. Iran cannot but perceive its strategic environment as highly threatening to its security: in particular, there is a risk of strategic encirclement by foreign powers[35] and by states in the region such as Pakistan, which has both nuclear weapons and a recent history of tense relations with Iran. In this framework, some American experts have suggested that the policy of isolating Iran should be reassessed and that consideration should be given to the possibility of inaugurating government-to-government dialogue with Teheran and of making efforts to 'reach out to the Iranian people'.[36] In the years of the Bush presidency this suggestion has in no way been adopted, and Washington's policy has remained concentrated on isolating Iran and blocking its nuclear programme. President Obama has indicated willingness to open the way for a diplomatic dialogue, but at the very early stages of his presidency it is still unclear what shape this new policy will take.

The EU, for its part, has consistently supported the idea of maintaining open channels of communication with Teheran. The policy of 'Critical Dialogue' with Iran had already been officially endorsed by the European Community at a meeting of the European Council in Edinburgh in December 1992. In the EU's intentions, the Dialogue should be a vehicle for raising concerns about Iranian behaviour and for demanding improvement on various issues, especially human rights and terrorism, areas in which progress is considered crucial for building closer relations (Rudolf 1999: 73). Europe's strategy, in contrast to the American punishment and containment policy, is once again to favour dialogue and trade, rather than coercion. The difference in approach is tied to the different perception of the dangers and of the most effective way to take on the issues, but also arguably to the different economic involvement in the region of the United States and of the European Union. In fact, while the United States has virtually no commercial relations with Iran, the volume of trade between European Union member states and Iran was, for example, almost 24 billion Euro in 2007.[37] European economic and political contacts with Iran are substantial, and have increased steadily; the EU is the first trade partner of Iran, accounting for almost a third of its exports. Close to 90% of EU imports from Iran are energy-related: Iran ranks as the sixth supplier of energy products to the EU.[38] Many European leaders advocate Iran's entry into the World Trade Organisation, suggesting that the integration of Iran into the world economy would foster greater transparency and allow the international community to monitor worrisome Iranian transactions more closely. European governments do not view engagement as endorsing the regime in question per se; rather, they believe that dialogue and trade relations allow them the leverage to moderate difficult government behaviour.

After Iran broke its 2003 agreement to suspend enrichment activities, Germany, France and the United Kingdom (in a group known as the EU3) took the leadership in talks with Iran about its nuclear programme. The EU, like the United States, is preoccupied by the possibility of an Iran armed with nuclear weapons and, despite Iranian assurances that the programme is intended solely for civilian purposes, has tried, through the EU3's diplomatic efforts, to stop it. The negotiations, however, have proceeded at a slow pace and have achieved few results. In 2006 the UN Security Council imposed sanctions against Iran and a restriction on trade with the country. As a result, EU exports to Iran decreased by about 10%, on average, in two years.

Further complexity is then generated by Iranian support of Hezbollah in Lebanon and of Hamas in the Gaza Strip. While both the EU and the United States, with varying degrees of commitment and success, have pushed for an advancement of the peace process, Iran has continued its political, military and economic support of forces that have acted as spoilers in the peace process and have contributed to maintaining the high instability in the region.

Threats to US and EU interests: The spread of terrorism

September 11th 2001 constituted a watershed in American perception of the risk of terrorism. Analysts had been suggesting well before 9/11 that the American homeland was increasingly likely to become the direct target of a terrorist strike (Lesser 1999: 88–9), but American perception and policy underwent a deep transformation after the New York and Washington attacks. Before 9/11, US perception of the terrorist threat was mainly linked to the possibility of American interests abroad – civilian, military or economic – being targeted. American soil was thought to be relatively safe from any immediate danger of retaliation for the harsh policy strategies pursued by the United States towards certain Middle East states, such as Iran, Iraq and Libya, or by American support of Israel.

Europeans, on the other hand, had a quite different view on the issue, having been the target of transnational terrorism (if on a lower scale than 9/11) since the 1970s – including Arab terrorist attacks against American and Israeli targets on European soil – and feeling highly exposed to this danger, given their geographical proximity to the Middle East (Hauser *et al.* 2002). Many governments were concerned that European cities could easily become a target for terrorism or retaliation by Arab states or radical groups, and that, with the advancement of military technology, cities in Southern Europe could become vulnerable to WMD attacks (Delpech 2002; Muller 2003). These fears were partly behind the more cautious and accommodating policy pursued by the EU towards the Arab states, behind the policy towards the Arab–Israeli peace process – in which the EU displayed far more attention to the claims of the Arabs than the United States did – and behind the attempts to build a critical dialogue with the very same countries which the United States wanted to isolate and contain through coercive diplomacy and even military intervention. These differences in approach have caused innumerable tensions between the United States and the EU, and accusations from Washington that the European allies were negotiating and trading with the enemy while America kept security and peace were recurrent. However, despite the fact that from the 1970s cooperation in the fight against terrorism developed among European governments – in time evolving into the formal third pillar of Justice and Home Affairs, now known as Police and Judicial Co-operation in Criminal Matters – it must be noted that terrorism and the proliferation of weapons of mass destruction have not for a long time been the object of a common strategy on prevention or coercion at the European level (Muller 2003: 5). Until December 2005, when the Council of Justice ministers approved a new strategy paper, a truly European threat assessment did not exist.[39]

The September 11th attacks drastically changed America's perception of its vulnerability to international terrorism; the US reaction can be summed up in three words: urgency, militarisation and unilateralism (Gnesotto 2002). The fight against terrorism and the protection of the American homeland became the strongest priority in US policy, relegating all other issues – such as the resolution of European crises or peacekeeping tasks – to secondary importance. The Pentagon's budget saw an increase of $48 billion for 2002, which brought it to a military expenditure of one billion dollars a day; furthermore, President Bush proposed a new cabinet-level Department of Homeland Security and requested $38 billion for this new department.[40] Finally, in a strong swing towards unilateralism, the United States adopted a policy of refusal of any form of external restraint on its strategies and actions, basing this choice on the need to have a free hand in effectively guaranteeing its security through whatever courses of action it saw fit – whether or not approved and supported by the international community. By the end of the Bush presidency, the expenditures for all projected defence-related spending for 2009 were $750 billion – almost a third of all US federal spending.[41]

European reaction to 9/11 was one of solidarity and support, as the invocation of Article 5 of the NATO Treaty showed,[42] but this did not mean total support of the anti-terrorism strategy adopted by the United States, an attitude that even the attacks in Madrid in 2004 and in London in 2005 did not quite change. In particular, most European governments believe that terrorism emanating from the region will never be destroyed by military action alone: without denying the need for military measures, they place the emphasis on prevention and non-military strategies and continue to view terrorism primarily as an issue for law enforcement and political action (Archick 2006). They see America's focus on the strengthening of its traditional military power as an inadequate reaction to a form of terrorism that has proved able to adopt a largely non-traditional, but lethal, *modus operandi*. In Europe's eyes, the West must think in terms of a more complex and multifaceted response: more substantial engagement with countries in the region should be attempted, and an improvement of the Western image should be pursued in the context of a comprehensive policy, aimed at preventing the surge of terrorism rather than repressing it, and which should include development aid, support of states in the region exposed to the risk of political instability, cooperation on the intelligence front to hit terrorist networks in Europe, and resolution of regional conflicts and in particular of the Arab–Israeli conflict (Gnesotto 2002: 101–2). On this last point it is worth underlining once more the different readings of the EU and the United States: while the European Union tends to see the resolution of the Arab–Israeli conflict as a crucial step in order to remove an issue that feeds discontent and radicalism and creates a breeding ground for terrorism, the United States tends to focus on the eradication of terrorism as a vital battle that the West must win and that will, in time, allow the resolution of the conflict between Israel and the Arabs.

Conclusion: Continuity and change in transatlantic relations in the Middle East

Given this analysis of American and European interests in the Greater Middle East, a number of elements, of both convergence and divergence, can be deemed to be long-term features in transatlantic relations in the Middle East, and have remained untouched by all the upheavals of the last decade, including George W. Bush's election, the September 11th attacks and the war in Iraq. They can be summarised as follows:

- EU's inability to overcome its internal divisions in formulating its Middle East policy

- EU reluctance to forsake the security umbrella offered by the United States in the region
- EU reliance on economic instruments as a means to obtain political influence
- US reliance on diplomatic instruments coupled with the credible threat of military force
- US reluctance to allow the EU to have a more prominent and independent political role in the region.

As Peter Rudolf has argued, 'the European approach [to the Middle East] is a mixture of widely shared political dispositions, distinctive national approaches and limited efforts at coordinating national policies at the intergovernmental level. Beneath the surface of coordination, there is unregulated economic and political competition. Critical dialogue remains largely a common declaratory policy with limited operational implications' (Rudolf 1999: 72).

A further crucial element of EU policy towards the Middle East that has not changed is the EU's reluctance to forsake the security umbrella offered by the United States: if the EU member states have made attempts to develop their own policy towards the Middle East, in order to protect their economic interests but also to pursue a strategy that they deemed more effective than American strategy to build relations with states in the region, this policy never went as far as implying a possible redefinition of EU and US roles and burden-sharing dynamics. The EU does not have the means, or indeed the political will, to contribute extensively to hard security in the area, which until now has been guaranteed by the United States through the Sixth Fleet stationed in the Mediterranean, massive military assistance to friendly countries, and the deterrence and power projection in the region implied by American military power and its readiness to use it.

The United States has, over the years, consistently shown great reluctance to allow the EU to have a prominent political role in the Middle East beyond that of agreeing with American policy. The priority that Washington gives to hard security concerns and instruments does not fit easily with European economic instruments, and the United States has repeatedly accused Europe of protecting and pursuing its own economic interests while exploiting the security cover offered by the Americans.

In short, the United States has defined political and security policy, backed up by military forces and active diplomacy. European governments have mostly attempted to use economic relations as an indirect route to political partnership. But they have stumbled over the conflicting interests of the EU's member states and their Mediterranean partners, over inconsistent attempts to introduce political conditionality into economic agreements, and, above all, over their own reluctance to endanger their relations with the United States, a risk that for most Europeans – except perhaps the French and, at least on the occasion of the attack on Iraq, the Germans – was a strong disincentive to attempt to develop more than a declaratory policy.

If all these elements have been consistently present in EU and US policies towards the Middle East, on the other hand, some events have indeed brought about significant changes in US and EU policies and have modified the trend of continuity in transatlantic relations in the region just described.

These events can be summarised as follows:

- The progressive building of a European political identity and the institutional consolidation of the EU with the introduction of new foreign policy instruments and of the role of High Representative and the creation of the European Security and Defence Policy.
- The failure of the Oslo process, which shifted European attitudes: the EU became less willing to follow the American lead when the Oslo process showed increasing weaknesses and finally collapsed.
- The apparent recent change in American strategy towards the Arab–Israeli peace process with the creation of the Middle East Quartet, which includes the EU, the United States, the UN and Russia, and seems to open the door to multilateralism in the negotiations.
- The adoption of the 'Bush Doctrine' and the strategy for the war on terror that have marked the adoption of a unilateral approach on America's part and have caused US–European relations to deteriorate from the surge of transatlantic sympathy and solidarity following September 11th 2001 to a climate of mutual distrust that arguably only a change of policy with a new American President will be able to reverse.

As emphasised in previous chapters, following the ratification of the Treaty of Maastricht the European Union gradually introduced new foreign policy instruments that would allow the EU to play a more relevant role in the international arena. The progressive development of the EU's identity as an international actor, coupled after 1995 with the failure of the Oslo Process and the increasingly important role of the EU in financing the Palestinian Authority, diminished European willingness to be constantly relegated to a secondary role and to accept America's exclusive role as mediator between the parties. During the two Clinton Presidencies, however, the US government did not accept the idea of conceding wider political responsibilities to the EU in the negotiations. Things changed to a certain degree with George W. Bush, particularly after the September 11th attacks. Having previously attempted to limit American involvement, the Bush Administration was forced back into the Middle East by 9/11 and compelled to devise new strategies to tackle the complex security issues arising from the region. The State Department seemingly decided to pursue a multilateral approach to the Arab–Israeli peace process, with cooperation with European governments as a key factor. The creation of the Middle East Quartet in 2002 (see Chapter 4) brought about a change in US policy, bringing it closer to the EU's policy and opening a new phase of transatlantic coordination and cooperation. As previously highlighted, however, this cooperation has been fairly limited, and the United States has not refrained from reverting to a bilateral approach when it deemed this necessary. The EU, however, has benefited from its membership of the Quartet, as the initiative has given more salience to the EU's role and has, to a certain degree at least, legitimated the EU as a credible actor.

While the creation of the Quartet has favoured a – limited – rapprochement between the EU and the United States on the issue of the Arab–Israeli conflict, the new unilateral policy guidelines elaborated by the Bush administration to fight the 'War on Terror' have brought about a rift between the allies that only President Obama might be able to repair. The war in Iraq, Guantanamo Bay, and the Abu Ghraib scandal all contributed to highlighting the difference between the European and the American approaches to threats arising from the region. If, on the one hand, the EU is not yet ready and willing to defy American supremacy in the

Middle East and push its own agenda in spite of US pressures, on the other hand the events of the past few years have increased EU member states' consciousness of the urgent need to find adequate strategies to protect not only their interests but also their policy preferences.

8
Conclusion

> There is only one way to see things, and it is to see them in their entirety.
>
> (J. Ruskin)

The balance of forty years of European involvement in the Arab–Israeli peace process is rather mixed. The then EC was first forced to consider the formulation of a policy towards the conflict by the recognition of the necessity to develop a coherent approach to international crises on the part of the burgeoning economic community. The failure of the six member states to react in a coordinated and consistent fashion to the 1967 Six-Days War was a strong indicator of the need to work towards political as well as economic integration, and contributed significantly to the establishment of the European Political Cooperation mechanism.

Geographical proximity, dependence on Middle Eastern oil and fear of insecurity spillover, as well as the historical role played by several European countries in the region, are just some of the reasons for the high importance accorded to the Arab–Israeli conflict by the European Union.

This conflict, however, has been insidious terrain not only for those directly involved in it, but also for the external powers that have tried to contribute to the achievement of a solution. In the past decade alone the end of two US presidencies has been marked by unsuccessful last-minute attempts at finding a solution, in Camp David (Bill Clinton) and in Annapolis (George W. Bush). It is perhaps to be expected, therefore, that the European Union, an organisation of sovereign states that have pooled some aspects of their sovereignty but continue to try to retain control over their foreign and security policy, would sink in the quicksands of this conflict, with its myriad of local, regional and international ramifications.

But what are the achievements, the limits and the failures of the EU's involvement in the Arab–Israeli conflict and peace process in the last forty years? Or rather, to put the question in a different – if rather blunt – way, why has the EU been unable to develop an autonomous and effective policy towards the Arab–Israeli conflict, despite its efforts and the inordinate amount of time and resources it has committed over the years?

This book set out to answer this question by verifying a number of working hypotheses. Firstly it examined convergence among EU member state policies, in order to establish whether they differ so profoundly as to make impossible the achievement of a common European policy towards the Middle East peace process. It then conducted a legal–institutional analysis of the instruments of the EU's Common Foreign and Security Policy, so as to verify the quantity, nature and effectiveness of these instruments, and what use the member states make of them in developing a common policy towards the peace process. Finally it focused on the issue of transatlantic relations, analysing how relations with the United States influence the elaboration of a common European policy towards the Middle East.

The first answer to the central question 'why has the EU spent so much time on Middle East policy, to so little effect?' is that the member states have indeed failed to reach a sufficiently convergent approach. A number of variables, both exogenous and endogenous, have actually led to a certain degree of convergence in the member states' approach to the Middle East. It is in fact within the context of the formulation of the policy towards the Middle East that European governments have frequently been able to reach an agreement and unify their position, as the large number of joint actions and common declarations approved over the years testifies. Since the issuing of the Venice declaration in 1980, the central tenets of European policy have been the recognition of the Palestinians' right to self-determination and of Israel's right to exist within secure borders, the support of a two-state solution and the reliance on UN resolutions as the basis for future agreement.

However, close scrutiny of the factors that have encouraged convergence also shows that, for each member state, the rationale behind the harmonisation of its policy with that of the other member states has differed. In other words, what has proven to be the driving force behind the formulation of a distinct EU policy towards the peace process is more a 'congruence' – defined, using Helen Wallace's (2000) words, as the compatibility of the policy actors' preferences as a basis for establishing a shared policy regime –than a real convergence capable of producing a truly collective policy, the expression of a unitary European political strategy. To give just a few examples, France's desire to develop a distinct European policy that would differ from the American one, Germany's efforts both to maintain a good relationship with Israel and to develop ties with Arab states, Italy's wish to maintain a strong Mediterranean focus in European policy, and Britain's sense of responsibility towards its former mandate (coupled, however, with the desire not to 'tramp on the US' feet') all combine to push EU member states towards the formulation of a specific 'European policy' towards the conflict, while at the same time individual national approaches and priorities remain distinct.

Time and again these differences have emerged, either in a very blatant and public way (for example, with individual member states trying to develop independent initiatives without consultation with other states, or with national representatives making political statements that differ from the official line of the Union expressed by the High Representative for CFSP) or in negotiations behind closed doors, the latter resulting in watered-down declarations and initiatives.

The undiminished strength of specific national preferences continues to pose a challenge to the consolidation of political convergence among the member states, generating what can be called a paradox of 'converging parallels'. EU member states have maintained, and struggle to maintain, tight control over their foreign policy in order to protect what they consider to be their national interests. Nonetheless, they increasingly find that those interests can be better protected through a common European action that is able to project into the international arena the combined weight of the now twenty-seven members of the Union. As a consequence, more and more national governments, often prompted by totally different reasons and agendas, turn to the EU and encourage the formulation of common European policies, creating the effect of a convergence of policies, which, however, in most cases will not intersect and will remain an equal distance apart, being in this sense a policy of converging parallels.

The second hypothesis explored is that the EU might lack the relevant levers and instruments to affect the Middle East peace process. In the years since the creation of EPC political integration, the EC/EU has taken huge steps forward. Discussions around foreign and security policy have gone from being taboo in the agendas of Brussels meetings to being everyday business. One after the other, new foreign policy instruments have been introduced and 'tested' in the international arena. All these instruments have been used in Europe's dealings with the peace process, from the issuing of common positions to the approval of joint actions, from the deployment of a Special Representative to the creation of a regional framework of cooperation with the Barcelona Process. In fact, the so-called reflexive dimension of European Middle East policy – what Greilsammer and Weiler (1987) have defined as a policy mainly concerned with the actual formation of a common policy as an integrative value per se – appears to have been rather important. The Middle East peace process has somehow offered the perfect stage to afford the EU international visibility as a global actor. The sensitivity of the issue, coupled on the other hand with the continuing involvement of the United States and its determination to maintain leadership and to prevent the EU from gaining significant influence, has presented the EU with the opportunity to experiment with new foreign policy instruments and to gain significant – and much needed – experience in foreign policy coordination while maintaining a secondary and less risky role. Rather than being interested in actually reshaping Arab–Israeli relations, European governments have often appeared, especially until the collapse of the Oslo process in 2000, more concerned with protecting themselves from any fallout from the Middle East conflict while at the same time 'flexing EU muscles' innocuously.

While, as mentioned, the EU has used all types of instruments in its dealing with the MEPP, the use of economic instruments is the one that has most characterised the Union's action. The EU's direct economic support of the peace process has been enormous: the EU is the largest donor of non-military aid to the MEPP, and it is also the first donor of financial and technical assistance to the Palestinian

Authority. Especially in the past eight years, the EU has tried, with some success, to use its generous support of the Palestinians to advance institution-building, accountability and transparency in the PA, especially after some reports suggested the possibility that EU funds had been misused. More recently, however, and especially after Hamas' electoral victory in 2006, EU support has been directed mainly at preventing the complete collapse of the PA and a humanitarian catastrophe in the Occupied Territories. The focus, in other words, has shifted from institution-building to crisis management, a situation that allows the Union very little room to exercise a significant political influence.

The EU's economic relations with Israel, unlike its political relations, are also quite solid: the Union is Israel's largest trading partner and the leading source of its imports. The relationship is based on an Association Agreement and has recently been enhanced and tightened through the Neighbourhood Policy and a specific Action Plan. In its dealings with Israel the EU has privileged the notion that economic relations can become the basis for political influence. On the other hand, frustration has been mounting in several European capitals at the realisation of the very little influence that Europe has on Israel's policies, and a consensus seems to be emerging that a further upgrade of economic ties with Israel will have to be conditional upon progress on the peace process front.

In the past few years the EU has tried to 'upgrade' its role in the peace process and to increase its ability to exercise a significant political influence; in other words, to use the well-known expression, to stop being just a payer and become a player.

Membership of the Middle East Quartet (with the United States, the UN and Russia) has been a step in that direction, as have been the first attempts to be involved in the security dimension of the peace process by putting 'boots on the ground'. This last aspect is crucial: for a long time the limited availability of military instruments has in fact hampered the EU's chances of influencing the peace process. Both Israel and the Arabs have continued to turn to the United States to guarantee security in the region and to reliably back up any political and security arrangement agreed upon during the negotiations, while the EU has remained relegated to a secondary role, limited to financing the Palestinian Authority, while lacking much influence on the actual peace process. The two occasions in which the EU has been involved in the hard security dimension of the peace process, however, have not been great successes. The 2005 EUBAM operation in Rafah was numerically very small (ninety personnel in the full operative phase) and had to be suspended after Hamas' takeover of Gaza in 2007. The European presence in UNIFIL 2, the beefed-up UN mission in Lebanon launched in 2006 after the Israel–Hezbollah war, is numerically substantial, but its deployment was preceded by tense negotiations amongst member states on the rules of engagement, resulting in a rather ineffective operation which is not succeeding in preventing Hezbollah from rearming.

Neither operation has really significantly managed to transform the nature of EU involvement in the peace process and its image as a security actor. Israel in particular remains convinced that the EU's commitment to offer military forces to guarantee peace should an agreement be found is more talk than substance. The refusal in 2006 to change the mandate of UNIFIL to include the active disarmament of Hezbollah (i.e. to carry out peace enforcement) is, in the eyes of Israel, an indication that the EU cannot be trusted actually to be ready to undertake a risky mission should an agreement be reached between Israel and the Palestinians. In this context the United States has remained until now the only accepted mediator in the peace process capable of backing up commitments with a credible military force.

In sum, what characterises EU policy is not a lack of policy instruments, but rather a lack of willingness to make full use of the numerous instruments that already exist. Member states are also reluctant to further develop instruments that could truly enhance the EU's chances of acting effectively in the peace process – such as the Special Representatives and the High Representative for CFSP – and, by keeping the actual decision-making powers in the framework of intergovernmental cooperation, have imposed strict limits on their scope of action.

This leads to the third hypothesis explored in the book, namely that US interests in the Middle East and the dynamics of EU–US relations have relegated the EU to a secondary role in the Middle East peace process.

The United States and the EU share a number of interests in the Middle East, including guaranteeing the free flow of oil; the promotion of regional stability and prosperity; and the fight against terrorism. Europe, however, does not always support the strategies adopted by Washington, nor does it always perceive the threats in the same way. For both, the resolution of the Arab–Israeli conflict, as one of the main sources of instability in the region, is a crucial interest. The diplomatic strategy proposed by the EU for the settlement of the conflict, however, differs significantly from that supported by the United States. While Washington has long backed the Israeli preference for bilateral talks and has worked as a mediator in this framework, the EU has consistently favoured a multilateral approach, insisting on the need to deal with all issues at stake (Jerusalem, the settlements, refugees, etc.) in the context of international conferences that would see the participation of all the relevant regional actors. The United States has jealously protected the primacy of its role as mediator and has actively discouraged a more significant European political involvement, while at the same time recognising the importance and welcoming the large financial assistance provided by the EU to the Palestinian Authority.

As well as a different European approach, not only to the Arab–Israeli peace process but to the Middle East in general, what has emerged clearly is the EU's unwillingness to endanger its relations with the United States by decisively promoting an independent European stance in the region. After the experiences of 1973–1974 and 1980–1981, it has become evident to all EU member states that an effective and autonomous policy towards the Middle East unavoidably carries with it disagreement with the United States – quite possibly involving active disapproval from Washington. For all member states – except France on some occasions – this has proved to be a strong disincentive against attempting to develop a policy that is more than declaratory. In most member states' foreign policy agendas, transatlantic relations are indeed a much higher priority than the formulation of a distinct EU policy towards the Middle East. Moreover, the security umbrella offered by the United States, which is the sole security manager of the region, is not something which any member state is able or prepared to renounce. Neither individual member states nor the EU as such can really protect Europe from insecurity spillover from the Middle East, or guarantee free access to the vital oil resources.

The creation of the Middle East Quartet in 2002 has established a formal framework for the EU and the United States to interact and coordinate their policies towards the peace process. Some ideas, including the concept of a 'Roadmap' and the idea of convening an international conference, originated in Europe but were then transformed into a Quartet strategy. This has seemingly brought about a convergence of strategy between the EU and the United States, and has also helped the EU to be for the first time accepted by Israel as a contributor to security arrangements, albeit in an extremely limited fashion. While the so-called Annapolis process did not really bring about any progress in the last year of the George W. Bush presidency, the first steps of the Obama presidency in Middle East diplomacy seem to suggest a further rapprochement of European and American strategies. Washington has in fact stepped up pressure on Israel to initiate a complete freeze on settlements in the West Bank, while at the same time working for inter-Palestinian reconciliation and attempting to revive and give operative substance to the 2002 Arab Peace Initiative. All these moves are much more in line with European preferences, and might open a new season of cooperation between the EU and the United States.

Europe will probably continue to play a secondary role in the peace process, especially given the limits to its foreign policy action imposed by the intergovernmental framework and by the need to constantly harmonise the policy preference of twenty-seven member states, but through coordination with the United States the EU's policy of contributing to institution-building and to the establishment of a functioning economy in the Palestinian territories can create the necessary conditions for a viable Palestinian state to be created. The emergence of Iran as a regional power, and the consequent alignment of Sunni Arab states to counter Teheran's bid for hegemony and its effort to develop nuclear capabilities, is creating a window of opportunity for an advancement of the peace process through the temporary convergence of Israeli and Arab states' interests. To return to the negotiating table, many steps have to be undertaken at the same time, including a tougher line vis-à-vis Israel to stop settlement growth, the construction of a credible interlocutor on the Palestinian side and the coordination of regional powers in support of the process. In this framework it is only through coordination with the United States that the European Union will be able to act effectively and to exercise its influence on the development of the negotiations.

Notes

1 Introduction

1. Henry Kissinger, US Secretary of State, quoted in the *Daily Telegraph*, 8 March 1974.
2. M.A. Moratinos, EU Special Envoy for the Middle East peace process: '*The evolution of European Common Foreign and Security Policy*', conference at the Helmut Kohl Institute for European Studies on 11 January 1998.
3. One preliminary clarification should be made at this point regarding the use of the terms 'European' and 'Europe', which may be misleading. In this book, 'Europe' will in effect mean the 'European Community' and, after 1993, the 'European Union'; where necessary reference will be made to the specific role played by individual member states, and to the internal dynamics of relations between the Union as such and individual member states.
4. Communiqué of the Conference of the Heads of State and Government of the Member States of the European Community (The Hague Summit Declaration), The Hague, 2 December 1969, paragraph 3.
5. Chris Patten, quoted in Howorth (2000b: 32).
6. *The Middle East Peace Process and the European Union*, European Parliament Working Paper, Directorate General for Research, Poli 115, 1999.
7. See also Select Committee on European Union (Sub-Committee C), Ninth Report: *The Common Strategy of the European Union in the Mediterranean Region*, House of Lords Reports, London, 2001.
8. Author's interview with Sir Brian Crowe, Former Director-General for External and Politico-Military Affairs, General Secretariat of the Council of the European Union.
9. Author's interview with Harry Kney-Tal, Israeli Envoy to the EC and to NATO.
10. Author's interview with Sir Malcolm Rifkind, former British Minister of Defence and Secretary of State for Foreign and Commonwealth Affairs.
11. Part of this chapter has been previously published as an article in the *European Foreign Affairs Review* (Musu 2003).
12. This chapter is partly based on a joint chapter written by the author and William Wallace (Musu and Wallace 2003).

2 European Political Cooperation and the Middle East conflict (1969–1990)

1. Communiqué of the Conference of the Heads of State and Government of the Member States of the European Community (The Hague Summit Declaration), The Hague, 2 December 1969, Paragraph 15.

2. Communiqué of the Conference of the Heads of State and Government of the Member States of the European Community (The Hague Summit Declaration), The Hague, 2 December 1969, Paragraph 3.

3. See the Communiqué of the Conference of the Heads of State and Government of the Member States of the European Community (The Hague Summit Declaration), The Hague, 2 December 1969, Paragraph 3: 'Entry upon the final stage of the Common Market not only means confirming the irreversible nature of the work accomplished by the Communities, but also means paving the way for a united Europe capable of assuming its responsibilities in the world of tomorrow and of making a contribution commensurate with its traditions and its mission.'

4. Ibid., Paragraph 4: '[The Heads of State or of Government] have a common conviction that a Europe composed of States which, while preserving their national characteristics, are united in their essential interests, assured of internal cohesion, true to its friendly relations with outside countries, conscious of the role it has to play in promoting the relaxation of international tension and the rapprochement among all people, and first and foremost among those of the entire European continent, is indispensable as a mainspring of development, progress and culture, world equilibrium and peace is to be preserved.'

5. First Report of the Foreign Ministers to the Heads of State and Government of the Member States of the European Community (The Davignon or Luxembourg Report), Luxembourg, 27 October 1970, Part Two, I.

6. Second Report of the Foreign Ministers to the Head of State and Government of the Member States of the European Community (The Copenhagen Report), Copenhagen, 23 July 1973, Part II art.11: 'On [all important foreign policy] questions each State undertakes as a general rule not to take up final positions without prior consultation with its partners within the framework of the political cooperation machinery.' Part II art. 12.b: 'The Political Cooperation machinery, which is responsible for dealing with questions of current interest and where possible for formulating common medium and long-term positions, must do this keeping in mind, *inter alia*, the implications for and the effects of, in the field of international politics, Community policies under construction.'

7. Second Report of the Foreign Ministers to the Head of State and Government of the Member States of the European Community (The Copenhagen Report), Copenhagen, 23 July 1973, Part II art.12.b.

8. German Foreign Minister Hans-Dietrich Genscher speaking, announcing the outcome of a foreign ministers' meeting, 10–11 June 1974, cited in Hill and Smith 2000: 97.

9. Tensions were also arising as a consequence of different US and European policies towards the Yom Kippur war and the subsequent conflict with OPEC.

10. Report issued by the Foreign Ministers of the Ten on European Political Cooperation (The London Report), London, 13 October 1981, Part II, 7: '[...] If necessary, and if the Ten so agree, the Presidency, accompanied by

representatives of the preceding and succeeding Presidencies, may meet with representatives of third countries'.

11. Ibid., Part II, 12: '[...] The Presidency will ensure that the discussion of the Community and Political Cooperation aspects of certain questions is coordinated if the subject matter requires this. Within the framework of the established rules and procedures the Ten attach importance to the Commission of the European Communities being fully associated with Political Cooperation at all levels'.
12. Ibid., Part II, 13.
13. Ibid., Part II, 10.
14. Ibid., Part I: 'The Foreign Ministers agree to maintain the flexible and pragmatic approach which has made it possible to discuss in Political Cooperation certain important foreign policy questions bearing on the political aspects of security.'
15. Resolution 242 of the United Nations was passed on 22 November 1967 and called, among other things, for the '(1) withdrawal of Israel armed forces from territories occupied in the recent conflict; (2) termination of all claims or states of belligerency and respect for and acknowledgement of the sovereignty, territorial integrity and political independence of every State in the area and their right to live in peace within secure and recognised boundaries free from threats or acts of force'. United Nations, Security Council, Official Records: Resolutions and Decisions of the Security Council, 1967.
16. Declaration of the Nine Foreign Ministers on the Situation in the Middle East, Brussels, 6 November 1973, Paragraph 3.
17. *EC Bulletin*, No. 12, 1973.
18. *The Middle East Peace Process and the European Union*, European Parliament Working Paper, Directorate General for Research, Poli 115, 1999.
19. United States, Canada, Norway, Japan and the EC Member States.
20. However, it must be noted that even the United States conducted some bilateral negotiations, for example with Saudi Arabia, and justified the subsequent agreements by their link to a Middle East settlement and an eventual moderation of oil prices.
21. The ECG was charged with the following tasks: (1) conservation of energy and restraint of demand; (2) setting up a system for allocating oil supplies in times of emergency or severe shortage; (3) acceleration of the development of additional energy sources in order to diversify energy supplies; (4) acceleration of energy Research and Development programmes through international cooperative efforts. *Bulletin of the European Communities*, No. 2, 1974.
22. *Department of State Bulletin*, 12 February 1974, cited in Feld (1978).
23. *The New York Times*, 16 March 1974, quoted in Ifestos (1987: 433).
24. *Daily Telegraph*, 8 March 1974.
25. It must also be noted that 'the gaping rift between European and US views robbed EC positions of much practical significance for the Arabs, for it was mainly the influence Europe could bring to bear in Washington that promised real advantage'.

26. Statement by the European Council on the Middle East, London, 29 June 1977.
27. Statement of the Nine Foreign Ministers on the Egyptian–Israeli Peace Treaty, Paris, 26 March 1979.
28. For an analysis of the Venice Declaration, see Ifestos (1987); Garfinkle (1983); Allen and Smith (1984); Greilsammer and Weiler (1987); *The Middle East Peace Process and the European Union*, European Parliament Working Paper, Directorate General for Research, Poli 115, 1999.
29. Declaration by the European Council on the Situation in the Middle East (Venice Declaration), Venice, 12–13 June 1980.
30. It must be recalled not only that the enlargement of the EC to the UK, Ireland and Denmark had increased the incoherence of Europe's policy towards the Middle East, considering that the three countries had three national policies differing from each other as much as from that of the original Member States, but that the entry of Greece into the EC in 1981 complicated things further, given Greece's strong ties with the Arab world and the fact that it had not yet recognised the State of Israel.
31. See, for example, the contradictory statements of the new Foreign Minister Claude Cheysson regarding the Venice Declaration, quoted in Greilsammer and Weiler (1987: 65).
32. Bahrain, Kuwait, Oman, Qatar, Saudi Arabia and the United Arab Emirates.
33. Cooperation was to take place in the field of economic affairs, agriculture and fisheries, industry, energy, science, technology, investment, the environment and trade. *Bulletin of the European Communities*, No. 3, 1988, p. 93.

3 The EU and the Middle East Peace Process: From Hope to Despair (1991–1999)

1. The legal instrument regulating the EU's pledge is Regulation (EC) No. 1734/94.
2. *The Middle East Peace Process and the European Union*, European Parliament Working Paper, Directorate General for Research, Poli 115, 1999, p. 17.
3. *The Middle East Peace Process and the European Union*, 1999, p. 42.
4. The Persian Gulf states cut off funds to the PLO and hundreds of thousands of Palestinians were forced out of the Gulf states.
5. *The Middle East Peace Process and the European Union*, 1999, p. 26.
6. Ibid.
7. However, in 1992 Israel lifted its veto on full EC participation in the Madrid Middle East Peace negotiations when the Labour Government took office, and consented to have the EC join the multilateral working groups in exchange for the EC's commitment to updating the 1975 EC–Israel Cooperation Accord.
8. Statement by the EC President-In-Office, Mr Hans Van Den Broek, to the Middle East Peace Conference, Madrid, 30 October 1991, quoted in *The Middle East Peace Process and the European Union* (1999).

9. Delors, J., *Le Nouveau Concert Européen*, Paris: Editions Odile Jacob, 1992, quoted in de Schoutheete de Tervarent (1997: 42).

10. See the letter of 19 April 1990 addressed by President Mitterrand of France and President Kohl of Germany to the Irish EC Presidency, quoted in de Schoutheete de Tervarent (1997: 44).

11. The three pillars are: (a) the first pillar, now referred to as the European Community (EC), made up of the three originally separate Communities: European Steel and Coal Community, European Economic Community and European Atomic Energy Community; (b) the second pillar for the development of a Common Foreign and Security Policy; (c) the third pillar for the development of cooperation in Justice and Home Affairs.

12. Israeli Ministry of Foreign Affairs, Information Division, *The Middle East Peace Process, An Overview*, Jerusalem, 1999.

13. *The Middle East Peace Process and the European Union* (1999).

14. *The Price of Non-peace: The Need for a Strengthened Role for the European Union in the Middle East*, European Parliament, Directorate General for Research, Political Series, Working Paper, Brussels, 1999.

15. Author's interviews with senior Israeli diplomats in Rome (May 2001) and Brussels (May 2002).

16. Ron Pundak was involved in the 1993 Oslo negotiations and helped prepare the framework agreement that formed the basis of the 1999–2001 Israeli–Palestinian final status negotiations.

17. *The Middle East Peace Process: Official Documents*, Israeli Ministry of Foreign Affairs, Information Division, Jerusalem, 1999.

18. Four hundred and forty-four million ECUs in grants from the EC budget, 100 million ECUs worth of EIB loans, and 156 million ECUs made available to the United Nations Relief and Works Agency for Palestinian Refugees. In total the EU contribution to the peace process from 1994 to 1997 amounted to over 1.68 billion ECUs (*The Middle East Peace Process and the European Union*, 1999, p. 32).

19. Regulation (EC) No. 1734/94.

20. The Committee comprised the US, the EU, Canada, Japan, Russia, Norway and Saudi Arabia. Associate Members were Israel, Egypt, Jordan and the PLO. The Committee was to convene under World Bank auspices.

21. *Agence Europe*, 19 January 1991, p. 3.

22. See 'The Role of the European Union in the Middle East Peace Process and its Future Assistance', *Executive Summary of the Communication to the Council of Ministers and the European Parliament made by Manuel Marin, Vice President of the European Commission*, European Commission, 26 January 1998.

23. 'The Role of the European Union in the Middle East Peace Process and its Future Assistance', 1998.

24. Joint Actions 95/205/CFSP, 1 June 1995, and 95/403/CFSP, 25 September 1995.

25. President Chirac's speech at Technion University, Haifa, 22 October 1996.

26. Joint Action no. 96/676/CFSP, 25 November 1996.

27. Collateral Letter of Assurances to the Palestinians, signed by Mr Hans van Merlo, President-in- Office of the European Union, January 1997.
28. Joint Action no. 97/289/CFSP, 29 April 1997.
29. Mr Arafat had on several occasions declared that he would proclaim a Palestinian State at the end of the interim period (i.e. five years after the Oslo Agreement) if no progress had been made.
30. Conclusions of the European Council in Berlin, 24–25 March 1999.
31. '[...] The European Union declares its readiness to consider the recognition of A Palestinian State in due course in accordance with the basic principles referred to above [...]', ibid.
32. The Berlin Declaration and the full political and legal implications of its content are discussed in depth in Chapter 6.
33. Conclusions of the European Council Meeting in Cologne, 3–4 June 1999, II, 4, Staffing decisions.
34. Declaration to the Final Act on the establishment of a Policy Planning and Early Warning Unit, Treaty of Amsterdam.
35. The tasks of the Policy Planning and Early Warning Unit include: (a) monitoring and analysing developments in areas relevant to the CFSP; (b) providing assessments of the Union's foreign and security policy interests and identifying areas on which the CFSP could focus in future; (c) providing timely assessments and early warning of events, potential political crises and situations that might have significant repercussions on the CFSP; (d) producing, at the request of either the Council or the Presidency, or on its own initiative, reasoned policy option papers for the Council.
36. Author's interview with Pascal Charlat, Head of the Middle East Task Force, Policy Planning Unit, Council Secretariat, May 2002.

4   The EU Strategy for the Middle East Peace Process in the Post-9/11 Era

1. See Sharm-el-Sheikh Fact Finding Committee (also known as Mitchell Committee), *Summary of Recommendations*. Available at http://usembassy-israel.org.il/publish/peace/archives/2001/may/mitchell.html.
2. Communiqué issued by the Quartet, New York, 17 September 2002. Available at http://www.un.org/news/dh/mideast/quartet_communique.htm.
3. The Treaty of Amsterdam introduced the Common Strategy as an additional foreign policy instrument. The Common Strategy can be defined as a framework that defines what the main EU interests in a region are, and by what general means they might be pursued. See Calleya, S., in *'The Common Strategy of the European Union in the Mediterranean Region'*, 2001.
4. See Musu, C., in *'The Common Strategy of the European Union in the Mediterranean Region'*, 2001.
5. European Council, *Common Strategy of the European Union on the Mediterranean Region*, European Council, Feira, June 2000, Paragraph 15.

6. See Chapter 6 for further details on the Association Agreement.
7. See http://www.whitehouse.gov/news/releases/2002/06/20020624-3.html.
8. See http://www.state.gov/r/pa/prs/ps/2003/20062.htm.
9. International Crisis Group Report, 2003. Available at http://www.crisisgroup.org:80/home/index.cfm?l=1&id=1659.
10. James Phillips for the Heritage Foundation, 2003. Available at http://www.heritage.org/Research/MiddleEast/wm287.cfm.
11. Shlomo Ben Ami in *The Guardian*, 2007. Available at http://www.guardian.co.uk/commentisfree/2007/feb/15/bushsroadmaptofailureint.
12. See 'Comments by Javier Solana, EU High Representative for the CFSP following the meeting between President Bush and Prime Minister Sharon', available at http://www.consilium.europa.eu/ueDocs/cms_Data/docs/pressdata/EN/declarations/79932.pdf.
13. See also Musu, C., 'The Middle East Quartet: A New Role for Europe?' in Möckli and Mauer (2009).
14. See the website of EUBAM Rafah: www.eubam-rafah.eu/portal. In the summer of 2009 a numerically rather small EU contingent of about thirty people under the command of the French Colonel Alain Faugeras remains on 'standby' in southern Israel, having relocated its headquarters from a hotel to offices in Ashkelon. Interview with a member of EUBAM Rafah, July 2009, Ashkelon, Israel.
15. Sven Biscop, 'For a "More Active" EU in the Middle East: Transatlantic Relations and the Strategic Implications of Europe's Engagement with Iran, Lebanon and Israel-Palestine', *Egmont Paper* no. 13, March 2007.
16. See Youngs, R., 'The EU and the Middle East Peace process: Re-engagement?', FRIDE Comment, March 2007. The Rafah crossing point was last opened with the presence of EUBAM Rafah on 9 June 2007. Since then, the mission has remained on standby, ready to re-engage but awaiting a political solution.
17. See, for example, 'Failure Risks Devastating Consequences', a letter to President Bush by Zbigniew Brzezinski, Lee H. Hamilton, Brent Scowcroft, Paul Volcker, and other former Washington officials from both parties published by *The New York Review* in its 8 November 2007 issue, just before the Annapolis conference.
18. On the concept of 'actorness', see Sjostedt (1977).

5 European Foreign Policy and the Arab–Israeli Peace Process: The Paradox of 'Converging Parallels'?

"A version of this chapter has been published in Musu, C. and Casarini, N. (eds) (2007), *EU Foreign Policy in an Evolving International System: The Road to Convergence*, Palgrave Macmillan. Musu, C.: 'The EU and the Arab-Israeli peace process,' 112–27.

1. In a speech to the Italian Parliament in July 1960, Christian Democrat Aldo Moro spoke of what he called 'parallel convergences', referring to

the parallel abstention of a left and a right Party (i.e. the Socialist Party and the Monarchic Party), which had allowed the formation of a new centrist government in Italy under the leadership of Mr Fanfani. *Italian Parliamentary Acts, Stenographical Reports*, 20–26 July 1960.

2. *The American Heritage Dictionary of the English Language*, 4th edn, copyright 2000 by Houghton Mifflin Company. Published by Houghton Mifflin Company.

3. Author's interviews with Harry Kney-Tal (Israeli Envoy to the EC and to NATO) and Yehuda Millo (Israeli Ambassador to Italy and the Holy See) in 2001 and 2002 and with senior Israeli diplomats in 2005 and 2006.

4. In a private communication with the author, Andrew Moravcsik has argued that 'we cannot entirely dismiss the "null hypothesis", namely that – absent a tie as close as US–Israel – ultimately European countries just do not care that much, which is why they do little and can afford to indulge parochial national interests'.

5. Author's interview with Harry Kney-Tal, Israeli Ambassador to the EC, May 2002.

6. Vedrine, H., *Les Mondes de Francois Mitterrand*, Paris: Fayard, 1996.

7. In October 1996 France's President Chirac visited Israel, the Palestinian Territories, Egypt, Jordan, Syria and Lebanon; during one of his speeches he suggested that the European Union should stand alongside the United States and Russia as co-sponsor of the peace process, and that the increased involvement of France and the EU would help restore confidence in the process. His trip was as much welcomed by the Arabs as it was received coldly by both Israel and the United States.

8. In January 2009, a few days after the end of France's semester of EU's Presidency, President Nicolas Sarkozy made a trip to the Middle East in the hope of negotiating a ceasefire after Israel had attacked Hamas in the Gaza Strip earlier in December. His visit coincided with one from an EU delegation formed by Karel Schwarzenberg, the Czech foreign minister and representative of the EU's Presidency, Javier Solana, the EU's foreign policy chief, and Benita Ferrero-Waldner, external relations commissioner. See 'Sarkozy's Middle East diplomacy ruffles a few feathers – in Europe', *Financial Times*, 6 January 2009.

9. Author's interview with Lord Weindefeld of Chelsea, member of the House of Lords and Vice-Chairman of the Europe–Israel Group (September 2003).

10. See Volker Perthes (2002), 'Germany and the Middle East Conflict: What Interests, If Any?' in Overhaus, Maull and Harnisch.

11. See, for example, Foreign Minister Joschka Fischer's shuttle diplomacy between Israel and Arafat after the June 2001 suicide bombing of a Tel Aviv nightclub, and his 2002 seven-point 'idea paper' for peace in the Middle East; more recently, see the intermediary role played by Germany in 2004 when Israel exchanged over 400 prisoners for an Israeli businessman and the remains of three Israeli soldiers held by Hezbollah (the exchange took place on German soil).

12. Author's interview with Sir Malcolm Rifkind, Former British Minister of Defence and Secretary of State for Foreign and Commonwealth Affairs (September 2003).
13. Author's interview with Gianni De Michelis.
14. Author's interview with Gianni De Michelis.
15. The annual mandate, successively prolonged by the Council of Ministers until today, gives wide-ranging responsibilities, which include among others:

    To establish and maintain close contact with all the parties to the peace process, and all other key regional and international countries and organisations;

    To observe negotiations and to be ready to offer the EU's advice and good offices should the parties request this;

    To contribute, where requested, to the implementation of agreements reached between the parties, and to engage with them diplomatically in the event of non-compliance with the terms of these agreements;

    To engage constructively with signatories to agreements within the framework of the peace process in order to promote compliance with the basic norms of democracy, including respect for human rights and the rule of law

16. The former President of the European Commission Jacques Delors, referring to the institutional set-up of the CFSP, has used the expression 'organised schizophrenia'. Quoted in Jorgensen, K.E. (2002), 'Making the CFSP work', in Peterson, J. and Shackleton, M. (eds), *The Institutions of the European Union*, Oxford University Press, p. 227.
17. Joint Declaration of the Nine Foreign Ministers on the Situation in the Middle East, Brussels, 6 November 1973.
18. With kind permission of the author.
19. Collins English Dictionary, Harper Collins Publishers, Glasgow, 2000 (emphasis added).

6 The Instruments of European Foreign Policy and Their Use in the Case of the Arab–Israeli Peace Process: A Case of Insufficiency, Inadequacy, Misuse or Underutilisation?

1. Other capabilities may include the right to establish diplomatic relations, the capacity to bring international claims or international procedural capacity.
2. The three pillars are: (a) the first pillar, now referred to as the European Community (EC), made up by the three originally separate Communities: European Steel and Coal Community, European Economic Community, and European Atomic Energy Community; (b) the second pillar for the development of a Common Foreign and Security Policy; (c) the third pillar for the development of cooperation in Justice and Home Affairs.

3. Report of the Reflection Group on the IGC, December 1995, cited in Wessel (1999).
4. 'When it is necessary to conclude an agreement with one or more States or international organisations [...] the Council, acting unanimously, may authorise the Presidency, assisted by the Commission as appropriate, to open negotiations to that effect'. Treaty of Amsterdam, Brussels, 1997, Article 24.
5. Declaration n. 4 adopted by the Amsterdam IGC.
6. Document CONV 305/02, 1 October 2002.
7. Document CONV 850/03, 18 July 2003.
8. Agreements have been concluded either with countries, such as Bosnia and Herzegovina, Macedonia, Indonesia or the Democratic Republic of Congo, where the Union was operating, or with third countries, such as Switzerland, Chile, Morocco or New Zealand, participating in peace-keeping operations led by the Union. More than sixty such agreements have been concluded (de Schoutheete and Andoura 2007).
9. See http://ec.europa.eu/external_relations/cfsp/intro/index.htm.
10. TEU, Article 4.
11. Treaty of Amsterdam, Article 26.
12. Treaty of Amsterdam, Article J5.
13. Treaty of Amsterdam, Article J4.
14. See http://europa.eu/scadplus/glossary/qualified_majority_en.htm.
15. That is, when the Council is adopting a decision defining a Union action or position, on the basis of a proposal 'which the High Representative of the Union for Foreign Affairs and Security Policy has presented following a specific request to him or her from the European Council, made on its own initiative or that of the High Representative'.
16. Such as the imposition of economic sanctions, the conclusion of association agreements, the extension of aid, etc.
17. TEU, Article 22.
18. Treaty of Amsterdam, Article 14.
19. TEU, Article 28, Paragraph 1.
20. Treaty of Amsterdam, Article 28, Paragraph 2.
21. Normally the GNP scale is used.
22. Communication from the Commission, A Project for the European Union, Brussels, 22 May 2002.
23. See Final Report of Working Group VII on External Action, European Convention, 17 December 2002, pp. 4–5. Available at http://ue.eu.int/pressdata/EN/conveur/73862.pdf.
24. See the speech made by US Secretary of State Madeleine K. Albright: 'NATO: Ready for the 21st Century', 12 July 1998. Available at http://www.usembassy.ro/USIS/Washington-File/100/98–12-07/eur107.htm.
25. Declaration by the Western European Union's Council of Ministers (The Petersberg Declaration), Bonn, 19 June 1992, Part II, Article 4.
26. Conclusions of the European Council Meeting, Cologne, 3–4 June 1999.
27. See http://ue.eu.int/uedocs/cmsUpload/2010%20Headline%20Goal.pdf; the WEU, although largely inactive, still remains in existence at the time of writing.

28. Declaration of the Nine Foreign Ministers on the Situation in the Middle East, Brussels, 6 November 1973.
29. In the case of Germany, for example, any deviation from a pro-Israeli position was very hard to realise without the excuse of European solidarity.
30. See Glossary of Institutions, Policies and Enlargement of the European Union: http://www.europa.eu.int/scadplus/leg/en/cig/g4000j.htm.
31. Council Decision on a joint action in support of the Middle East peace process, 94/276/CFSP; Council Decision supplementing Joint Action 94/276, 95/205/CFSP.
32. Council Decision 95/403/CFSP, 25 September 1995.
33. See 'The Role of the European Union in the Middle East Peace Process and its Future Assistance', *Executive Summary of the Communication to the Council of Ministers and the European Parliament made by Manuel Marin, Vice President of the European Commission*, European Commission, 26 January 1998.
34. The Israeli–Palestinian Interim Agreement on the West Bank and the Gaza Strip; Annex II: Protocol Concerning Elections, Article V, Paragraph 4. Available at http://www.israel-mfa.gov.il/mfa/go.asp?MFAH00qc0
35. In his article Wessel recalls the definition of 'treaty' provided in Article 2 of the Vienna Convention on the Law of Treaties between States and international Organisations or between International Organisations (1986). A treaty is defined as 'an international agreement governed by international law and concluded in written form [...] between international organisations, whether that agreement is embodied in a single instrument or in two or more related instruments and whatever its particular designation'.
36. The first appointed Special Representative was Mr Miguel Angel Moratinos, who was succeeded in 2003 by Mr Marc Otte.
37. Continuing the application of Joint Action 96/676/CFSP, 22 July 1997 (no. 97/475/CFSP). Modifying and continuing Joint Action 96/676/CFSP (extension of mandate: security questions), 26 October 1998 (no. 98/608/CFSP). Modifying and continuing Joint Action 96/676/CFSP (extension of mandate: EU–Israel Forum), plus rectification, 11 October 1999 (no. 99/664/CFSP). Modifying Joint Action 96/676/CFSP, 17.12.1999 (no. 99/843/CFSP). Marc Otte's appointment and mandate are set out in Joint Actions: 2008/133/CFSP, 2006/119/CFSP, 2005/99/CFSP, 2004/534/CFSP and 2003/537/CFSP.
38. The annual mandate, successively prolonged by the Council of Ministers until today, gives wide-ranging responsibilities (see http://consilium.europa.eu/cms3_fo/showPage.asp?id=452&lang=EN), which include, among others:

    To establish and maintain close contact with all the parties to the peace process, and all other key regional and international countries and organisations;

    To observe negotiations and to be ready to offer the EU's advice and good offices should the parties request this;

To contribute, where requested, to the implementation of agreements reached between the parties, and to engage with them diplomatically in the event of non-compliance with the terms of these agreements;

To engage constructively with signatories to agreements within the framework of the peace process in order to promote compliance with the basic norms of democracy, including respect of human rights and the rule of law.

39. Interviews with senior Israeli policymakers, Brussels, April 2008 and Jerusalem, July 2009.
40. Joint Action 97/289/CFSP, subsequently extended in 1999 to 31 May 2002.
41. See http://www.consilium.europa.eu/ueDocs/cms_Data/docs/pressData/en/declarations/84603.pdf.
42. See Council Joint Action 2005/889/CFSP of 12 December 2005 on establishing a European Union Border Assistance Mission for the Rafah Crossing Point (EUBAM Rafah) and Council Joint Action 2007/359/CFSP of 23 May 2007 amending and extending Joint Action 2005/889/CFSP on establishing a European Union Border Assistance Mission for the Rafah Crossing Point (EUBAM Rafah).
43. See 'EUBAM head: Keeping Rafah open is the trick', Jerusalem Post, 6 February 2009, at http://www.consilium.europa.eu/uedocs/cmsUpload/090206JerusalemPostEUBAMHEADKeepingGazabordeopenisthetrick.pdf.
44. The partners are Algeria, Egypt, Israel, Jordan, Lebanon, Morocco, Syria, Tunisia, Turkey and the Palestinian Authority.
45. The provisions of the Euro-Mediterranean Association Agreements governing bilateral relations vary from one Mediterranean Partner to the other, but have certain aspects in common: (a) political dialogue; (b) respect for human rights and democracy; (c) establishment of WTO-compatible free trade over a transitional period of up to twelve years; (d) provisions relating to intellectual property, services, public procurement, competition rules, state aids and monopolies; (e) economic cooperation in a wide range of sectors; (f) cooperation relating to social affairs and migration (including readmission of illegal immigrants); (g) cultural cooperation.
46. Until 2007 the MEDA programme has been the principal financial instrument of the European Union or the implementation of the Euro-Mediterranean Partnership. The Programme offers technical and financial support measures to accompany the reform of economic and social structures in the Mediterranean partner countries. The first legal basis of the MEDA programme was the 1996 MEDA Regulation (Council Regulation no1488/96) for the period of 1995–1999, when the programme accounted for €3.435 million. On November 2000 a new improved regulation (Nr. 2698/2000) establishing MEDA II for the period of 2000–2006 was adopted. The funding of the new programme amounted to € 5.35 billion. Source: European Commission.
47. The Committee is chaired by the EU Presidency and consists of the EU Troika, Mediterranean Partners, and European Commission

representatives (member states not in the EU Troika also participate). The Committee acts as an overall steering body for the regional process, with the right to initiate activities to be financed in accordance with the MEDA Regional Indicative Programme.

48. See http://ec.europa.eu/external_relations/euromed/index_en.htm.
49. See http://europa.eu.int/comm/external_relations.
50. See http://www.delwbg.ec.europa.eu/en/funding/pegas_documents.htm.
51. See http://ec.europa.eu/external_relations/occupied_palestinian_territory/ec_assistance/index_en.htm.
52. See EU–Israel Action Plan http://ec.europa.eu/world/enp/pdf/action_plans/israel_enp_ap_final_en.pdf.
53. Source: European Commission. See http://ec.europa.eu/trade/issues/bilateral/countries/israel/index_en.htm.
54. See, for example, 'Israel: Divest, Boycott, Sanction', by Naomi Klein, 26 January 2009 edition of *The Nation*, http://www.thenation.com/doc/20090126/klein, or 'The case for sanctions against Israel.What worked with apartheid can bring peace to the Middle East', by Gerald Kaufman, *The Guardian*, 12 July 2004.
55. On 10 April 2002, for example, the European Parliament called for suspending the trade agreement with Israel with a non-binding resolution backed by 269 votes to 208.
56. See http://www.delwbg.ec.europa.eu/en/faq/index.htm.
57. See 'Spanish EU Presidency threatens sanctions against Israel', http://www.euractiv.com/en/security/spanish-eu-presidency-threatens-sanctions-israel/article-112743.
58. See 'The offer on the table' by Benita Ferrero-Waldner, http://ec.europa.eu/commission_barroso/ferrero-waldner/speeches/speeches/2009_04_17_haaretz_article.pdf and 'Statement of the European Union', 9th Meeting of the EU–Israel Association Council Luxembourg, 15 June 2009, http://www.delisr.ec.europa.eu/docs/Statement%20of%20the%20European%20Union.doc.
59. See 'EU mulls trade sanctions against Israel over settlements', Reuters 06 June 2009, http://www.worldbulletin.net/news_detail.php?id=42936.
60. See Musu, C., in 'The Common Strategy of the European Union in the Mediterranean Region', Select Committee on European Union (Sub-Committee C), Ninth Report, House of Lords Reports, London, 2001. It should be noted that the Document of the Common Strategy was drafted in June, when there were still high hopes that the Peace Process was at a turning point and that the Camp David talks would eventually bring the parties closer to a peaceful agreement .
61. Available at http://ec.europa.eu/world/enp/pdf/country/enpi_euromed_rsp_en.pdf.
62. See 'Europe's Collective Inaction in Lebanon', by James Graff, *Time Magazine*, 20 August 2006, http://www.time.com/time/magazine/article/0,9171,1229066,00.html.
63. Conversation with a high-ranking officer of UNIFIL, Montreal, November 2008. See also Kern, S. 'Fear Factor: Lebanon and the European Way of

Peacekeeping', *The Brussels Journal*, September 2007, http://www.brussel-sjournal.com/node/2477.

64. Interviews with Israeli politicians, diplomats and military.

7   Transatlantic Relations and the Middle East: Patterns of Continuity and Change

1. One preliminary clarification should be made at this point: the expression 'Greater Middle East' in this context refers to a region that also embraces the Maghreb, the Mashreq and the Persian Gulf, but not Afghanistan or Pakistan. For convenience, throughout the chapter the expression 'Middle East' will be used, and specific references to single countries in the region will be made when necessary.

2. Given the size of the Jewish population in the US, of approximately 5,700,000 people, the biggest Jewish communities being in New York (1,900,000), Los Angeles (585,000) and Miami (535,000), such lobbies can rely on extensive resources. Source of the figures: World Jewish Congress, www.wjc.org.il.

3. See *Navigating through Turbulence. America and the Middle East in a New Century,* Report of the Presidential Study Group written under the auspices of The Washington Institute for Near East Policy, December 2000, pp. 65–9.

4. See 'U.S. Middle East Policy and the Peace Process', Report of an Independent Task Force sponsored by the Council on Foreign Relations, Henry Siegman, Project Coordinator, 1997.

5. Quoted in Friedman, T.L., 'Passion for Peace', Op-Ed, *New York Times*, 28 June 2003.

6. The British Jewish community amounts to ca. 280,000 people, the French to ca. 600,000, the German to 100,000. Source of the figures: World Jewish Congress, www.wjc.org.il.

7. See for example the surge of anti-Semitic attacks in France (Daniel Ben Simon, 'Beyond the bounds', *Ha'aretz Daily*, 18 May 2003), or the suicide attack in Tel Aviv by two British nationals (Sarah Lyall, 'What Drove 2 Britons to Bomb a Club in Tel Aviv?', *New York Times*, 12 May 2003). Numerous demonstrations and attacks against Jewish property also took place in various European countries during the Israeli attack on Gaza of December 2008 ('U.K. anti-Semitism on the rise after Israel's Gaza operation', *Ha'aretz Daily*, 14 February 2009).

8. Thus, for instance, strong reproof over the construction of Jewish settlements in the West Bank, request for the withdrawal of Israel from the Golan Heights and Lebanon, support of Palestinian presence in East Jerusalem.

9. Author's interviews with senior Israeli diplomats in Rome and Brussels.

10. A senior Israeli diplomat, interviewed in Rome in 2001, underlined that 'Israel wants face to face talks. Negotiation with Egypt and later with Jordan started both with bilateral contacts, and saw the involvement

of the Americans only in a second phase. The same happened in Oslo, where the Norwegians acted only as messengers; the Americans themselves where called in when talks were well under way'.

11. In 1979 at Camp David, for instance, talks revolved around negotiating peace, the restitution of Sinai and the diplomatic recognition of Egypt, while completely neglecting the Palestinian question.

12. See 'France acknowledges contacts with Hamas', *International Herald Tribune*, 19 May 2008.

13. The operation was originally to be called Operation Iraq Liberation, but the acronym (i.e. OIL) was thought to be inappropriate and the name was therefore changed. See Press Briefing by Ari Fleischer, Office of the Press Secretary, 24 March 2003.

14. *International Petroleum Statistics Report*, US Department of Energy, 1996.

15. See Policy Brief No. 3: Congressional Staff Briefing on *U.S. Challenges and Choices in the Gulf: Energy Security*, jointly sponsored by the Atlantic Council of the United States, the Middle East Institute, the Middle East Policy Council and the Stanley Foundation, 10 May 2002.

16. Source: Monthly Energy Review: *US Crude Oil imports by Area of Origin, 1973–2004*.

17. In other words, there is an inability of supply and demand to respond quickly to shocks; this explains why prices can double or triple as a result of very small changes in supply.

18. Source: *Monthly Energy Review*, US Department of Energy/Energy Information Administration, August 2002. See www.eia.doe.gov (Official Energy Statistics from the US Government).

19. See Policy Brief No. 1: Congressional Staff Briefing on *U.S. Challenges and Choices in the Gulf: Saudi Arabia*, jointly sponsored by the Atlantic Council of the United States, the Middle East Institute, the Middle East Policy Council and the Stanley Foundation, 14 December 2001.

20. The US is also Saudi Arabia's largest trading partner, and Saudi Arabia is the largest US export market in the Middle East. Source: globalsecurity. org; for an analysis of US Central Command (CentCom) facilities and of American relations with the countries of the area see http://www.globalsecurity.org/military/facility/saudi-arabia.htm.

21. Bahrain, Kuwait, Oman, Qatar and United Arab Emirates.

22. See http://ec.europa.eu/external_relations/gulf_cooperation/index_en.htm.

23. In 2005 the EU 25 imported 10.63% of its oil from Saudi Arabia, 9.01% from Libya, 6.11% from Iran, and 2.21 from Iraq. Source: European Commission Services.

24. For example, through the Euro-Mediterranean Partnership and the Common Mediterranean Strategy: see *Reshaping European Policy in the Middle East and North Africa*, Discussion Paper presented by The Bertelsmann Group for Policy Research, Centre for Applied Policy Research, Munich, to the VI Kronengberg Talks, 26–28 October 2000, organised by the Bertelsmann Foundation, Gutersloh.

25. 'The Role of the European Union in the Middle East Peace Process and its Future Assistance', *Executive Summary of the Communication to the Council of Ministers and the European Parliament made by Manuel Marin, Vice President of the European Commission*, European Commission, 26 January 1998.

26. See *Muslims in Europe: The State of Research*, paper prepared for the Russell Sage Foundation, New York, by Buijs, F.J. and Rath, J., Dept of Political Science/Institute for Migration and Ethnic Studies, University of Amsterdam, October 2002, p. 3.

27. See *Congressional Presentation, Summary Tables Fiscal Year 1998*, Washington DC: US Agency for International Development, 1998.

28. An important pillar of the bilateral relationship between the US and Egypt remains US security and economic assistance to Egypt, which expanded significantly in the wake of the Egyptian–Israeli Peace Treaty in 1979. US military aid to Egypt totals over $1.3 billion annually. In addition, the US Agency for International Development (USAID) provided over $24 billion in economic and development assistance to Egypt between 1975 and 2000. See http://www.globalsecurity.org/military/facility/egypt.htm.

29. Since 1952, the United States has provided Jordan with economic assistance totalling more than $2 billion, including funds for development projects, health care, support for macroeconomic policy shifts toward a freer market system, and both grant and loan acquisition of US agricultural commodities. See http://www.globalsecurity.org/military/facility/jordan.htm.

30. These states (together with Nicaragua, Cuba and North Korea) were named in a 1985 speech made by President Ronald Reagan, quoted in Klare 1995.

31. The policy was termed Dual Containment in a speech delivered on 13 May 1993 by Martin Indyk, Director for Near East and South Asia at the National Security Council.

32. As usual, it is necessary to differentiate between different member states' policies: the Critical Engagement approach is shared by most states, but the UK is clearly more supportive of the more intransigent American approach.

33. See http://www.consilium.europa.eu/uedocs/cmsUpload/78367.pdf.

34. See Policy Brief No. 2: Congressional Staff Briefing on *U.S. Challenges and Choices in the Gulf: Iran*, jointly sponsored by the Atlantic Council of the United States, the Middle East Institute, the Middle East Policy Council and the Stanley Foundation; 8 March 2002.

35. It should not be forgotten that, since the war on Afghanistan, US forces are based in Saudi Arabia, Kuwait, Turkey, Bahrain, Qatar, the United Arab Emirates, Oman, Yemen, Afghanistan, Pakistan, Uzbekistan, Tajikistan and elsewhere in central Asia.

36. Policy Brief No. 5: Congressional Staff Briefing on *U.S. Challenges and Choices in the Gulf: Iran and Proliferation Concerns*, sponsored by the

Atlantic Council of the United States, the Middle East Institute, the Middle East Policy Council and the Stanley Foundation, 12 July 2002.

37. Source: European Commission, http://trade.ec.europa.eu/doclib/docs/2006/september/tradoc_113392.pdf.
38. Source: European Commission, http://ec.europa.eu/trade/issues/bilateral/countries/iran/index_en.htm.
39. See *The European Union Counter-Terrorism Strategy*, available at http://ue.eu.int/uedocs/cms_Data/docs/pressdata/en/jha/87257.pdf.
40. The new Department brought together elements of various agencies previously working separately, such as the Coast Guard, the Border Patrol, the Custom Service and Immigration. Source: The Transportation Security Administration and the Federal Emergency Management Agency, *The Military Balance, 2002–2003*, The International Institute for Strategic Studies, Oxford University Press, 2002, pp. 240–7.
41. See Guy Raz, 'What Drives Record Spending on Defense?', 7 February 2008, http://www.npr.org/templates/story/story.php?storyId=18764753.
42. The Alliance central article of collective defence, which makes an attack on one of the signatories an attack on the entire Alliance.

Bibliography

Adler, E. and Barnett, M. (eds) (1998), *Security Communities*, Cambridge: Cambridge University Press.

Adler, J. (1998), 'The Political Role of the European Union in the Arab-Israel Peace Process: An Israeli Perspective', *The International Spectator*, 33(4), October–December.

Agate, P. and Imperiali, C. (1984), 'National Approaches to the Arab-Israeli Conflict: France', in Allen, D. and Pijpers, A. (eds) *European Foreign Policy-Making and the Arab-Israeli Conflict*, The Hague: Martinus Nijhoff Publishers.

Aggestam, L. (2000), 'Germany', in Manners, I. and Whitman, R. (eds) *The Foreign Policies of European Union Member States*, Manchester: Manchester University Press.

Aliboni, R. (2000), *The Role of International Organisations in the Mediterranean*, paper prepared for the Halki International Seminar on 'The Mediterranean and the Middle East: Looking Ahead', Halki, 13–18 September.

Aliboni, R. (2002), *After September 11th: Europe, the Mediterranean and the Middle East in a Transatlantic Perspective*, paper presented at the workshop on 'Trans-Atlantic and Trans-Mediterranean Relations: Perceptions in the Aftermath of September 11th', sponsored by the German Marshall Fund of the United States and by the NATO Office of Information and Press, IAI, Rome, 1 October.

Aliboni, R. (2004), *Promoting Democracy in the EMP. Which Political Strategy?*, Working Group I, Third Year Report, Euromesco, Lisbon.

Aliboni, R. (2005), 'The Geopolitical Implications of the European Neighbourhood Policy', *European Foreign Affairs Review*, 10(1): 1–16.

Aliboni, R. (ed.) (1998), *Partenariato nel Mediterraneo. Percezioni, politiche, istituzioni*, Milano: Franco Angeli.

Aliboni, R. and Said Aly, A.M. (2000), 'Challenges and Prospects', in Joffé, G. and Vasconcelos, A. (eds) *The Barcelona Process. Building a Euro-Mediterranean Regional Community*, London: Frank Cass, pp. 209–23.

Allen, D. (1978), 'The Euro-Arab Dialogue', *Journal of Common Market Studies*, 16(4), June, Blackwell Publishers.

Allen, D. (1998), ' "Who Speaks for Europe?": The Search for an Effective and Coherent External Policy', in Peterson, J. and Sjursen, H. (eds) *A Common Foreign Policy for Europe? Competing Visions of the CFSP*, London: Routledge.

Allen, D. and Pijpers, A. (eds) (1984), *European Foreign Policy-Making and the Arab-Israeli Conflict*, The Hague: Martinus Nijhoff Publishers.

Allen, D. and Smith, M. (1984), 'Europe, the United States and the Arab-Israeli Conflict', in Allen, D. and Pijpers, A. (eds) *European Foreign Policy-Making and the Arab-Israeli Conflict*, The Hague: Martinus Nijhoff Publishers.

Allen, D. and Smith, M. (1990), 'Western Europe's Presence in the Contemporary International Arena', *Review of International Studies*, 16(1): 19–37.

Allen, D. and Smith, M. (1998), 'The EU's Security Presence: Barrier, Facilitator or Manager?', in Rhodes, C. (ed.) *The European Union in the World Community*, Boulder, CO: Lynne Rienner.

Allen, D. and Smith, M. (2001), 'External Policy Developments', *Annual Review of the EU 2000–2001, Journal of Common Market Studies*, 39, Blackwell Publishers.

Allen, D., Rummel, R. and Wessels, W. (1982), *European Political Cooperation: Towards a Foreign Policy for Western Europe?*, London: Butterworths.

Almond, G.A. (1956), 'Comparing Political Systems', *Journal of Politics*, 18(2).

Ambrosetti, M. (2001), 'NATO's Mediterranean Dialogue', *The International Spectator*, 36(1): January–March.

Andreani, G. (2000), 'Why Institutions Matter', *Survival*, 42(2): Summer, IISS.

Aoun, E. (2003), 'The European Foreign Policy and the Arab-Israeli Dispute: Much Ado about Nothing?', *European Foreign Affairs Review*, 8(3): Fall, 289–31.

Archick, K. (2006), 'US-EU Cooperation against Terrorism', *Congressional Research Report for Congress*, The Library of Congress.

Art, R.J. and Cronin, P.M. (eds) (2003), *The United States and Coercive Diplomacy*, Washington, DC: United States Institute of Peace Press.

Asseburg, M. (2003), 'From Declarations to Implementation? The Three Dimensions of European Policy towards the Conflict', in Ortega, M. (ed.) *The European Union and the Crisis in the Middle East*, Chaillot Paper No. 62, Paris, July, Institute for Security Studies.

Asseburg, M. (2009), 'European Conflict Management in the Middle East. Towards a More Effective Approach', *SWP Research Paper*, German Institute for International and Security Affairs and Carnegie Endowment for International Peace, Berlin, February.

Bail, C., Reinicke, W.H. and Rummel, R. (eds) (1997), *EU-US Relations: Balancing the Partnership: Taking a Medium-Term Perspective*, Baden-Baden: Nomos.

Barbé, E. (1998), 'Balancing Europe's Eastern and Southern Dimensions', in Zielonka, J. (ed.) *Paradoxes of European Foreign Policy*, The Hague: Kluwer Law International.

Barbé, E. and Izquierdo, F. (1997), 'Present and Future of Joint Actions for the Mediterranean Region', in Holland, M. (ed.) *Common Foreign and Security Policy. The Record and Reforms*, London: Pinter.

Behrendt, S. and Hanelt, C.H. (2000), *Bound to Cooperate – Europe and the Middle East*, Gutersloh: Bertelsmann Foundation Publishers.

Bekker, P.H.F. (1994), *The Legal Position of Intergovernmental Organisations: A Functional Necessity Analysis of Their Legal Status and Immunities*, Dordrecht: Martinus Nijhoff.

Biscop, S. (2005), *The European Security Strategy. A Global Agenda for Positive Power*, Aldershot: Ashgate.

Blackwill, R. and Sturmer, M. (eds) (1997), *Allies Divided. Transatlantic Policies for the Greater Middle East*, CSIA Studies in International Security, Cambridge, MA: MIT Press.

Blunden, M. (2000) 'France', in Manners, I. and Whitman, R. (eds) *The Foreign Policies of European Union Member States*, Manchester: Manchester University Press.

Bonvicini, G. and Coffey, J.I. (eds) (1989), *The Atlantic Alliance and the Middle East*, London: Macmillan Press.

Bonvicini, G., Maurizio Cremasco, M., Reinhardt, R. and Schmidt, P. (eds) (1995), *A Renewed Partnership for Europe: Tackling European Security Challenges by EU-NATO Interaction*, in cooperation with the Istituto Affari Internazionali, Rome, Baden-Baden: Nomos Verlagsgesellschaft.

Brands, H.W. (1994), *Into the Labyrinth. The United States and the Middle East: 1945–1993*, New York: McGraw-Hill.

Bretherton, C. and Vogler, J. (1999), *The European Union as a Global Actor*, London: Routledge.

Bronstone, A. (1997), *European Union-United States Security Relations: Transatlantic Tensions and the Theory of International Relations*, New York: St. Martin's Press.

Brown, M.E., Lynn-Jones, S.M. and Miller, S.E. (eds) (1996), *Debating the Democratic Peace*, Cambridge, MA: MIT Press.

Buijs, F.J. and Rath, J. (2002), *Muslims in Europe: The State of Research*, paper prepared for the Russell Sage Foundation, New York, Department of Political Science/Institute for Migration and Ethnic Studies, University of Amsterdam.

Bull, H. (1982), 'Civilian Power Europe: A Contradiction in Terms?', *Journal of Common Market Studies*, 21(1/2): September–December.

Bulmer, S., Jeffery, C. and Paterson, W.E. (2000), *Germany's European Diplomacy: Shaping the Regional Milieu*, Manchester: Manchester University Press.

Buzan, B. and Waever, O. (1999), *Europe and the Middle East: An Inter-Regional Analysis. NATO's New Strategic Concept and the Theory of Security Complexes*, working paper presented to the Workshop of the Bertelsmann Foundation, 'A Future Security Structure for the Middle East and the Eastern Mediterranean', Frankfurt, 3–5 October.

Calleya, S. (2001) in *"The Common Strategy of the European Union in the Mediterranean Region"*, Select Committee on European Union (Sub-Committee C), Ninth Report:, House of Lords Reports, London.

Calleya, S. (2002), 'Conflict Prevention in the Mediterranean: A Regional Approach', in Huldt, B. Engman, M. and Davidson, E. (eds) *Euro-Mediterranean Security and the Barcelona Process. Strategic Yearbook 2003*, Swedish National Defence College, Stockholm, pp. 41–59.

Cameron, F. (1997), 'Where the European Commission Comes In: From the Single European Act to Maastricht', in Regelsberger, E., de Schoutheete de Tervarent, P. and Wessels, W. (eds), *Foreign Policy of the European Union: From EPC to CFSP and Beyond*, Boulder, CO: Lynne Rienner.

Cameron, F. (1998), 'Building a Common Foreign Policy: Do Institutions Matter?', in Peterson, J. and Sjursen, H. (eds) *A Common Foreign Policy for Europe? Competing Visions of the CFSP*, London: Routledge.

Cameron, F. (1999), *The Foreign and Security Policy of the European Union. Past, Present and Future*, Sheffield: Sheffield Academic Press.

Caporaso, J. (1992), 'International Relations Theory and Multilateralism: The Search for Foundations', *International Organisation*, 46(3).

Caporaso, J. (1996), 'The European Union and Forms of State: Westfalian, Regulatory or Postmodern?', *Journal of Common Market Studies*, 34(1): March, Blackwell Publishers.

Carlsnaes, W., Sjursen, H. and White, B. (eds) (2004), *Contemporary European Foreign Policy*, London, Sage.

Christiansen, T. (1996), 'A Maturing Bureaucracy? The Role of the Commission in the Policy Process', in Richardson, J. (ed.) *European Union. Power and Policy-Making*, London: Routledge.

Claes, D.H. (2001), *The Politics of Oil-Producer Cooperation. The Political Economy of Global Interdependence*, Boulder, CO: Westview.

Cofman Wittes, T. and Youngs, R. (2009), 'Europe, the United States, and Middle Eastern Democracy: Repairing the Breach', *Analysis Paper*, No. 18, The Brookings Institution.

Coker, C. (2003), *Empires in Conflict. The Growing Rift between Europe and the United States*, Whitehall Paper Series, No. 58, London: Royal United Services Institute.

Corbett, R., Jacobs, F. and Shackleton, M. (eds) (1995), *The European Parliament*, London: Cartermill.

Cornish, P. (1997), *Partnership in Crisis: The United States, Europe, and the Fall and Rise of NATO*, London: Royal Institute of International Affairs.

Cornish, P. and Edwards, G. (2001), 'Beyond the EU/NATO Dichotomy: The Beginning of a European Strategic Culture', *International Affairs*, 77(3): 587–603.

Covarrubias, J. and Lansford, T. (2007), *Strategic Interests in the Middle East. Opposition or Support for US Foreign Policy*, Aldershot: Ashgate.

Croft, S. (2000), 'The EU, NATO and Europeanisation: The Return of Architectural Debate', in *European Security*, 9(3): Autumn, London: Frank Cass, pp. 1–20.

Crowe, B. (2003), 'Europe's CFSP after Iraq', *International Affairs*, 79(3).

Daalder, I., Gnesotto, N. and Gordon, P. (2006), *Crescent of Crisis. US-European Strategies for the Greater Middle East*, Washington: Brookings Institution Press.

Dassù, M. and Missiroli, A. (2002), 'More Europe in Foreign and Security Policy: The Institutional Dimension of CFSP', *The International Spectator*, 37(2): April–June.

De Michelis, G. and Kostner, F. (2003), *La lunga ombra di Yalta. La specificità della politica italiana*, Venezia: I Grilli per Marsilio.

de Schoutheete de Tervarent, P. (1997), 'The Creation of the Common Foreign and Security Policy', in Regelsberger, E., de Schoutheete de Tervarent, P. and Wessels, W. (eds) *Foreign Policy of the European Union: From EPC to CFSP and Beyond*, Boulder, CO: Lynne Rienner.

de Schoutheete de Tervarent, P. and Andoura, S. (2007), 'The Legal Personality of the European Union', *Studia Diplomatica*, 60(1).

de Vasconcelos, A. (2004), *Launching the Euro-Mediterranean Security and Defence Dialogue*, EUROMESCO Brief, Lisbon: Instituto de Estudos Estratégicos e Internacionais.

Deighton, A. (2000), 'The Military Security Pool: Towards a New Security Regime for Europe?', *The International Spectator*, 35(4): October–December.

Del Sarto, R.A. and Schumacher, T. (2005), 'From EMP to ENP: What's at Stake with the European Neighbourhood Policy towards the Southern Mediterranean?', *European Foreign Affairs Review*, 10(1): 17–38.

Delpech, T. (2002), *International Terrorism and Europe*, Chaillot Paper No. 56, Paris: Institute for Security Studies.

Dembinski, M. and Kinka, G. (eds) (1998), *Cooperation or Conflict? Transatlantic Relations in Transition*, New York: St. Martin's Press.

Den Boer, M. and Monar, J. (2002), '11 September and the Challenge of Global Terrorism to the EU as a Security Actor', in Edwards, G. and Wiessala, G. (eds) *Annual Review of the EU 2001/2002*, Oxford: Blackwell.

Den Boer, M. and Wallace, W. (2000), 'Justice and Home Affairs. Integration through Incrementalism?', in Wallace, H. and Wallace, W. (eds) *Policy-Making in the European Union*, 4th edn, Oxford: Oxford University Press.

Deutsch, K.W. Burrell, S.A. and Kann, R.A. (1957), *Political Community and the North Atlantic Area. International Organization in the Light of Historical Experience*, Princeton, NJ: Princeton University Press.

Deutsch, K.W., Edinger, L.J., Macridis, R.C. and Merritt, R.L. (1967), *France, Germany and the Western Alliance: A Study of Elite Attitudes on European Integration and World Politics*, New York: Charles Scribner's Sons.

DiGeorgio-Lutz, J.A. (2003), 'The U.S.-PLO Relationship. From Dialogue to the White House Lawn', in Lesch, D.W. (ed.) *The Middle East and the United States. A Historical and Political Reassessment*, Boulder, CO: Westview.

Dinan, D. (1999), *Ever-Closer Union: An Introduction to the European Union*, London: Macmillan.

Dosenrode, S. and Stubkjaer, A. (2002), *The European Union and the Middle East*, Sheffield: Sheffield Academic Press.

Drozdiak, W., Geoffrey Kemp, G., Leverett, F.L., Makins, C.J. and Stokes, B. (2004), *Partners in Frustration: Europe, the United States and the Broader Middle East*, policy paper of the Atlantic Council of the United States.

Duchene, F. (1972), 'Europe's Role in World Peace', in Mayne, R. (ed.) *Europe Tomorrow: Sixteen Europeans Look Ahead*, London: Fontana/Collins for Chatham House.

Easton, D. (1957), 'An Approach to the Study of Political Systems', *World Politics*, 9(5): 383–400.

Echague, A. (2007), *The European Union and the Gulf Cooperation Council*, working paper, Fundación para las Relaciones Internacionales y el Diálogo Exterior (FRIDE).

Edwards, G. (1984), 'National Approaches to the Arab-Israeli Conflict: Britain', in Allen, D. and Pijpers, A. (eds) *European Foreign Policy-Making and the Arab-Israeli Conflict*, The Hague: Martinus Nijhoff Publishers.

Edwards, G. (1989), 'Multilateral Coordination of Out-of-Area Activities', in Bonvicini, G. and Coffey, J.I. (eds) *The Atlantic Alliance and the Middle East*, London: Macmillan Press, pp. 237–8.

Edwards, G. (1996), 'National Sovereignty vs. Integration? The Council of Ministers', in Richardson, J.J. (ed.) *European Union. Power and Policy-Making*, London: Routledge.

Edwards, G. (2000), 'Europe's Security and Defence Policy and Enlargement: The Ghost at the Feast?', RCS No. 2000/69, Florence, EUI Working Paper.

Edwards, G. and Philippart, E. (1997a), 'The Euro-Mediterranean Partnership: Fragmentation and Reconstruction', *European Foreign Affairs Review*, The Hague: Kluwer Law International, 4, pp. 465–89.

Edwards, G. and Philippart, E. (1997b), 'The EU Mediterranean Policy: Virtue Unrewarded or ...?', *Cambridge Review of International Affairs*, 11(1): Summer/Fall.

Edwards, G. and Spence, D. (eds) (1994), *The European Commission*, London: Cartermill.

Edwards, G. and Wiessala, G. (eds) (2002), *The European Union. Annual Review of the EU 2001/2002*, Oxford: Blackwell.

Eliassen, K.A. (ed.) (1998), *Foreign and Security Policy in the European Union*, London: Sage.

Emerson, M. (2008), 'Making Sense of Sarkozy's Union for the Mediterranean', *CEPS Briefs*, No. 155, March.

Emerson, M. and Tocci, N. (2003), *The Rubik Cube of the Wider Middle East*, Brussels: Centre for European Policy Studies.

European Council (2003), *A Secure Europe in a Better World: European Security Strategy*, Brussels, 12 December.

Everts, S. (2001), *Unilateral America, Lightweight Europe? Managing Divergence in Transatlantic Foreign Policy*, London: Centre for European Reform.

Falke, A. (2000), 'The EU-US Conflict over Sanctions Policy: Confronting the Hegemon', *European Foreign Affairs Review*, The Hague: Kluwer Law International, 5.

Feld, W.J. (1978), 'West European Foreign Policies: The Impact of the Oil Crisis', *Orbis: A Journal of World Affairs*, Spring.

Forster, A. (2000), 'Britain', in Manners, I. and Whitman, R. (eds) *The Foreign Policies of European Union Member States*, Manchester: Manchester University Press.

Forster, A. and Wallace, W. (2000), 'Common Foreign and Security Policy: From Shadow to Substance?', in Wallace, H. and Wallace, W. (eds) *Policy Making in the European Union*, Oxford: Oxford University Press.

Freedman, L. (ed.) (2002), *Superterrorism. Policy Responses*, Oxford: Blackwell Publishing.

Frellesen, T. and Ginsberg, R.H. (1994), *EU-US Foreign Policy Cooperation in the 1990s: Elements of Partnership*, Brussels: CEPS Publications.

Fuller, G.E. (2004), *Islamists in the Arab World: The Dance around Democracy*, Carnegie Paper No. 49, Washington DC: Carnegie Endowment for International Peace.

Gardner, A.L. (1997), *A New Era in US-EU Relations? The Clinton Administration and the New Transatlantic Agenda*, Aldershot: Avebury.

Garfinkle, A. (1983), *Western Europe's Middle East Diplomacy and the United States*, Philadelphia Policy Papers, Philadelphia, PA: Foreign Policy Research Institute.

Gebhard, P.R.S. (1994), *The United States and European Security*, Adelphi Paper 286, International Institute for Strategic Studies, Brassey's.

Gervasoni, M. (2003), *Storia dei paesi europei nel secolo XX. La Francia*, Milano: Unicopli.

Giegerich, B. and Wallace, W. (2004), 'Not Such a Soft Power: The External Deployment of European Forces', *Survival*, 46(2): Summer, 163–82.

Gillespie, R. (ed.) (1997), *The Euro-Mediterranean Partnership*, Ilford: Frank Cass.

Ginsberg, R.H. (1999), 'Conceptualising the EU as an International Actor: Narrowing the Theoretical Capability-Expectations Gap', *Journal of Common Market Studies*, 37(3): Autumn.

Ginsberg, R.H. (2001), *The European Union in International Politics. Baptism by Fire*, Boulder, CO: Rowman & Littlefield Publishers.

Gnesotto, N. (1998), *La Puissance et l'Europe*, Paris: Presses de La Fondation National des Sciences Politiques.

Gnesotto, N. (2002), 'Reacting to America', *Survival*, The IISS Quarterly, 44(4): Winter.

Gomez, R. (1998), 'The EU's Mediterranean Policy: Common Foreign Policy by the Back Door?', in Peterson, J. and Sjursen, H. (eds) *A Common Foreign Policy for Europe? Competing Visions of the CFSP*, London: Routledge.

Gompert, D. and Larrabee, S. (eds) (1998), *America and Europe. A Partnership for a New Era*, RAND Studies in Policy Analysis, Cambridge: Cambridge University Press.

Gordon, P.H. (1998), *The Transatlantic Allies and the Changing Middle East*, Adelphi Paper 322, International Institute for Strategic Studies, Oxford: Oxford University Press.

Gordon, P.H. (2003), 'Bush's Middle East Vision', *Survival*, The IISS Quarterly, 45(1): Spring.

Greene, D.L. and Leiby, P.N. (1995) *The Outlook for US Oil Dependence*, report prepared for the Office of Transportation Technology, US Department of Energy, May.

Greilsammer, I. (1981), *Israël et l'Europe*, Lausanne: Fondation Jean Monnet pour l'Europe, Centre des Recherches Européennes.

Greilsammer, I. and Weiler, J. (1987), *Europe's Middle East Dilemma: The Quest for a Unified Stance*, Boulder, CO: Westview.

Greilsammer, I. and Weiler, J. (1988), *Europe and Israel: Troubled Neighbours*, New York: de Gruyter.

Grevi, G. (2007), 'Pioneering Foreign Policy: The EU Special Representatives', Chaillot Paper No. 106, October.

Guay, T.R. (1999), *The United States and the European Union. The Political Economy of a Relationship*, Sheffield: Sheffield Academic Press.

Haass, R.N. (ed.) (1999), *Transatlantic Tensions: The United States, Europe, and Problem Countries*, Washington, DC: Brookings Institution.

Hadar, L.T. (1996), 'Meddling in the Middle East? Europe Challenges U.S. Hegemony in the Region', *Mediterranean Quarterly*, Fall.

Hagman, H.C. (2002), *European Crisis Management and Defence: The Search for Capabilities*, Adelphi Paper 353, International Institute for Strategic Studies, Oxford: Oxford University Press.

Hanelt, C.P. (2008), *Bound to Cooperate. Europe and the Middle East II*, Gutersloh: Bertelsmann Foundation Publishers.

Hannay, D. (2000), 'Europe's Common Foreign and Security Policy: Year 1', *European Foreign Affairs Review*, The Hague: Kluwer Law International, 5: 275–80.

Harpaz, G. (2004), 'The Dispute over the Treatment of Products Exported to the European Union from the Golan Heights, East Jerusalem, the West Bank and the Gaza Strip – the Limits of Power and the Limits of the Law', *Journal of World Trade*, 38(6): 1049–58.

Hauser, R., Robertson West, J., Ginsburg, M.C., Kemp, G., Kennedy, C., Makins, C.J. and Steinberg, J. (2002), *Elusive Partnership: US and European Policies in the Near East and the Gulf*, policy paper, The Atlantic Council of the United States, September.

Heisbourg, F. (2000), 'Europe's Strategic Ambitions: The Limits of Ambiguity', *Survival*, 42(2): Summer.

Heisbourg, F., Houben, M., Becher, K. and Emerson, M. (eds) (2002), *Readings in European Security*, 1, Brussels: Centre for European Policy Studies and London: International Institute for Security Studies.

Heller, M.A. (2003), 'The "Trans-Atlantic Rift", Iraq and Israel', *Strategic Assessment*, Jaffee Centre for Strategic Studies, Tel Aviv University, 6(1): May.

Heuser, B. (1996), *Transatlantic Relations: Sharing Ideals and Costs*, London: Royal Institute of International Affairs.

Hill, C. (1990), 'European Foreign Policy: Power Bloc, Civilian Model – or Flop?', in Rummel, R. (ed.) *The Evolution of an International Actor: Western Europe's New Assertiveness*, Boulder, CO: Westview.

Hill, C. (1993), 'The Capability-Expectations Gap, or Conceptualising Europe's Foreign Policy', *Journal of Common Market Studies*, 31(3): September.

Hill, C. (1997), *Convergence, Divergence and Dialectics: National Foreign Policies and the CFSP*, Florence: European University Institute.

Hill, C. (1998), 'Closing the Capability-Expectations Gap?', in Peterson, J. and Sjursen, H. (eds) *A Common Foreign Policy for Europe? Competing Visions of the CFSP*, London: Routledge.

Hill, C. (2001), 'The EU's Capacity for Conflict Prevention', *European Foreign Affairs Review*, The Hague: Kluwer Law International, 6: 315–33.

Hill, C. (2002), *EU Foreign Policy since 11 September 2001: Renationalising or Regrouping?*, First Annual EWC Guest Lecture, 'Europe in the World Centre', University of Liverpool, 24 October.

Hill, C. (2003), *The Changing Politics of Foreign Policy*, Basingstoke: Palgrave Macmillan.

Hill, C. (ed.) (1996), *The Actors in Europe's Foreign Policy*, London: Routledge.

Hill, C. and Smith, K.E. (2000), *European Foreign Policy: Key Documents*, London: Routledge.

Hill, C. and Smith, K.E. (eds) (2005), *International Relations and the EU*, Oxford: Oxford University Press.

Hix, S. (1999), *The Political System of the European Union*, Houndmills: Palgrave.

Holland, M. (1995), 'Bridging the Capability Expectations Gap: A Case-Study of the CFSP Joint Action on South Africa', *Journal of Common Market Studies*, 33(4): December.

Holland, M. (ed.) (1997), *Common Foreign and Security Policy. The Record and Reforms*, London: Pinter.

Hollis, R. (1997), 'Europe and the Middle East: Power by Stealth?', *International Affairs*, 73(1).

Hollis, R. (1999), *Barcelona's First Pillar: An Appropriate Concept for Security Relations?*, working paper presented to the Workshop of the Bertelsmann Foundation, 'A Future Security Structure for the Middle East and the Eastern Mediterranean', Frankfurt, 3–5 October.

House of Lords (2007), European Union Committee, 'The EU and the Middle East Peace Process', 26th Report of Session 2006–07.

Howorth, J. (2000a), 'Britain, France and the European Defence Initiative', *Survival*, 42(2): Summer.

Howorth, J. (2000b), *European Integration and Defence: The Ultimate Challenge?*, Chaillot Paper, No. 43, Paris: Institute for Security Studies.

Howorth, J. (2003), 'Foreign and Defence Policy Cooperation', in Peterson, J. and Pollack, M.A. (eds) *Europe, America, Bush: Transatlantic Relations after 2000*, London: Routledge.

Huntington, S. (1993), 'The Clash of Civilisations?', *Foreign Affairs*, 72(3): Summer.

Ifestos, P. (1987), *European Political Cooperation. Towards a Framework of Supranational Diplomacy?*, Aldershot: Avebury.

Jawad, H.A. (1992), *Euro-Arab Relations. A Study in Collective Diplomacy*, Reading: Ithaca Press.

Joffé, G. and Vasconcelos, A. (eds) (2000), *The Barcelona Process. Building a Euro-Mediterranean Regional Community*, London: Frank Cass.

Johansson-Nogués, E. (2004), 'A "Ring of Friends"? The Implications of the European Neighbourhood Policy for the Mediterranean', *Mediterranean Politics*, 9(2): 240–7.

Jørgensen, K.E. (1997a), *The European Union's Performance in World Politics: How Should We Measure Success?*, Florence: European University Institute.

Jørgensen, K.E. (2002), 'Making the CFSP Work', in Peterson, J. and Shackleton, M. (eds) *The Institutions of the European Union*, Oxford: Oxford University Press.

Jørgensen, K.E. (ed.) (1997b), *Reflective Approaches to European Governance*, Basingstoke: Macmillan.

Jünemann, A. (2003), 'Repercussions of the Emerging European Security and Defence Policy on the Civil Character of the Euro-Mediterranean Partnership', *Mediterranean Politics*, 8(2/3): 37–53.

Kagan, R. (2002), 'Power and Weakness', *Policy Review*, No. 113.

Kemp, G. and Harkavy, R.E. (1997), *Strategic Geography and the Changing Middle East*, Washington, DC: Carnegie Endowment for Peace in cooperation with Brookings Institution Press.

Kennedy, P. (2000), 'Spain', in Manners, I. and Whitman, R. (eds) *The Foreign Policies of European Union Member States*, Manchester: Manchester University Press.

Keohane, R.O. (1989), *International Institutions and State Power*, Boulder, CO: Westview.

Keohane, R.O. (2003), 'Ironies of Sovereignty: The EU and the US', in Weiler, J., Begg, I. and Peterson, J. (eds) *Integration in an Expanding European Union. Reassessing the Fundamentals*, Oxford: Blackwell.

Khalilzad, Z. (1998), 'Challenges in the Greater Middle East', in Gompert, D. and Larrabee, S. (eds) *America and Europe. A Partnership for a New Era*, RAND Studies in Policy Analysis, Cambridge: Cambridge University Press.

Klare, M. (1995), *Rogue States and Nuclear Outlaws: America's Search for a New Foreign Policy*, New York: Hill and Wang.

Kodmany-Darwish, B. (1995), 'La France et le Moyen-Orient: entre nostalgie et réalisme', *Politique Etrangère*, 4.

Kohler, B. (1982), 'Euro-American Relations and European Political Cooperation', in Allen, D., Rummel, R. and Wessels, W. (eds) *European Political Cooperation*, London: Butterworths.

Kupchan, C.A. (1998), 'From European Union to Atlantic Union', in Zielonka, J. (ed.) *Paradoxes of European Foreign Policy*, The Hague: Kluwer Law International.

Kupchan, C.A. (2000), 'In Defence of European Defence: An American Perspective', in *Survival*, 42(2): Summer.

Laatikainen, K.V. and Smith, K.E. (eds) (2006), *The European Union at the United Nations. Intersecting Multilateralisms*, New York: Palgrave Macmillan.

Laffan, B. and Shackleton, M. (2000), 'The Budget. Who Gets What, When, and How', in Wallace, W. and Wallace, H. (eds) *Policy-Making in the European Union*, 4th edn, Oxford: Oxford University Press.

Lansford, T. (2000), *Evolution and Devolution: The Dynamics of Sovereignty and Security in Post-Cold War Europe*, Aldershot: Ashgate.

Laurent, P.H. and Maresceau, M. (eds) (1998), *The State of the European Union*, Vol. 4, Boulder, CO: Lynne Rienner.

Layne, C. (1996), 'Kant or Cant: The Myth of the Democratic Peace', in Brown, M.E., Lynn-Jones, S.M. and Miller, S.E. (eds) *Debating the Democratic Peace*, Cambridge, MA: MIT Press.

Lenzi, G. (1997), *Defining the European Security Policy*, Florence: European University Institute.

Lesch, D.W. (ed.) (2003), *The Middle East and the United States. A Historical and Political Reassessment*, Boulder, CO: Westview.

Lesser, I.O. (1998), 'The Changing Mediterranean Security Environment: A Transatlantic Perspective', *Journal of North African Studies*, London: Frank Cass, 3(2): Summer.

Lesser, I.O. (1999), 'Countering the New Terrorism: Implications for Strategy', in Lesser, I.O., Hoffman, B., Arquilla, J., Ronfeldt, D.F., Zanini, M. and Jenkins, B.M. (eds) *Countering the New Terrorism*, Santa Monica, California: RAND Publications.

Lesser, I.O., Hoffman, B., Arquilla, J., Ronfeldt, D.F., Zanini, M. and Jenkins, B.M. (1999), *Countering the New Terrorism*, Santa Monica, California: RAND Publications.

Lia, B. (1999), 'Security Challenges in Europe's Mediterranean Periphery – Perspectives and Policy Dilemmas', *European Security*, London: Frank Cass, 8(4): 27–56, Winter.

Lieber, R.J. (1997), 'U.S. Middle East Policy in the Clinton Second Term', *Middle East Review of International Affairs*, 1(1): January.

Lieber, R.J. (2002), 'A New Era in U.S. Strategic Thinking', in *September 11 One Year Later*, A Special Electronic Journal of the US Department of State, September.

Long, D. (1997), 'Multilateralism in the CFSP', in Holland, M. (ed.) *Common Foreign and Security Policy. The Record and Reforms*, London: Pinter.

Luif, P. (2002), *The Voting Behaviour of the EU Member States in the General Assembly of the United Nations: An Indicator for the Development of the Common Foreign and Security Policy*, paper presented at the 1st Pan-European Conference on European Union Politics, Bordeaux, 26–28 September.

Luif, P. (2003), 'EU Cohesion in the UN General Assembly', Occasional Paper No. 49, Paris: European Union Institute for Security Studies (http://www.iss.europa.eu/uploads/media/occ49.pdf).

Majone, G. (1996), 'A European Regulatory State?', in Richardson, J.J. (ed.) *European Union. Power and Policy-Making*, London: Routledge.

Mammarella, G. and Cacace, P. (1998), *Storia e Politica dell'Unione Europea*, Bari: Laterza.

Manners, I. and Whitman, R. (eds) (2000), *The Foreign Policies of European Union Member States*, Manchester: Manchester University Press.

Marescau, M. and Lannon, E. (eds) (2001), *The EU's Enlargement and Mediterranean Strategies. A Comparative Analysis*, New York: Palgrave.

Marin, M. '*The Role of the European Union in the Middle East Peace Process and its Future Assistance*', communication made by Mr Manuel Marin, Vice-President of the European Commission, on 26/01/1998. Available at http://www.medea.be/index.html?page=&lang=en&doc=866&highlight=manuel%20marin.

Marks, G., Scharpf, F.W., Schmitter, P.C. and Streeck, W. (1996), *Governance in the European Union*, London: Sage.

Marr, P. (1994),'The United States, Europe, and the Middle East: An Uneasy Triangle', *Middle East Journal*, 48(2): Spring.

Mearsheimer, J.J. (2001), *The Tragedy of Great Powers Politics*, New York: Norton.

Merand, F. (2008), *European Defence Policy: Beyond the Nation*, Oxford: Oxford University Press.

Merand, F. (ed.) (2010), '*European Security since the Fall of the Berlin Wall* ', European Union Series, University of Toronto Press.

Missiroli, A. (2000), 'Italy', in Manners, I. and Whitman, R. (eds) *The Foreign Policies of European Union Member States*, Manchester: Manchester University Press.

Missiroli, A. (2003), 'Ploughshares into Swords? Euros for European Defence', *European Foreign Affairs Review*, The Hague: Kluwer Law International, 8(1): Spring.

Missiroli, A. (ed.) (2002), *Bigger EU, Wider CFSP, Stronger ESDP? The View from Central Europe*, Occasional Paper No. 34, Paris: European Union Institute for Security Studies, April.

Möckli, D. and Mauer, V. (eds) (2009), '*A Strained Partnership: European-American Relations and the Middle East from Suez to Iraq*', London: Routledge.

Moens, A. (2003), 'ESDP, the United States and the Atlantic Alliance', in Howorth, J. and Keeler, J.T.S. (eds) *Defending Europe: The EU, NATO and the Quest for European Autonomy*, New York: Palgrave Macmillan, pp. 25–37.

Moisi, D. (2001), 'Europe's Role in Making Middle East Peace', *Middle East Times*.

Moisi, D. (2003), 'Europe and the "Universality" of the Israeli-Palestinian Conflict', in Ortega, M. (ed.) *The European Union and the Crisis in the Middle East*, Chaillot Paper No. 62, Paris: Institute for Security Studies, July.

Monar, J. (1997a), 'The EU's Foreign Affairs System after the Treaty of Amsterdam: A "Strengthened Capacity for External Action"?', *European Foreign Affairs Review*, The Hague: Kluwer Law International, 1(2).

Monar, J. (1997b), 'The Financial Dimension of the CFSP', in Holland, M. (ed.) *Common Foreign and Security Policy: The Record and Reforms*, London: Pinter.

Monar, J. (1998a), 'Institutional Constraints of the European Union's Mediterranean Policy', in *Mediterranean Politics*, London: Frank Cass, 3(2): Autumn.

Monar, J. (ed.) (1998b), *The New Transatlantic Agenda and the Future of EU-US Relations*, London: Kluwer Law International.

Moratinos, M.A. (2000), *European Union-Middle East: Developing Societies for Peace*, Distinguished Lecture Series, European University Institute, Florence.

Moravcsik, A. (1993), 'Preferences and Power in the European Community: A Liberal Intergovernmental Approach', *Journal of Common Market Studies*, 31(4): 473–524.

Moravcsik, A. (1994), 'Why the European Union Strengthens the State: Domestic Politics and International Cooperation', Paper No. 52, Boston, MA: Harvard University Centre for European Studies.

Moravcsik, A. (1998), *The Choice for Europe: Social Purpose and State Power from Messina to Maastricht*, Cornell, NY: UCL Press.

Moravcsik, A. (2003), 'Reassessing Legitimacy in the European Union', in Weiler, J., Begg, I. and Peterson, J. (eds) *Integration in an Expanding European Union. Reassessing the Fundamentals*, Oxford: Blackwell.

Muller, H. (2003), *Terrorism, Proliferation: A European Threat Assessment*, Chaillot Paper No. 58, Paris: Institute for Security Studies, March.

Musu, C. (January 2001), in *"The Common Strategy of the European Union in the Mediterranean Region"*, Select Committee on European Union (Sub-Committee C), Ninth Report: House of Lords Reports, London.

Musu, C. (2003), 'European Foreign Policy: A Collective Policy or a Policy of "Converging Parallels"?', *European Foreign Affairs Review*, 8(1): Spring, 35–49.

Musu, C. (2006a), 'Profile. NATO's Mediterranean Dialogue: Recent Developments', *Mediterranean Politics*, London: Routledge, 11(3): November.

Musu, C. (2006b), 'The Madrid Quartet. An Effective Instrument of Multilateralism?', in *Europe-Israel Monitor*, Berlin/Tel Aviv: Friedrich-Ebert-Stiftung.

Musu, C. (2007), 'The EU and the Middle East Peace Process: A Balance', *Studia Diplomatica, The Brussels Journal of International Relations*, in 'Global Europe', Special Issue on the Occasion of the 50th Anniversary of the Treaty of Rome and the 60th Anniversary of the Royal Institute for International Relations, Brussels.

Musu, C. (2009), 'The Middle East Quartet: A New Role for Europe?', in Möckli, D. and Mauer, V. (eds) *A Strained Partnership: European-American Relations and the Middle East from Suez to Iraq*, London: Routledge.

Musu, C. and Casarini, N. (eds) (2007), *EU Foreign Policy in an Evolving International System: The Road To Convergence*, New York: Palgrave Macmillan.

Musu, C. and Wallace, W. (2003), 'The Focus of Discord? The Middle East in US Strategy and European Aspirations', in Peterson, J. and Pollack, M.A. (eds) *Europe, America, Bush: Transatlantic Relations after 2000*, London: Routledge.

Nabulsi, K. (2004) 'The Peace Process and the Palestinians. A Roadmap to Mars', *International Affairs*, 80(2), 221–231.

Neugart, F. (2003), *Conflict in the Middle East – Which Role for Europe?*, Impulse Paper, Bertelsmann Group for Policy Research, Centre for Applied Policy Research, Ludwig-Maximilians-University, Munich.

Nonneman, G. (2003), 'A European View of the US Role in the Israeli-Palestinian Conflict', in Ortega, M. (ed.) *The European Union and the Crisis in the Middle East*, Chaillot Paper No. 62, Paris: Institute for Security Studies, July.

Nonneman, G. (ed.) (1993), *The Middle East and Europe: The Search for Stability and Integration*, London: Federal Trust for Education and Research.

Nuttall, S. (1992), *European Political Cooperation*, Oxford: Clarendon Press.

Nuttall, S. (1994), 'The Commission and Foreign Policy Making', in Edwards, G. and Spence, D. (eds) *The European Commission*, London: Cartermill.

Nuttall, S. (2000), *European Foreign Policy*, Oxford: Oxford University Press.

Nuttall, S. (2001/3), ' "Consistency" and the CFSP: A Categorisation and Its Consequences', London School of Economics and Political Science,

Department of International Relations, European Foreign Policy Unit Working Paper.

Nye, J. (2000), 'The US and Europe: Continental Drift?', *International Affairs*, 76(1): January.

Ortega, M. (2003), 'A New EU Policy on the Mediterranean?', in Batt, J., Lynch, D., Missiroli, A., Ortega, M., Triantaphyllou, D. (eds) *Partners and Neighbours: A CFSP for a Wider Europe*, Chaillot Paper No. 64, Paris: EU Institute for Security Studies, pp. 86–101.

Overhaus, M., Maull, H.W. and Harnisch, S. (eds) (2002), 'German Foreign Policy and the Middle East Conflict', *German Foreign Policy in Dialogue: Newsletter*, 3(7) (http://www.deutsche-aussenpolitik.de/newsletter/issue7.pdf).

Pardo, S. and Zemer, L. (2005), 'Towards a New Euro-Mediterranean Neighbourhood Space', *European Foreign Affairs Review*, 10: 39–77.

Park, W. and Wyn Rees, G. (eds) (1998), *Rethinking Security in Post-Cold War Europe*, London: Addison Wesley Longman.

Perthes, V. (2000), 'The Advantages of Complementarity: US and European Policies towards the Middle East Peace Process', *The International Spectator*, 33(2): April–June.

Perthes, V. (2002), 'Germany and the Middle East Conflict: What Interests, If Any?', in Overhaus, M., Maull, H.W. and Harnisch, S. (eds) 'German Foreign Policy and the Middle East Conflict', *German Foreign Policy in Dialogue: Newsletter*, 3(7) (http://www.deutsche-aussenpolitik.de/newsletter/issue7.pdf).

Peters, J. (1999), 'Europe and the Middle East Peace Process: Emerging from the Sidelines', in Stavridis, S., Couloumbis, T., Veremis, T. and Waites, N. (eds) *The Foreign Policies of the European Union's Mediterranean States and Applicant Countries in the 1990s*, Houndmills: Macmillan.

Peterson, J. (1993), *Europe and America in the 1990s: Prospects for Partnership*, Aldershot: Edward Elgar.

Peterson, J. and Pollack, M.A. (eds) (2003), *Europe, America, Bush: Transatlantic Relations after 2000*, London: Routledge.

Peterson, J. and Shackleton, M. (eds) (2002), *The Institutions of the European Union*, Oxford: Oxford University Press.

Peterson, J. and Sjursen, H. (eds) (1998), *A Common Foreign Policy for Europe? Competing Visions of the CFSP*, London: Routledge.

Philippart, E. (2003), 'The Euro-Mediterranean Partnership: A Critical Evaluation of an Ambitious Scheme', *European Foreign Affairs Review*, The Hague: Kluwer Law International, 8: 201–20.

Philippart, E. and Winand, P. (2001), *Ever Closer Partnership: Policy-Making in US-EU Relations*, Bruxelles/Oxford: Presses Interuniversitaires Européennes.

Piening, C. (1997), *Global Europe: The European Union in World Affairs*, Boulder, CO: Lynne Rienner.

Pollack, M.A. (2000), *International Relations Theory and European Integration*, RCS No. 2000/55, EUI Working Paper, Florence.

Pollack, J. (2002), 'Saudi Arabia and the United States, 1931–2002', *Middle East Review of International Affairs*, 6(3): September, 77–102.

Pollack, M.A. (2003), 'Unilateral America, Multilateral Europe?', in Peterson, J. and Pollack, M.A. (eds) *Europe, America, Bush: Transatlantic Relations after 2000*, London: Routledge.

Prados, A.B. (2006), *Saudi Arabia: Current Issues and U.S. Relations*, Issue Brief for Congress, Congressional Research Service.

Pundak, R. (2001), 'From Oslo to Taba: What Went Wrong?', *Survival*, 43(3): Autumn.

Putnam, R.D. (1988), 'Diplomacy and Domestic Politics', *International Organisation*, 42.

Quandt, W. (2003), 'New U.S. Policies for a New Middle East?', in Lesch, D.W. (ed.) *The Middle East and the United States. A Historical and Political Reassessment*, Boulder, CO: Westview.

Rama-Montaldo, M. (1970), 'International Legal Personality and Implied Powers of International Organisations', *British Yearbook of International Law*, 44.

Regelsberger, E. and Wessels, W. (1996), 'The CFSP Institutions and Procedures: A Third Way for the Second Pillar', *European Foreign Affairs Review*, The Hague: Kluwer Law International, 1.

Regelsberger, E., de Schoutheete de Tervarent, P. and Wessels, W. (eds) (1997), *Foreign Policy of the European Union: From EPC to CFSP and Beyond*, Boulder, CO: Lynne Rienner.

Reich, B. (2003), 'The United States and Israel: The Nature of a Special Relationship', in Lesch, D.W. (ed.) *The Middle East and the United States. A Historical and Political Reassessment*, Boulder, CO: Westview.

'Reshaping European Policy in the Middle East and North Africa' (2000), discussion paper presented by The Bertelsmann Group for Policy Research, Centre for Applied Policy Research, Munich, to the VI Kronengberg Talks, organised by the Bertelsmann Foundation, Gutersloh, 26–28 October.

Richardson, J.J. (ed.) (1996), *European Union: Power and Policy-Making*, London: Routledge.

Richmond, O.P. (2000), 'Emerging Concepts of Security in the European Order: Implications for "Zones of Conflict" at the Fringes of the EU', *European Security*, London: Frank Cass, 9(1): Spring, 41–67.

Risse-Kappen, T. (1996), 'Exploring the Nature of the Beast: International Relations Theory and Comparative Policy Analysis Meet the European Union', *Journal of Common Market Studies*, Oxford: Blackwell, 34(1): March.

Roberson, B.A. (ed.) (1998), *The Middle East and Europe*, London: Routledge.

Rosamond, B. (2000), *Theories of European Integration*, European Union Series, London: Macmillan Press.

Rosecrance, R.N. (1997), *The European Union: A New Type of International Actor*, Florence: European University Institute.

Rudolf, P. (1999), 'Critical Engagement: The European Union and Iran', in Haass, R.N. (ed.) *Transatlantic Tensions: The United States, Europe, and Problem Countries*, Washington, DC: Brookings.

Ruggie, J.G. (1993), *Multilateralism Matters: The Theory and Praxis of an Institutional Form*, New York: Columbia University Press.

Rummel, R. (1997), 'The CFSP's Conflict Prevention Policy', in Holland, M. (ed.) *Common Foreign and Security Policy: The Record and Reforms*, London: Pinter.

Rummel, R. (ed.) (1990), *The Evolution of an International Actor: Western Europe's New Assertiveness*, Boulder, CO: Westview.

Rummel, R. and Wiedemann, J. (1998), 'Identifying Institutional Paradoxes of CFSP', in Zielonka, J. (ed.) *Paradoxes of European Foreign Policy*, The Hague: Kluwer Law International.

Russett, B. (1996), 'Why Democratic Peace?', in Brown, M.E., Lynn-Jones, S.M. and Miller, S.E. (eds) *Debating the Democratic Peace*, Cambridge, MA: MIT Press.

Saltiel, D.H. and Purcell, J.S. (2002), 'Moving Past Dual Containment. Iran, Iraq, and the Future of US Policy in the Gulf', *Bulletin of the Atlantic Council of the United States and The Stanley Foundation*, 13(1): January.

Sayigh, Y. (1991), 'The Gulf Crisis: Why the Arab Regional Order Failed', *International Affairs*, 67(3).

Schmid, D. (2003), *Interlinkages within the Euro-Mediterranean Partnership: Linking Economic, Institutional and Political Reform: Conditionality within the Euro-Mediterranean Partnership*, EUROMESCO Paper No. 27, Lisbon: Instituto de Estudos Estratégicos e Internacionais.

Select Committee on European Union (Sub-Committee C) (2001), *The Common Strategy of the European Union in the Mediterranean Region*, Ninth Report, House of Lords Reports, London.

Serfaty, S. (2000), 'Europe, the Mediterranean, and the Middle East', *Joint Force Quarterly Forum*, No. 24, Spring.

Shaked, H. and Rabinovich, I. (eds) (1980), *The Middle East and the United States, Perceptions and Policies*, London: Transaction Books.

Shlaim, A. (1994), *War and Peace in the Middle East: A Critique of American Policy*, New York: Whittle Books in association with Viking.

Sicherman, H. (1980a), 'The United States and Israel: A Strategic Divide?', *Orbis: A Journal of World Affairs*, Summer.

Sicherman, H. (1980b), 'Politics of Dependence: Western Europe and the Arab-Israeli Conflict', *Orbis: A Journal of World Affairs*, Winter.

Sick, G. (2003), 'The United States in the Persian Gulf: From Twin Pillars to Dual Containment', in Lesch, D.W. (ed.) *The Middle East and the United States: A Historical and Political Reassessment*, Boulder, CO: Westview.

Siegman, H. (1997), *U.S. Middle East Policy and the Peace Process*, Report of an Independent Task Force sponsored by the Council on Foreign Relations.

Silvestri, S. (1998), 'Il nuovo quadro strategico del mediterraneo. La collocazione dell'Italia', in Aliboni, R. (ed.) *Partenariato nel Mediterraneo. Percezioni, politiche, istituzioni*, Milano: Franco Angeli.

Silvestri, S. (2003), 'The European Union, the United States and the Middle East: Some Scenarios', in Ortega, M. (ed.) *The European Union and the Crisis in the Middle East*, Chaillot Paper No. 62, Paris: Institute for Security Studies, July.

Sjostedt, G. (1977), *The External Role of the European Community*, Farnborough: Saxon House.

Sjursen, H. (1998), 'Missed Opportunity or Eternal Fantasy? The Idea of a European Security and Defence Policy', in Peterson, J. and Sjursen, H. (eds) *A Common Foreign Policy for Europe? Competing Visions of the CFSP*, London: Routledge.

Skidmore, D. and Hudson, V. (eds) (1993), *The Limits of State Autonomy: Societal Groups and Foreign Policy Formulation*, Boulder, CO: Westview.

Sloan, S.R. (2000), *The United States and European Defence*, Chaillot Paper No. 39, Paris: Institute for Security Studies, Western European Union.

Smith, H. (2002), *European Union Foreign Policy: What It Is and What It Does*, London: Pluto Press.

Smith, K.E. (1998), 'The Instruments of European Union Foreign Policy', in Zielonka, J. (ed.) *Paradoxes of European Foreign Policy*, The Hague: Kluwer, pp. 67–85.

Smith, K.E. (1999), *The Making of EU Foreign Policy: The Case of Eastern Europe*, London: Macmillan.

Smith, K.E. (2003), 'Understanding the European Foreign Policy System', *Contemporary European History*, Cambridge: Cambridge University Press, 12(2): 239–54.

Smith, M. (1996a), 'The European Union and a Changing Europe: Establishing the Boundaries of Order', *Journal of Common Market Studies*, Blackwell, 34(1): March.

Smith, M. (1996b), 'The EU as an International Actor', in Richardson, J. (ed.) *European Union. Power and Policy-Making*, London: Routledge.

Smith, M. (2003), 'Sovereignty, Responsibility and World Order', in Weiler, J., Begg, I. and Peterson, J. (eds) *Integration in an Expanding European Union. Reassessing the Fundamentals*, Oxford: Blackwell.

Smith, M.E. (2004), *Europe's Foreign and Security Policy: The Institutionalization of Cooperation*, Cambridge: Cambridge University Press.

Soetendorp, B. (2002), 'The EU's Involvement in the Israeli-Palestinian Peace Process: The Building of a Visible International Identity', *European Foreign Affairs Review*, The Hague: Kluwer Law International, 7: 283–95.

Soltan, G. (2004), *Southern Mediterranean Perceptions and Proposals for Mediterranean Security*, EUROMESCO Brief, Lisbon: Instituto de Estudos Estratégicos e Internacionais.

Spencer, C. (1998), 'Rethinking or Reorienting Europe's Mediterranean Security Focus', in Park, W. and Wyn Rees, G. (eds) *Rethinking Security in Post-Cold War Europe*, London: Addison Wesley Longman.

Spencer, C. (2001), 'The EU and Common Strategies: The Revealing Case of the Mediterranean', *European Foreign Affairs Review*, The Hague: Kluwer Law International, 6.

Stavridis, S. and Hutchence, J. (2000), 'Mediterranean Challenges to the EU's Foreign Policy', *European Foreign Affairs Review*, The Hague: Kluwer Law International, 5.

Stavridis, S., Couloumbis, T., Veremis, T. and Waites, N. (eds) (1999), *The Foreign Policies of the European Union's Mediterranean States and Applicant Countries in the 1990s*, Houndmills: Macmillan Press.

Stein, K.W. (2002), 'The Bush Doctrine: Selective Engagement in the Middle East', *Middle East Review of International Affairs*, 6(2): June.

Steinbach, U. (1980), 'The European Community and the United States in the Arab World – Political Competition or Partnership?', in Shaked, H. and Rabinovich, I. (eds) *The Middle East and the United States, Perceptions and Policies*, London: Transaction Books.

Steinberg, G.M. (1999), 'The European Union and the Middle East Peace Process', *Jerusalem Letter*, Jerusalem Centre for Public Affairs, 15 November.

Steinberg, G.M. and Etengoff, A. (2002), *Arms Control and Non-Proliferation: Developments in the Middle East*, The Begin-Sadat Centre for Strategic Studies, Bar-Ilan University.

Steinberg, J.B. (2003), 'An Elective Partnership: Salvaging Transatlantic Relations', *Survival*, The IISS Quarterly, 45(2): Summer.

Strategic Survey 2002/3: An Evaluation and Forecast of World Affairs (2003), Oxford: Oxford University Press for the International Institute for Strategic Studies.

Taylor, P. (1982), 'The European Communities as an Actor in International Society', *Journal of European Integration*, 6(1).

Taylor, P. (1983), *The Limits of European Integration*, London: Croom Helm.

Taylor, P. (1991), 'The European Community and the State: Assumptions, Theories and Propositions', *Review of International Studies*, 17(2): April.

Taylor, P. (1996), *The European Union in the 1990s*, Oxford: Oxford University Press.

Thomas, J.P. (2000), *The Military Challenges of Transatlantic Coalitions*, Adelphi Paper 333, International Institute for Strategic Studies, Oxford: Oxford University Press.

Tietje, C. (1997), 'The Concept of Coherence in the Treaty on European Union and the Common Foreign and Security Policy', *European Foreign Affairs Review*, The Hague: Kluwer Law International, 2.

Tilikainen, T. (2001), 'To Be or Not to Be? An Analysis of the Legal and Political Elements of Statehood in the EU's External Identity', *European Foreign Affairs Review*, The Hague: Kluwer Law International, 6.

Tocci, N. (2005), 'The Widening Gap between Rhetoric and Reality in EU Policy towards the Israeli-Palestinian Conflict', *CEPS Working Documents*, Brussels.

Tocci, N. (2007), *The EU and Conflict Resolution: Promoting Peace in the Backyard*, London: Routledge.

Tonra, B. (2001), *The Europeanisation of National Foreign Policy: Dutch, Danish and Irish Foreign Policy in the European Union*, Aldershot: Ashgate.

Vaisse, J. (2008), 'Muslims in Europe: A Short Introduction', *US – Europe Analysis Series*, Washington, DC: Brookings Institution, September.

Vasconcelos, A. and Joffe, G. (eds) (2000), 'Special Issue on the Barcelona Process', *Mediterranean Politics*, 5(1): Spring.

Vedrine, H. (1996), *Les Mondes de François Mitterrand*, Paris: Fayard.

Volpi, F. (2004), 'Regional Community Building and the Transformation of International Relations: The Case of the Euro-Mediterranean Partnership', *Mediterranean Politics*, 9(2): 145–64.

Von Bogdandy, A. (1999), 'The Legal Case for Unity: The European Union as a Single Organisation with a Single Legal System', *Common Market Law Review*, No. 36.

Waever, O. (1996), 'European Security Identities', *Journal of Common Market Studies*, Blackwell, 34(1): March.

Waever, O. (1998), 'Insecurity, Security and Asecurity in the West European Non-War Community', in Adler, E. and Barnett, M. (eds) *Security Communities*, Cambridge: Cambridge University Press.

Wallace, H. (1996a), 'The Institutions of the EU: Experience and Experiments', in Wallace, W. and Wallace, H. (eds) *Policy-Making in the European Union*, 4th edn, Oxford: Oxford University Press.

Wallace, H. (2000), 'The Policy Process. A Moving Pendulum', in Wallace, W. and Wallace, H. (eds) *Policy-Making in the European Union*, 4th edn, Oxford: Oxford University Press.

Wallace, H. and Wallace, W. (2000), *Policy-Making in the European Union*, 4th edn, Oxford: Oxford University Press.

Wallace, H., Wallace, W. and Webb, C. (eds) (1977), *Policy Making in the European Community*, Chichester: Wiley.

Wallace, W. (1990), *The Transformation of Western Europe*, London: Pinter (for the Royal Institute of International Affairs).

Wallace, W. (1996b), *Opening the Door: The Enlargement of NATO and the European Union*, London: Centre for European Reform.

Wallace, W. (1999a), 'The Sharing of Sovereignty: The European Paradox', *Political Studies*, 47, Blackwell.

Wallace, W. (1999b), 'Europe after the Cold War: Interstate Order or Post-Sovereign Regional System?', *Review of International Studies*, 25.

Weiler, J., Begg, I. and Peterson, J. (eds) (2003), *Integration in an Expanding European Union: Reassessing the Fundamentals*, Oxford: Blackwell.

Werner, R.A. (1977), 'Oil and U.S. Security Policies', *Orbis: A Journal of World Affairs*, Fall.

Wessel, R.A. (1999), *The European Union's Foreign and Security Policy. A Legal Institutional Perspective*, The Hague: Kluwer Law International.

Wessel, R.A. (2000), 'Revisiting the International Legal Status of the EU', *European Foreign Affairs Review*, The Hague: Kluwer Law International, n. 5.

Whetten, L.L. (1977), *The Arab-Israeli Dispute: Great Power Behaviour*, Adelphi Paper 128, London: International Institute for Strategic Studies.

White, B. (2001), *Understanding European Foreign Policy*, Basingstoke: Palgrave.

White, B. (2004), 'The European Union as a Foreign Policy Actor', in Hermann, M. and Sundelius, B. (eds) *Comparative Foreign Policy Analysis: Theories and Methods*, New Jersey: Prentice Hall.

White, N.D. (1996), *The Law of International Organisations*, Manchester: Manchester University Press.

Whitman, R. (1998), *From Civilian Power to Superpower? The International Identity of the European Union*, Basingstoke: Macmillan.

Whitman, R. (2002), *The Fall and Rise of Civilian Power Europe*, paper presented to the conference on 'The European Union in International Affairs', National Europe Centre, Australian National University, 3–4 July.

Whitman, R. (2008/1), 'Foreign, Security and Defence Policy and the Lisbon Treaty: Significant or Cosmetic Reforms?', *Global Europe Papers*, University of Bath.

Wittes, T.C. and Yerkes, S.E. (2006), *What Price Freedom? Assessing the Bush Administration's Freedom Agenda*, Analysis Paper, No. 10, Washington, DC: Brookings Institution.

Wittes, T.C. and Youngs, R. (2009), *Europe, the United States, and Middle Eastern Democracy: Repairing the Breach*, Analysis Paper, No. 18, Washington, DC: Brookings Institution.

Wright, V. (1996), 'The National Coordination of European Policy-Making: Negotiating the Quagmire', in Richardson, J.J. (ed.) *European Union: Power and Policy-Making*, London: Routledge.

Yacobi, H. and Newman, D. (2008), 'The EU and the Israel-Palestine Conflict', in Diez, T., Albert, M. and Stetter, S. (eds) *The European Union and Border Conflicts: The Power of Integration and Association*, Cambridge: Cambridge University Press.

Yorke, V. (1999), 'The European Union and the Israeli-Palestinian Peace Process: The Need for a New Approach', *Saferworld Reports*, October.

Youngs, R. (2004), *Europe's Uncertain Pursuit of Middle East Reform*, Carnegie Paper No. 45, Washington, DC: Carnegie Endowment for International Peace.

Youngs, R. (2005), *Ten Years of the Barcelona Process: A Model for Supporting Arab Reform?*, Working Paper No. 2, Madrid: FRIDE.

Youngs, R. (2006), *Europe and the Middle East: In the Shadow of September 11*, Boulder, CO: Lynne Rienner.

Zielonka, J. (1998a), *Explaining Euro-Paralysis: Why Europe Is Unable to Act in International Politics*, New York: St. Martin's Press.

Zielonka, J. (ed.) (1998b), *Paradoxes of European Foreign Policy*, The Hague: Kluwer Law International.

Zielonka, J. (2001), 'How New Enlarged Borders Will Reshape the European Union', *Journal of Common Market Studies*, 39(3): 507–36.

Index

217